GEORGE MONK
Duke of Albemarle.

M.V. der Gucht Sculp.

THE LIFE

OF

GENERAL *MONK:*

Duke of *Albemarle,*

CONTAINING,

I. A faithful Account of his unparallel'd Conduct, surprizing Actions, and Providential Success in accomplishing the RESTORATION of MONARCHY.

II. A particular Relation of that most memorable March from *Cildstream* to *London*; the Preparations for it in *Scotland,* and the Happy Consequences of it in *England.*

III. Many Mistakes committed by our Historians, (particularly the Earl of *Clarendon*) concerning the General's Administration, rectified.

Publish'd from an Original MANUSCRIPT of *THOMAS SKINNER.* M. D.

With a PREFACE in Vindication of General *Monk*'s Conduct; and giving some Account of the Manuscript. By WILLIAM WEBSTER, M. A. Curate of St. *Dunstans,* in the *West.*

The SECOND EDITION, corrected.

LONDON:

Printed for J. GRAVES in St. *James's-Street*: J. ISTED and J. HOOKE, in *Fleet-Street.* M.DCC.XXIV.

The Naval & Military Press Ltd

in association with

The National Army Museum, London

Published jointly by

The Naval & Military Press Ltd
Unit 10 Ridgewood Industrial Park,
Uckfield, East Sussex,
TN22 5QE England

Tel: +44 (0) 1825 749494
Fax: +44 (0) 1825 765701

www.naval-military-press.com
www.military-genealogy.com
www.militarymaproom.com

and

The National Army Museum, London
www.national-army-museum.ac.uk

In reprinting in facsimile from the original, any imperfections are inevitably reproduced and the quality may fall short of modern type and cartographic standards.

TO

The Right Honourable the

Counteſs *Granville*

AND

JOHN Lord GOWER,

Baron of *Sittenham* in the County of *York*.

MADAM,

HE following Life claims the Protection of Your LADYSHIP'S Name, in Right of Relation and Friendſhip; the Loyal and Antient Families of the GRAN-

A VIL-

DEDICATION.

VILLES and the MONKS being nearly ally'd by Birth, and an Agreement in Principles. But the DUKE of ALBEMARL and Your Great Father the EARL of BATH were more intimately united by an early Acquaintance in their Youth; and in their riper Years, by a happy Concurrence of Counsels and Actions, in the Accomplishment of the truly Glorious RESTORATION. But,

MADAM,
Besides the Consideration of Piety to Your deceased Father, who bears so Honourable a Part in the ensuing History, and Affection to the Memory of an Illustrious RELATION, who is the chief Subject of it; give me leave to say, Your LADYSHIP appears

DEDICATION.

pears to be under a further and more particular Obligation to encourage a faithful Account of the Life and Actions of the DUKE of ALBEMARLE; forasmuch as the Honour of Your Family must necessarily partake of the Injury he has suffered from the Misrepresentations of his Enemies. And,

MY LORD,

To the Honour of YOUR LORDSHIP'S Patronage this History seems equally entitled, your LORDSHIP being also descended from the GRANVILLES, and thereby related to the MONKS: But not more nearly related by Blood, than by an Affinity of high Qualities and noble Endowments. The Wisdom, Courage, and constant Adherence to the Interest of their

King

DEDICATION.

King and Country, with other Virtues so conspicuous in your ANCESTORS, shine, in their full Perfection, in Your LORDSHIP's Character. As a good Subject, You think it Your Duty to encourage *Monarchical Men*, and *Monarchical Principles*, not having learned the Maxims of some *modern* Politicians, who shew their Loyalty to his MAJESTY, by an habitual Aversion to *Kingly* Government, and an idustrious Zeal, upon all Occasions where they can do it with impunity, to propagate *Republican* Notions: As an ENGLISHMAN, You are equally careful to preserve the invaluable Blessings of *Liberty* and *Property*; as a Member of the CHURCH, You esteem it neither *Popery* nor *Superstition*, to assert her *Doctrines* and

In-

DEDICATION.

Inſtitution, to ſupport her *Rights*, and protect her *Clergy*.

But beſides theſe excellent Qualities which ſhew themſelves in a more publick manner, Your LORDSHIP's private Virtues are made ſubſervient to the Good of Your COUNTRY: That eaſy Addreſs and flowing Affability, That engaging Condeſcenſion, as well as graceful Dignity in all Your Actions, have my LORD, in Your early Years, given You ſuch a Share of the general Eſteem and Affections of Your Countrymen, as very few have ever lived to attain to. Thoſe who have the Happineſs to live near You, feel no other Effects of the Man of Quality, than his Bounty and Hoſpitality, and a Readineſs to protect them from the Injuries of other Men. As all theſe

DEDICATION.

these happy Talents have been conducted with the most honest Skill, 'tis hoped, the World will learn from Your LORDSHIP's Example, how unnecessary Party Rage, and an unneighbourly Resentment towards such as differ from You are to the carrying on a good Cause successfully.

I hope, my LORD, I shall one Day see Your LORDSHIP in full Power at the Head of that Interest (the Interest of our Constitution in Church and State) which no Man has more effectually promoted. This, my LORD, is the proper Reward of the Virtues You have already shewn, and in wishing it, I give a Proof of my Zeal for the Happiness of my *Country*, and the Honour of the *Crown*.

DEDICATION.

I muſt now humbly beg your Honours to accept of this plain Addreſs, and my inconſiderable Share in the Performance I here preſent You with. It is a great Advantage to the Memory of the Author, that his Patrons, are proper Judges of juſt and elegant Writing. The Editor has no Hopes, but in your wonted Candor, and Condſecention. I have engaged in a good Cauſe, and with a good Intention which is all I have to plead in Excuſe for an *Introduction* ſo much below the Dignity of the Subject. Had I vindicated the Conduct of General Monk as juſtly as Dr. Skinner has related it faithfully, the *Stateſman*, the *Hero*, the *Patriot*, would all appear in their proper Luſtre, and reflect

DEDICATION.

as much Honour upon the Relations of the DUKE, as can be derived to them from the Virtue and Nobility of their PROGENITORS.

I am,

    May it please Your Honours,

        With great Esteem,

    Yours Honours most obedient

    And devoted humble Servant.

        William Webster.

THE EDITOR'S PREFACE.

*I*N *this Prefatory Discourse, wherein I propose to make some Reflections upon the Conduct of* GENERAL MONK, *in Vindication of him from some Aspersions of his Enemies, or the less malicious, but equally injurious Mistakes of those, who would be thought at least to be favourable to his Character; I shall not detain the Reader upon the common Subject of Biographers, the delightful and profitable Nature of History in general, but confine my self directly to the Matter and Sence of Action before us. A Scene equally wonderful and surprising, in the Formation, in the Conduct, in the Accomplishment, and happy Effects of it. A Scence which open'd in reducing this Part of the World we inhabit, out of the dismal Confusion and Anarchy, wherein, like the primitive Choas, it lay involv'd, into a State so well inform'd and regular, that perhaps no Constitution of Govern-*

ment

ment upon Earth ever subsisted upon a more wise, equitable, or well-tempered Model.

In reference to foreign History, I shall only observe, that if Facts, wherein the several Ages and Nations of the World would have been interested, if Revolutions respecting the Government of Greece, *or* Rome, *are thought useful and entertaining to Men of polite Literature, especially when set in a proper and good Light, though we are no further affected by them, than as they discover to us the Arts aud Errors of Government, and the common Events of civil Life; certainly a Desire of being acquainted with the History of our own Nation, or with any momentous Part of it, will not only be allowed natural, but highly laudable and instructive.*

Now if we carry our Enquiries into the English *History as high as we have any Authentick Records to direct us, we shall find no Period, since we were known to live under a regular Form of Government, more memorable for the Variety of surprizing and important Incidents, or accompanied with more legible Marks of a Divine Superintendency, than what the Author of the following Life has undertaken to relate. And as it has been thought a common Act of Justice in all Parts of the World, I may say the Barbarous, as well as the more civiliz'd, to celebrate the Memory of those who have perform'd any extraordinary and meritorious Actions in their Service; so brave and generous a People as the* English *must necessarily be pleas'd with an History intending to do Honour to one of the greatest Ornaments and Supports of the* English *Nation; and to whose Merit it is owing nnder the good Providence of* GOD, *that we now subsist as a Nation, governed by our own Laws, under a Limited Monarchy, which is the most excellent Form of Goverment, and best a-*

dapted

PREFACE. iii

dapted to the Genius of the People; that his present Majesty, for his Royal Relation to the Family then restor'd, now possesses the Crown; and that we enjoy the Benefit of his Administration, with the Prospect of a Succession of Kings, of his Race, to set upon his Throne to latest Posterity. A Consideration, one would think, sufficient to endear the Memory of GENERAL MONK *to some of his most inveterate Enemies; at least to deter them from shewing their Malice to him, because it will at the same time discover a Disaffection, where they pretend the most inflam'd Zeal.*

I do not mean that a bare Design of honouring the Memory of GENERAL MONK, *is sufficient to to recommend every Narrative of his Life. To approve a Design of that Nature to the Taste of the present Age, it must be well and happily executed: And I dare presume to say, that every impartial Reader, allowing for some Variations in the Phraseology of our Biographer from the modern Diction, will allow, that he has acquitted himself not only as a Man of Probity, but as an elegant, and especially as a most clear and methodical Writer, and one that was as a Master of his Subject.*

Yet it cannot be deny'd, whatever Justice this Author has done to the Memory of GENERAL MONK, *or how much soever the* English *Nation is indebted to that great Man, he has met with most injurious Treatement; and, as it will appear in the Sequal of this Preface, some Authors of Credit and Distinction in the World, have not been altogether so tender of his Reputation, as might have been expected from the general Character of their Probity and Candor.*

In Reference to several of his gallant Actions, the Notoriety whereof was too evident to be deny'd

the

the Merit of them has yet been ascrib'd to indirect and ignoble Motives; to the Direction and Influence of a particular Providence, without allowing any Thing to him, as an intelligent and free Agent, voluntarily concurring with the Divine Will; and, as the most extraordinary Instance of their Envy, even to the Direction of those very subordinate Persons, who were manifestly the Creatures of his Power and Interest, and entirely directed by him. I am sensible, and so was the GENERAL *himself, how much was owing to the over-ruling Hand of* GOD, *that the wisest of human Counsels were not equal to a Success so very wonderful and unexpected, and that the Wisdom and Advice of those Persons who were admitted into the Secrecy of his Counsels, though those were but very few, were of Use to him? but I can see no Reason for supposing him the Property of his Assistants, or merely passive to an irresistible Direction of Providence; any more than I can agree in Opinion with my Lord* Clarendon, That it would be Glory enough to his Memory, to have been such an unwilling Instrument.

They, who have been averse to any Impressions to his Advantage, have been very forward to credit, and propagate the most groundless Insinuations. Ludlow (*whom yet I would not be thought to include among my Authors of Probity and Candor*) *charges* GENERAL MONK *with making it a Condition of his restoring the King, that his Majesty should* give him the Lieutenancy of *Ireland. And yet in another Place he says,* The General promis'd to restore the King without any Conditions at all; *assigning this extraordinary Reason for it, that he was in Hopes* by not articling to have the better Terms. *Whereas if he had really intended to ca-*

pitulate

PREFACE.

pitulate with the King, he could hardly have ask'd any thing, besides the Crown it self, or something very prejudicial to the Dignity of it, which his Majesty would not have granted.

But the most popular and odious Charge which has been brought against the GENERAL, is that of Dissimulation and Insincerity: And, to aggravate it, nothing has been omitted which the common Places upon these Heads could supply. To make good his Charge, *it is said* he had a secret Intention to bring in the King, while he was in the Interest of the Common-wealth; *but then again, to deprive him of the Credit and Reward of such an Intention, they labour as industriously to prove, that* he intended no such thing.

But though it may be thought a sufficient Answer to the Enemies of GENERAL MONK, that they are so contradictory and inconsistent in their Charge against him; may there not yet be some Difficulty in accounting for his Conduct, to Persons more equally dispos'd to form a Judgment of it? What Proof have we that he had a real Intention to restore the King? Or, if he had such an Intention, how shall we reconcile his Dissembling, after the manner he is acknowledged to have done, to the strict Rules of Honour, or Moral Vertue.

I shall answer to these Questions, first, in more general Observations; and then particularly, in a Recapitulation of the most considerable and important Passages of his Conduct.

Concerning the GENERAL's Inclinations and Intentions towards the Restoration, the learned World has been very much divided in their Opinion; more, I think, than they needed to have been in a Matter where the Evidence is so clear and strong.
Some

Some ascribe the Origin of his Loyal Purposes to the Resentment of a Disgrace put upon him by the Parliament, wherein it was moved, and debated, whether he should answer for the Peace concluded between him and O Neal, *General of the* Irish *Rebels. This Opinion, tho' it blemishes his Designs with a dishonourable Motive, yet gives them a much earlier Date than others are willing to allow.* Mr. Echard *says indeffinitely,* That his Intentions to settle the general Quiet of the Land were very early, and that he all along fram'd his Designs suitable to the Opportunities that were given him. *My Lord* Clarendon *represents him as* entirely devoted to the Person and Fortunes of *Cromwel,* otherwise better inclin'd to serve the King, than any Man in Power of the three Kingdoms; but not to have taken up any settled Purpose or Resolution of restoring him; till about the Time of the Conference between the *General* and Sir *John Greenvil*; and that he was then forc'd upon that sudden Resolution by the impetuous Torrent of Loyalty, which had almost overflow'd the Nation, or was gradually led into it by a Concurrence of unforeseen Accidents.

Now that the GENERAL *did intend to restore the King, and fram'd his Measures suitable to such a Design, tho' it has been, and is still represented as a Question of great Uncertainty, yet, the several Circumstances of his Conduct being distinctly consider'd, we may collect Evidence enough to prove it highly probable; as probable as we could suppose it to be, if he did really proceed upon such an Intention.*

His Concurrence and Engagements with Oliver, *and the Common-wealth Party, all his Arts of Concealment and Caution, which have been objected against his having any Intention towards the Restoration,*

PREFACE.

tion, were absolutely necessary to the effecting it. He could never have been in any Capacity of serving his Majesty, without continuing his Power and Interest with his Enemies, nor have maintain'd himself in Power without those Compliances. And is it not very unreasonable, when he us'd all the proper and necessary Measures which could possibly have restor'd the King, to turn all those Measures into Arguments to prove that he really did not intend it? Is it not a more just Way of reasoning, to conclude from his uniform and regular Conduct, in the same manner as we must suppose him to have conducted himself, upon the Supposition of his intending the Restoration, that he really did intend, what he prosecuted seemingly by such probable Means, and at last really effected?

My Lord Clarendon *has observ'd, and frequently repeated the Observation, as if he laid a great* **Stress** *upon it,* That they could never draw from him any plain and open Declaration, that he never gave any publick Proof of his having this End in View. *But to make the* GENERAL *some Amends for this groundless Objection, he has himself most effectually answer'd it, by confessing, that* it was happy for the King he never did discover his Intentions, because such a Discovery must necessarily have destroy'd the Design. *His Silence, where Silence was necessary can never be drawn into an Argument. And it is the same Thing as to the other Objections commonly urg'd,* his frequent Declarations both publick and private; *and above all,* his advising the Parliament to use all proper Means to prevent the King's Restoration. *They were necessary Artifices to conceal his Design, and therefore can never carry any Proof of his not having had such an Intention. The particular Circumstances*

cumstances of his *Conduct* I have reserved for a distinct *Consideration*; at present I am arguing from the *Concessions* of his Enemies, who grant, that if the GENERAL intended to restore the King, he took the most probable, if not the only possible Methods of doing it. *And I desire the Reader, as he peruses the History, carefully to weigh the several Steps of his Proceedings, and endeavour to contrive any other more probable, or indeed possible Means. I have impartially try'd the Experiment myself, and the Result has been in favour of the* GENERAL.

But it may, perhaps, be more difficult to reconcile some Parts of his Conduct to the strict Rules of Simplicity and godly Sincerity: *In particular his Dissimulation with the Party whose Interest he seem'd to espouse, under whom he certainly served.*

As much as I honour the Memory of GENERAL MONK, *and as great an Inclination as I really have to favour his Character, in pure Gratitude for his most extraordinary Services to my Country, I must have that Regard to my own Character, whose proper Office it is to assert Truth as laid down in the most authentick Rule of it, the Gospel, as not to disserve the Cause of Virtue, by favouring a loose Morality. I willingly therefore allow, that Dissimulation, especially Dissimulation in so many repeated Instances of it, is immoral, and unworthy the Dignity of a Man. But then where a Person was an Instrument of so much Good, where there appeared to be a particular Designation of Providence to make him that happy Instrument, and there was no visible Prospect of effecting our Deliverance by any other Hand, let us not preclude him from the common Allowances, which have been usually*

made

PREFACE.

made to Heroes, by whose Means any great Revolutions have been wrought for the Benefit of Mankind, tho' every Step taken in order to accomplish them, could not be perfectly justify'd.

Nay, I may. challenge the most virulent Adversaries of the GENERAL, *to instance in any Revolution, how glorious soever in their own Judgment of it, where the like Arts of Dissimulation have not been used, tho' perhaps neither upon Motives more incontestably good, nor for Ends more necessary and beneficial to the State.*

Why then should GENERAL MONK *be singled out as the only Person to whom no Quarter is to be given, because he conducted himself by the same political Maxims which some of the most celebrated Heroes of Antiquity, whether recorded in profane or sacred History, would have made no Scruple of, if we may judge from the History of their Actions under the like Circumstances.*

I am not at all surpriz'd to find Ludlow, *and other hot* Republicans, *precipitated from a height of Power and Greatness, and expos'd to the just Indignation of an injur'd Prince,* and *of a long abus'd and oppress'd People, inclin'd, at any Rate, to traduce the great Instrument of their Ruin and Infamy. Neither are we to wonder, if we still find Men of rigid* Republican *Principles, equally violent in their Expressions of Rage and Malice against the Hand which pull'd down their beloved Idol of Anarchy and Confusion. Of these Malignants I can only desire, that they would be consistent with* common *Sense, and not affect to recommend themselves to the Favour of a* King, *or his* Ministers, *by the Defence of such Principles and Practices, as are utterly destructive of* Monarchy *in general. But from all true* Englishmen, *from the*

Friends

Friends of our happy Constitution in Church and State, the Restorer of Religious and Civil Liberties may demand a Readiness, an Alacrity, in celebrating his undoubted Virtues, a favourable Construction of what is doubtful, and the Forgiveness of what is criminal in his Conduct.

How far he is capable of being defended from the Charge of Hypocrisy and Dissimulation, will appear more distinctly upon a Review of his History. However, some general Remarks may here be made to his Advantage.

Though he was sometimes more free than Christian Simplicity will justify, (though not more than the Necessity of his Affairs requir'd) in his Professions of Affection to their Cause; yet several of his Declarations and Promises are express'd in ambiguous Terms, and capable of another Sense than what they understood him in. Particularly when he profess'd, that he did not intend to set up a single Person, *but to settle the* Nation upon Commonwealth Principles; *it was so far true, that he did not intend* immediately *and* directly to restore the King, *but to restore a* free and full Parliament, *and to have the Restoration of the King the immediate Act of the* Nation, *of the whole* Nation *by their Representatives.*

Where his Expressions are too strong and full to be softened by a charitable Construction, some Allowance ought to be made on Account of his unhappy Circumstances, by which he was cast among a Set of People, whom he neither lov'd, nor could trust, as Dr. Skinner *observes; and whom he look'd upon as common Villains and Robbers, who had no manner of Right to the strict and rigid Observance of Truth from him. I am not now considering whether he was a good Casuist: I only observe*

PREFACE. xi

obferve, in Vindication of his Sincerity, that he feem'd to act upon Principle ; upon an Opinion, which I allow to be erroneous, that he might take greater Liberties in impofing upon them, by Reafon of their having forfeited their Right to an open and ingenuous Treatment.

That he was not naturally of a collufive and treacherous Temper, appears from the reft of his Behaviour, and from undeniable Teftimonies. My Lord Clarendon * *confeffes*, That throughout his whole Life he was never fufpected of Diffimulation. Dr. † Skinner *takes particular Notice, upon the Occafion of his going to the* King *at* Oxford, *to clear himfelf from a Sufpicion of Difloyalty, that the Lord* Hawley, *then Governor of* Briftol, took his Parole of Honour, knowing him to be a Perfon of Integrity, and that would not falfify his Word. *Plainnefs in his Dealing, and a certain Franknefs in his Behaviour, were fo much his proper Character, that he obtain'd among the Soldiers the vulgar, but honourable Title of* Honeft George. *And it cannot efcape the Notice of the moft negligent Obferver, how different his Carriage was to thofe whom he thought to carry honeft Purpofes, and to thofe Rebels, who had ufurp'd and tyrannically abus'd the Royal Authority; how great and uneafy a Reftraint his Behaviour towards the latter was upon his natural Temper. And which, I think, is an undeniable Confirmation of his acting upon a fettled Principle, tho' a miftaken one, in his fallacious Conduct towards*

---

* Vol. III. 8vo. p. 700. † p. 23. Sect. 8.

the Common-wealth; though he did not scruple to make Declarations and Promises repugnant to his real Sentiments and Intentions, he absolutely refus'd ever to abjure the King *or* Monarchy, *when the Abjuration-Oath was tender'd to him as a Test of his Affection; and when the Refusal of it much endanger'd not only his Interest, his Commission, and thereby his whole Scheme, but his Life too; an undeniable Argument, both of his conscientious Regard to the Sacredness of an Oath, and of his loyal Intentions. It does not indeed appear that he ever took any Oath at all, but the* Covenant, *which declar'd expresly for the* King *and* Monarchy. *Dr.* Gumble *questions whether he took even That; but an Author of* * *good Credit affirms it. A scurrilous Writer without a Name,* † *pretends to give us the Copies of several Letters, wherein the General calls* GOD *to witness in the same solemn Manner as in an Oath. But Anonymous Authors have but little Credit in Matters of Fact, the Truth of which depends upon their own Veracity. He does not tell us how he came by those Letters, where they may be seen, or how the World is to be satisfy'd of the Faithfulness of his Transcripts; only that they were before him, whether upon the Table, or in his Imagination, we are left to the Liberty of a Conjecture. If we judge from the Character of the* * *suppos'd Author, who made no scruple of falsifying the sacred Writings, or from his Design, which was to vilify a great Man by the Comparison of a perjur'd Villain, we may imagine he would form a Character to his Purpose.*

---

* Whitlock. † The Art of Restoring. * Toland.

PREFACE. xiii

It is certain that the GENERAL *did write several Letters, both from* Coldstream *to the* Juncto, *and afterwards from* London *to the Army and Garrisons, and that in those Letters he did dissemble his real Intention; but that he did it in a manner as solemn and sacred as an Oath, and yet that in a Time of the greatest Danger, he should refuse an Oath, it is the most absurd Supposition.*

I have been particular upon this Charge of Dissimulation, because it has been aggravated with a particular Industry, and received with an uncommon Credulity. Neither can I yet leave it without observing, to the eternal Infamy of his Accusers, that these religious Pretenders to Simplicity *and* godly Sincerity, *who represent* GENERAL MONK *as a Person wholly abandon'd, for departing sometimes from the strict Rules of them, though driven to that Necessity by their Rebellion against their* King *and* Country, *did not scruple themselves to falsify the most solemn Oaths and Engagements to both.* Ludlow *in particular had taken the Covenant, which oblig'd him to declare for the* King *and* Monarchy, *and at the same time was a notorious* Republican; *and boasted of it as the greatest Glory of his Life, that he was one of the* King's *Judges.*

I have argued hitherto upon the Supposition, that GENERAL MONK *was as deep in the Republican Schemes, as he has been maliciously represented by some, and implicity believed by others, to have been. But the Matter of Fact appeared otherwise to those who had the best Oppertunities of knowing the Truth of it. Dr.* Skinner

* *says*

* *says very justly*, that he was unlickily cast among those People, rather by his ill Fate, than any Choice of his own, but was still especially careful to keep himself from their greater Guilts. *Which is agreeable to what the* GENERAL *profess'd to Sir* John Greenvil, *That* his Heart and Affections were always true; and tho' he had been passive to some of their Directions, yet he neither had, nor would act by them in Prejudice to the real Interest of the King. *Dr.* Gumble *and Dr.* Price, *who attended him during the most exceptionable Part of his Conduct, assert, That* he never acted directly against any Persons who had the King's Commission. *The King himself so far acquitted him as to declare, That* GENERAL MONK had no Malice against him, nor had done any thing but what he could easily forgive: *The manner of which Expression at least imports, that he was not* deep *in the Projects of the Common-wealth, or that he was free from their* greater *Guilts. And in a Letter from* Breda *to the* GENERAL, *dated* May 20. *before the Restoration, he has this remarkable Passage :* I must ever acknowledge your extraordinary Affection to me and your discreet Conduct of this great Work, in which you have had to do with Persons of such different Humours, and contrary Affections, which you have wonderfully compos'd.
†.

My Lord Clarendon *also, in a Letter to Dr.* Barwick, *expresses a different Opinion of* GENERAL MONK's *Conduct from what he had enter-*

---

* Pag. 62. Sect. 9.
† Life of Dr. *Barwick*, p. 438.

PREFACE.

tain'd before. Says he, The Prospect of your Affairs looks very well towards us; and I am perſuaded that MONK will appear to have acted like a ſober Man †. *The Original of this Letter, under my Lord's own Hand, Mr. Bedford, who publiſhed that Life in* Latin, *and is now preparing a Tranſlation of it, by Subſcription, has in his Cuſtody. My Lord, in ſome preceding Letters, had complained of the* GENERAL'*s Conduct for being ſo myſterious and unintelligible*; *and in his Hiſtory he ſpeaks of it with the ſame Uncertainty and Doubt*; *rather giving an Account of the various Reports and Imaginations of others about the* GENERAL'*s Intention, than any ſettled Opinion of his own. But towards the Dawn of the Reſtoration, his Purpoſes began to be more clear and manifeſt from his Proceedings, while the Wiſdom and Regularity of his Proceedings appear'd equally clear from his Purpoſes. So that I hope, for the future, after ſo fair a Confeſſion, upon better Information, and a clearer Inſight into* GENERAL MONK'*s Deſigns, my Lord* Clarendon's *Authority will be no longer inſiſted upon. His Lordſhip has been ſo juſt to the* GENERAL, *as to acknowledge his own Conviction*; *and whoever has been miſled by his Doubts or Miſinformation, ought to follow his generous and ingenuous Example.*

I come now to make ſome particular Remarks upon the principal Stages, and moſt important Actions GENRAL MONK; *which I belive will ſtill give a better Light into his Character and Deſigns.*

---

† p. 427.

It

*It ought in the first Place to be remember'd, tho'
it be sufficiently known, that* GENERA MONK
was of Royal *Extraction, descended from the
Blood of the* Plantagenets, *and educated in a Family for many Generations eminent for their Loyalty to the Crown, and their Affection to the
Church of of* England; *under the Influence of
whose Instructions and Example, he must needs
have imbib'd early, and therefore lasting, Impressions of Duty and Allegiance to his King and Country.*

*With these inbred Sentiments and Inclinations
he went, at the Age of twenty one, into the Service of the* States *of* Holland, *where he continued
ten Years. Which Circumstance of his Life my
Lord* Clarendon *turns to his Disadvantage, insinuating that he then contracted a settled Affection for their Form of Government, which might
incline him afterwards the more readily to come
into the Plan of the Common-wealth in* England: *Notwithstanding he left their Service for
ill Usage, and how unlikely it is, that unjust
Administration, especially such Instances of it as
reflect any Dishonour or Injury upon our selves,
should give a Biass in Favour of a Government.*

*And if to the Affronts he receiv'd from the
Common-wealth in* Holland, *we add the Experience he had, for several Years, of the fatal Effects of that Government in* England, *more expensive in its Taxes, and in its Administration
more oppressive and injurious to the Rights and
Liberties of the People, than ever* Monarchy *had
been, under the most arbitrary of its Kings; we
can hardly imagine that* GENERAL MONK *should
so far have defac'd the yearly Impressions of his
Youth,*

PREFACE.

Youth, so wholly forgot his Obligations to this Crown, and the miserable Confusions wherein the Republick *had involv'd the Nation, as to desire the Continuance of it. So that I wonder my Lord* Clarendon *should draw any Consequences from the* GENERAL's *Residence in* Holland, *for a Proof of his Affection to* Republican *Principles, in Opposition to so many stronger Circumstances inclining him to prefer* Monarchy.

Upon his Return from Holland, *he was employ'd in the Expedition against the* Scots, *having been recommended to that Employment by the Earl of* Leicester, *as a Person of known Affection to the Interest of his Majesty; and he acquitted himself therein with much Honour and Fidelity.*

A Peace being concluded with those infamous Rebels, very dishonourable to the English *Nation, and such as gave Encouragement to a new Rebellion in* Ireland; *the Earl of* Leicester, *who was nominated by the King and Parliament, to the Lieutenancy of that Kingdom, made him Colonel of his own Regiment; in which Employment he still preserved the Character of a loyal and dutiful Subject, and for his eminent Services against those Rebels, was thought worthy of the Government of* Dublin.

Upon a Cessation of Arms with the Irish, *his Majesty recall'd the* English *Forces to his Assistance against a more dangerous Rebellion at home. Several Officers belonging to these Regiments, were suspected of an Inclination to serve the Parliament against the King. Among the rest was* GENERAL MONK, *who, upon his Arrival at* Bristol, *by Order from the Secretary of State, was secured, and sent to the King at* Oxford.

xviii The EDITOR's

This is the first Ground of Distrust concerning GENERAL MONK's *Loyalty; which my Lord* * Clarendon, *who never was thought partial to his Character, ascribes* " *rather to the want of Bitterness in his Discourses against the Parliament, than to any Inclination towards them.*" *Dr.* Skinner † *imputes it,* "*to his being one of the Earl of* Leicester's *own Officers, in particular Trust and Confidence with him.*" *If I may be allow'd the Liberty of a Conjecture in this Matter, the true Reason of his Disgrace might be this: The Successes of the Parliament's Forces in* England *had oblig'd the King to recall those Forces from* Ireland; *which was a Step, irregular in Strictness of Law, tho' apprehended necessary to his own Safety; he having before agreed to an Act of Parliament, whereby the Commons were empower'd to prosecute that War, and himself oblig'd not to make Peace without the Consent of Parliament. The Earl therefore being nominated to the Lieutenancy by the immediate Authority of the Parliament, it was natural enough for the Court to fear the Earl and his Officers, might still look upon themselves as the Servants of the Parliament, by Virtue of the foremention'd Act.*

But whatever were the Grounds of the King's Distrust; upon Mr. Monk's *Appearance before the King at* Oxford, *his Majesty was so entirely satisfy'd, that he made him Major-General to the* Irish *Brigade then commanded down to* Cheshire. *A Circumstance wherein my Lord* Clarendon * *is mistaken; for he represents him as going thither*

---

* Vol. III. pag. 699.   † Chap. 2. Sect. 7.   * Vol. III. p. 700.

only

PREFACE. xix

only in Quality of a Voluntier, his own Regiment having been dispos'd of.

In this Expedition he was taken Prisoner, and committed to the Tower; *where he continu'd till the Conclusion of the War between the King and Parliament, notwithstanding the great Hardships he suffer'd in his Imprisonment, and the many inviting Offers from the Parliament, if he would engage in their Cause. My Lord* Clarendon's *Testimony in this Case is very honourable to him:*
" He was no sooner in the Tower, than the Lord
" Lisle, who had great Kindness for him, and
" good Interest in the Parliament, with much Im-
" portunity endeavour'd to persuade him to take a
" Commission in that Service, and offer'd him a
" Command superior to what he had ever had be-
" fore; which he positively and disdainfully refu-
" sed to accept, tho' the Streights he suffer'd in
" Prison were very great, and he thought himself
" neglected, that there was no Care taken for his
" Exchange, nor Money sent for his Support."

The Truth of this Account, which my Lord Clarendon *here gives of the* GENERAL's *hard Circumstances during his Confinement in the* Tower, *and the great Desire he had to be releas'd from it, is confirm'd by a* LETTER *from the* GENERAL *to his Elder Brother: This* LETTER *is now in the Possession of Sir* Nicholas Morrice, *and a Friend of his and mine, procur'd me a Copy of it.*

A LETTER *from* GENERAL MONK *to his Elder Brother,* THOMAS MONK, *Esq.*

" I Wrote unto you by Captain *Bley*, in which
" LETTER, I did desire you to send me
" some Money: I have receiv'd Fifty Pounds
" by

"by your Order long since, for which I return
"you many Thanks. My Necessities are such,
"that they enforce me to intreat you to furnish
"me with Fifty Pounds more, as soon as pos-
"sible you may, and you shall very much oblige
"me in it. I shall intreat you to be mindful of me,
"concerning my Exchange, for, I doubt, all my
"Friends have forgotten me. I earnestly in-
"treat you therefore, if it lies in your Power,
"to remember me concerning my Liberty; and
"so, in haste, I rest,

From the Tower, *this*   *Your Faithful Brother*
6th *of* November.
1644.

and Servant,

GEORGE MONK.

Does this Conduct agree with the same noble Historian's Opinion in another Place, of which I have already taken notice, that he contracted an Inclination to a Common-wealth during his Residence in *Holland? Or rather is it not an undeniable Instance of an unshaken and immoveable Attachment to the Royal Cause?*

When the War was at an End, and the King himself a Prisoner, the whole Power of the Nation in the Hands of the Parliament, and no Possibility of doing his Majesty any Service in England, *the Lord* Lisle *prevail'd upon him to serve in* Ireland; *a War in which he had been engaged before, and which was agreeable to his Principles, the* Irish *being declared Enemies to* England, *and to the King, as well as to the Parliament: So that by this Expedition he did not properly serve the Parliament in Opposition to the King, but more properly the*
Nation

PREFACE. xxi

Nation in Opposition to the common Enemies of it, and by Commission from the Parliament, who were empowered by a publick Act of the Legislature, to grant Commissions for that Purpose.

So far was the GENERAL *from being conscious of any Disservice to the King from his Acceptance of that Commission, that besides his Declaration to the Bishop of* Ely, *then in the* Tower, *he told the Parliament it self,* That he was going to fight against the *Irish* Rebels, but not against the King, whom he was resolv'd never to oppose: *Whence it appears, that a positive Reserve of his Allegiance was an express Condition of his accepting the Commission, and that the Parliament comply'd with it. This remarkable Passage we meet with in the Life of Dr.* Barwick, *with relation to the Grounds of that good Man's Confidence in the* GENERAL'*s Loyalty, from what he had often heard the Bishop of* Ely *relate, as the Foundation of the same Confidence his Lordship had in him too.*

" *That that great Man, having been formerly*
" *taken Prisoner when fighting with signal Bra-*
" *very for the King, and that in no mean Post,*
" *and after a long and severe Confinement in the*
" Tower *with his Lordship, no Hopes left of*
" *recovering his Liberty,* (*the King's Cause grow-*
" *ing daily more desperate*) *when* Cromwel, *who*
" *knew his Courage and Experience in Military*
" *Affairs, had long courted him to come over to*
" *his Side, and at last offer'd him a Command in*
" *the* Irish *Service ; to obtain his Liberty, was*
" *persuaded to accept the Offer, but with this Pro-*
" *testation, that he would bear Arms against the*
" Irish *Rebels, but by no means against his King ;*
" *and when all Matters were agreed, and he was*
" *going to take leave of his Friends, he came to*
" *this*

" *this Bishop, and throwing himself at his Feet,*
" *begg'd the venerable Prelate's Benediction; bin-*
" *ding himself at the same time with this solemn*
" *Engagement, that he never would be an Enemy*
" *to the King.*

" * Nempe cum in Bello olim captus fuisset
" vir in paucis insignis Regi fortissimè dimicans,
" & squalore vinculorum in Arce Londinensi,
" juxta cum venerando Episcopo diu maceratus
" fuisset, nec ulla spes Libertatis recuperandæ,
" (rebus Regiis inndies labentibus) ipsi affulge-
" ret; diu à Cromwello, qui hominis fortitudi-
" nem, & rei Militaris peritiam probè noverat,
" in suas partes solicitatus est; tandemque ut
" Libertate suâ unà cum præfecturâ in Bello Hi-
" bernico frueretur persuasus, contra Rebelles
" Hibernicos, minimè verò contra Regem suum,
" se armaturum protestans. Cumque, jam accep-
" tis conditionibus, suis valedicturus esset, ad
" hunc † Episcopum accessit, ad cujus pedes
" provolutus, venerandi patris benedictionem
" petiit, hæc sanctè in se recipiens, Regi suo se
" hostem nunquam futurum.

An undeniable Testimony of his generous and open Dealing with the Parliament, and of his uncorrupted Fidelity to the King!

Accordingly the Writer of that Life asserts it
" *as a Fact most undoubted, that the* GENERAL
" *never fought either in* Ireland, *or* Scotland, *for*
" *his Deliverers in* England, *but employ'd all his*
" *Force against those who had formerly created the*
" *King all this Trouble and Disturbance.* * Hoc
" autem certissimum est, Virum illustrissimum

---

* Pag. 185—5.   † Dr. *Wren.*   * *Ibidem.*

" Libe-

"Liberatoribus suis in Angliâ nunquam mili-
"tâsse, vel in Hiberniâ, vel in Scotiâ; contra
"Gentes eas, quæ has Turbas Regi olim con-
"citaverant, omnem operam impendentem.

And this I conceive was the true Reason of the GENERAL'*s being so averse to any Employment in the Civil Wars at home, where he must una-voidably and directly have oppos'd his Majesty's Inte-rest, contrary to his own stedfast Resolution, and open Declaration. Neither can it remain any longer a Question, whether his being employ'd afterwards a-gainst the* Scots, "*was at his own particular De-*
"*sire and Request, or whether his good Fortune so*
"*far befriended him, as to rescue him from an*
"*Employment he so much dislik'd, that of fighting*
"*in* England;" * *tho'* Dr. Skinner *could not absolutely determine this Question.*

As a further Evidence that GENERAL MONK *chose, for his Provinces, the remoter Places of* Ireland *and* Scotland, *as judging them to be equal-ly the Enemies both of the King and Parliament, we find King* CHARLES II. *corresponding with the* GENERAL, *and directing him to those very Mea-sures he pursued, in relation to his serving in* Scotland, *where the King thought him most ca-pable of doing him effectual Service. For the Au-thor beforemention'd says,*

"After I had wrote this, his Grace, Christo-
"pher, *Duke* Albemarle, *did me the Honour to*
"*shew me a Letter written by the King, all in*
"*his own Hand, to his Grace's Father command-*
"*ing in* Scotland, *at least four Years before the*
"Restoration; *in which his Majesty earnestly ad-*
"*vis'd him to take particular Care not to suffer*

---
* Chap. 3. Sect. 15.   † Life of Dr. *Barwick.* p. 186.

"*him-*

" *himself, by any Artifice of* Cromwel's, *to be*
" *drawn out of* Scotland, *leaving him in other*
" *Things to the Direction of his own Judgment,*
" *not in the least doubtful of his Fidelity and O-*
" *bedience, when Opportunity should offer. This*
" *Letter he preserv'd among his most valuable*
" *Treasures; yet seems to have wrote no Answer*
" *to it, thinking it much better, and in that dan-*
" *gerous Conjuncture by all Means safer, to an-*
" *swer by some Heroick Undertaking, than by bare*
" *empty Words; yet from this profound and per-*
" *petual Silence, those Doubts I have mention'd*
" *above, without all peradventure, had their*
" *Rise.*

" Postquam hæc scripseram, illustrissimus Prin-
" ceps Christophorus Dux Albemarliæ ostende-
" re mihi Literas dignatus est, ad patrem suum,
" in Scotiâ imperantem, quadriennio saltem an-
" te Regnum restituum à Serenissimo Rege da-
" tas, & Regiâ manu exaratas, in quibus serio
" monuit, ut Vir illustrissimus id unice curaret,
" ne se Cromwelli Artibus è Scotiâ divelli pate-
" retur; cætera de ejus fide atque obsequio, quâ
" datâ opportunitate, præstando minime dubius.
" Has ille Literas inter lectissima κειμήλεια re-
" posuit; scribenti tamen nihil rescripsisse visus est;
" omnino satius, & in isto Rerum discrimine
" omnino tutius existimans, Heroico aliquo faci-
" nore, quam nudis & jejunis verbis respondere.
" Ex hâc tamen altâ & perpetuâ taciturnitate,
" dubia illa, de quibus supra diximus, procul
" omni dubio ortum sortiebantur.

*From the Tenor and Date of this Letter, there
is no room to doubt, but it was the very same which
is publish'd in the Appendix to* Dr. Barwick's *Life,*
No. I. *as it was communicated to the Editor by*
Sir

Sir Hans Sloan, *and had been transcrib'd by him from the Original in the Duke of* Albemarle's *Cabinet, in these Words:*

Collen, Aug. 12. 1655.

ONE who believes, he knows your Nature and Inclinations, very well assures me, that notwithstanding all ill Accidents and Misfortunes, you retain still your *old* Affection to me, and resolve to express it upon the seasonable Opportunity; which is as much as I look for from you. We must all patiently wait for that Opportunity, which may be offer'd soonner than we expect: When it is, let it find you ready; and in the meanTime have a care to keep yourself out of their Hands, who know the Hurt you can do them in a good Conjuncture; and can never but suspect your Affection to be, as I am confident it is, towards

Your, &c.
CHARLES REX.

To return to the Connection of our History: The GENERAL *came from his last Expedition in* Ireland *in* 1649, *and was out of all Employment till* 1650, *when the Scots enter'd into a Treaty with King* CHARLES II. *for restoring him to his Kingdom of* Scotland.

In the Expedition of Cromwel *against the Scots,* GENERAL MONK *accepted a Commission. And how difficult soever it may seem, at first Sight, to reconcile his opposing the Scots, who were endeavouring to restore the King, with his former Resolutions,*

lutions, That he never would oppose the King, yet *he might have very good Reasons to justify himself in that Part of his Conduct*; at least his declining any further Service under them, *from his Return to* England, *to the breaking out of this War, plainly shews it to be so in his Opinion.*

In my Judgment neither Dr. Gumble, *nor Dr.* Skinner *do Justice to the* GENERAL, *in giving the following Reasons for his engaging in this Expedition:* 1. The Rebellion and Insolence of the *Scots* against King CHARLES I. *and,* 2. Their perfidious treatment of himself in *Ireland*. Dr. Skinner *had taken notice before, that when the* Scots *enter'd into this Treaty with his Majesty, it* was concluded upon such Terms as *Goths* and *Vandals* would have been asham'd to offer to an hereditary Prince. *As the Motives to their Insurrection were an Impatience under the Government of* Independency, *and an intemperate Zeal for the* Presbyterian Model; *the Establishment of which both in* Scotland *and* England, *first induc'd them to take up Arms against their Sovereign: So they intended to restore their Religion, by making* That *Establishment a necessary Condition of restoring the* King. *I have not Time to recapitulate the Particulars of their religious Pretences, and Treachery, from the first Tumults in the Reign of* CHARLES I. *to the Death of that excellent Prince: But a Person so well acquainted with that People as* GENERAL MONK, *had too much Reason to conclude, they would not restore his Majesty upon honourable Terms. My Lord* * Clarendon *tells us,* "They were so careful in modelling this Army

---

* Page 375. Vol. III.

which

" which they had rais'd, that they suffer'd few or
" no Officers, or common Soldiers, who had been in
" the Engagement of Duke Hamilton, or who gave
" the least Occasion to be suspected to wish well to
" the King, to be receiv'd into their Service."
And when they were totally defeated by Cromwel,
the noble Historian * assures us, the King thought
it a Matter of Triumph, and the greatest Happiness that could befall him, *in that* he had thereby lost so great a Body of his Enemies; who, if they had prevail'd, would have shut him up in Prison. *In short, it was an Army neither rais'd nor govern'd by the* King: *They were not properly his Subjects, but he rather subject to them, being oblig'd to receive, instead of having the Power to give Laws. The Restoration they chiefly aim'd at was, that of their* Spiritual Dominion. *The* Royal Cause *was only the Pretence, as being apprehended a Means subservient to it. In what Light this Matter will appear to the Reader, I know not; to me it seems very clear, that the* Scots *would not have restor'd the* King *upon such Conditions as were consistent with the Dignity and Prerogative of the Crown, and the Rights and Liberties of the People; and that the Government could not have been settled upon any lasting Foundation by a foreign Force, much less by a Nation so obnoxious to the* English, *and so devoted to their own particular Interests, as the* Scots *were at that Time.*

The Parliament *having entirely reduc'd* Scotland, *resov'd upon an Act of* Coalition, *for uniting both Kingdoms into one Common-wealth.* GENE-

---

* Page 377.

RAL MONK *was one of the Commissioners sent down to* Scotland *to negotiate this Business: Which being intended as a Design, not only against the* King's *personal Interest, but to extirpate Monarchy out of that Kingdom, it may be wondred at, that if the* GENERAL *carry'd any good Inclinations towards the* King, *or Kingly Government, he should be concern'd in so wicked a Scheme.*

It is very difficult, at this Distance of Time, and upon an imperfect Knowledge of Circumstances, to form a Judgment of all the Motives and Reasons upon which the GENERAL *acted in every Part of his Conduct. The Urgency and Necessity of certain critical Conjunctures might oblige him to some Measures, which, for want of knowing the true Situation Things were then in, do now carry the Appearance of quite different Purposes, than those whereby he really govern'd himself. This, however, we may affirm with some Certainty, that the* **Danger** *of resisting the Importunities of the Party must have been great; that his Interest among them would have been impair'd, if not wholly destroy'd, and, by that Means, all future Power of serving the* King, *entirely lost; that they could have effected their Design without his Assistance: Very probably too the* GENERAL *might not think their Measures would prove effectual to the wicked Purposes intended by them. But after all, we must not argue from one single Passage of a Man's Life, in Opposition to the general Tenor of it, but account for the more ambiguous Parts whereof it is composed, by those which are plain and indisputable. Since therefore we have found him so very vigilant in what related to the* King's *Interests, so studious to avoid all Occasions of disserving him, we ought to conclude in Favour of his good and ge-*

neral

neral Intentions, *notwithstanding the Appearance of some few particular Instances (if such could really be assign'd) to the contrary.*

In 1655, *upon another Insurrection in* Scotland, GENERAL MONK *went thither again, and in a little Time compos'd those Disturbances. My Observations upon the last Expedition into that Kingdom, will sufficiently obviate any Inferences which may be drawn from hence.*

From this Time to the Message from the **KING** *to the* GENERAL *by Mr* Monk, *there is little which requires any Animadversions*; *only I shall wipe off an Imputation of Cruelty during his Administration in* Scotland. *My Lord* Clarendon * *terms it a* Rod of Iron, *and a* Yoke very grievous to the whole Nation; *an Expression which implies every Thing that is ignoble, tyrannical, and oppressive. But how shall we reconcile these Representations to what he says in another* † *Place,* " *That he,* (GENERAL MONK) " *had exercis'd no other Power over them* " *than was absolutely necessary to reduce that Peo-* " *ple to an entire Obedience*; *and that in all his o-* " *ther Carriage towards them he was friendly and* " *companionable*; *and as he was feared by the No-* " *bility, and hated by the Clergy, so he was not* " *unbelov'd by the common People, who receiv'd* " *more Justice, and less Oppression from him, than* " *they had been accustom'd to, under their own* " *Lords.*" Dr. Skinner's *Account of this Matter will be seen at* Chap. 3. Section 19. *and more at large at* Sect. 4, 7, 8. *of* Chap. *VII*; *with whom* Dr. Gumble *agrees.*

I shall now attend Mr. Monk, *the Clergyman, with his Majesty's Message to the* GENERAL, *and*

---

* Pag. 467. 555. † Page 702.

see what Disposition it found him in, and what Reception is met with from him.

My Lord Clarendon * *says*, "That the GENERAL *dismiss'd* him (his Brother) "without discovering to him any Inclination to the Business he came about." The ninth Chapter of the following Sheets gives a *satisfactory Account* of this *Transaction*, and a full Confutation of my Lord Clarendon's Opinion concerning it. A Declaration for a free and a full Parliament was immediately drawn up, and *sign'd* by the GENERAL *and his Officers*, (though *suppress'd* afterwards, upon the Defeat of Sir George Booth) *in the same Stile with that of Sir* George, *and the Lord* Fairfax, *without any mention made of the* King, *or Monarchy*; *and we may as well conclude from their Silence and Caution, as from the* GENERAL'S, *that they intended no more than they expresly declar'd.* And here it was that the GENERAL *seems to have form'd the particular Scheme for the Restoration, by reducing the* Military Power *to the Obedience of the Civil, which he so successfully executed, and which alone could have succeeded.* They were so afraid of uniting his Majesty's Enemies by an open Declaration for him, that in Sir George Booth's *Insurrection*, the first Appearance was only of such Persons as had not been engag'd on the King's side. † *Whereas the* GENERAL *was continually filling up his Army with Persons of known Affection to the* King. And Dr. Barwick tells us, in his Brother's Life, p. 149. "That in reforming the Officers of his Army, the GENERAL chose the rather to employ Colonel Cloberry, be-

---

* Page 702. † Skinner, Chap. 9. Sect. 1.

cause

PREFACE.

" *cause he knew him to be in the King's Interest,*
" *and that Mr.* Otway *(afterwards Sir* John)
" *Brother-in-Law to that Colonel, and most inti-*
" *mately concern'd with him in the Prosecution of*
" *that Interest, was so well assur'd of this, that*
" *when almost every one else despair'd of the Royal*
" *Cause, he had still great Hopes in the General,*
" *purely upon this Account.*" Illud saltem unum judicium ab eo captabat Otwayus animi in Regem minimè malevoli, cùm cæteri ferè omnes de rerum summa desperarent; quod Cloburii Operâ & Consilio ad eliminandos ab Exercitu Duces omnes, de quorum fide meritò dubitabat, eò libentius uteretur, quò hominem rei Regiæ studiosiorem noverat. *And if from this Time, we find him more frequent and warm in his Letters, his Conferences, his publick Speeches and Declarations, for the Commonwealth, it was because all his Actions and Proceedings began now to speak more plainly and openly for the* King

To prevent a Restoration, of which the several Enemies to it were apprehensive, from the Temper and Disposition of the Body of the Nation, and from the manifest Tendency of GENERAL MONK'S *Proceedings, notwithstanding his artful Disguises to conceal it; among other Stratagems employ'd by them to frustrate his Purposes, they made him an Offer, first, of the Palace and Estate of* Hampton-Court, *and then of the Government itself. Dr.* Skinner *seems* * *to think they were not in earnest in their Compliment, but meant it only as a secret Contrivance to ruin the* GENERAL ; *for which Opinion the Doctor does not assign any Reason, nei-*

---

* Pag. 277. Sect. 8.

ther am I capable of proposing a satisfactory one. For however bigotted they might be to their Republican *Schemes, which I am apt to think was owing to the Consideration of their own Safety, more than to the Conviction of their Judgment; or how averse soever they might be to the personal Interest of the* GENERAL; *the main Point they then aim'd at was, to prevent the Restoration of a Family they had so much injur'd and provok'd, and from whom their own guilty Conscience could expect nothing but a just Revenge. The* King *was to be kept out upon any Terms; the several Interests and Factions among themselves, and the united Wishes of the rest of the Nation were such, that they could not think of any probable Means of excluding him, but by the Advancement of* GENERAL MONK. *Upon this View, which was truly the State of the Case, it was necessary to their Interest, (the Principle which actuated and govern'd all their Measures) to augment his Power. No doubt Sir* Arthur Hazlerig *knew the Sentiments of the Party, when he offer'd to procure a hundred thousand Hands that should subscribe to his Title. So terrifying were the Apprehensions of another Person; so great the* GENERAL'S *Interest, that, had he not been so faithful a Subject, he might, to all human Appearance, with very little Difficulty, have assumed the Name and Power of a* King. *Concerning the Time of this Offer to the* GENERAL, *there is a Disagreement between my Lord* Clarendon *and the rest of our Historians; the one making it antecedent, the other subsequent to Sir* John Greenvil's *Application to him.* * *But the common Account, as it is the truest, so it seems to be most to the Honour of the* GENERAL'S *Refusal. My Lord* Cla-

---

* Clar. p. 734, 5.

PREFACE. xxxiii

rendon *is also mistaken in a material Circumstance relating to the Conference between Sir* John *and the* GENERAL; *who*, when Sir *John* came to him, after he had solemnly conjur'd him to Secrecy, upon the Peril of his Life, told him, he meant to send him to the King* *. *The* GENERAL *is here represented as first proposing the Business to Sir* John; *whereas Sir* John *with great Difficulty, by the Interest of Mr.* Morrice, *gain'd Access to the* GENERAL, *and boldly declar'd his Commission, without any other Encouragement to use that Freedom, than what he had drawn from the* GENERAL'*s Measures, whose Caution was so great that he did not think it safe to reveal a Secret of so much Danger to himself, and to the Success of his Designs, till Sir* John *had shewn himself, by an extraordinary Instance of Prudence and Courage, a Person fit to be trusted with such a Secret. A Mistake which diminishes the Glory due to the Character of that Excellent Person, and the noble Part he acted; and gives my Lord* Clarendon *an Occasion to make an Observation equally injurious to the Modesty and Humility of the* GENERAL; *that, as soon as he determin'd to advance the Design, he consulted how he might manage it in such a manner, before the Meeting of the Parliament, that what followed might be imputed to his Counsels and Contrivance* †. *My Lord* Clarendon *indeed has related the Conduct of* GENERAL MONK, *throughout the whole Affair of the Restoration, with less Accuracy and Clearness than was usual with that noble and excellent Historian. The Reason of which I hinted at before; that* here

---

* p. 735. † Pag. 734

C

he

he wrote at a *Distance from the Scene of Action*, and from the confus'd *Informations*, if not arbitrary *Conjectures* of other *People*, and upon *Things* wherein the *Person*, who is the *Subject* of the *Narration*, studiously conceal'd his *Proceedings*, and *Motives* from the *Knowledge* of the *World*. I have lately seen a memorable *Passage* in some *Remarks* upon our English *History*, *That when Sir* John Greenvil *return'd to the King with* GENERAL MONK's *Answer to his Majesty's Letter*; *the* GENERAL *enjoin'd him to conceal the Knowledge of their Conference from Chancellor* Hyde.

Having mention'd GENERAL MONK's *Refusal* of such great *Offers*, it gives me a proper *Occasion* to take notice of the *Malice*, or *Ignorance* of those, who resolve his *Part in the Restoration* into Self-interest, or Self-preservation.

He was in so much *Credit* with all *Parties*, by the *Reputation* of his extraordinary *Wisdom* and *Courage*, and the *Command* of an *Army* affectionately devoted to him, that he could at any *Time* have united himself to either of them upon his own *Terms*, whether in respect to *Honour*, to *Power*, or *Riches*. By *Overtures* of this kind, which he was continually sollicited to accept, he might have been secure of greater *Advantages*, than were even possible for the King to grant. Could he expect the *Royal Palace* and *Estate* of Hampton-Court, the *Authority* which Cromwel enjoy'd, the *Title* of King *from the* KING? *And* yet all these were offered him, and offer'd directly, to prevent his adhering to the King's *Interest*.

But if he went over to the King, as they represent, upon the *Prospect of a better Bargain*, how did he so resolutely decline any *Bargain* at all? If *Interest* was

the

PREFACE. xxxv

the Motive to his Loyalty, undoubtedly 'twas his Interest to secure to himself and Friends the Advantages he propos'd, by an express Stipulation. Is it natural or customary for selfish Men to prefer a precarious and uncertain Reward, to one that is determinate and secure? Especially considering, that Services have generally a larger Value set upon them, when wanted, than after they are effected. Nothing can be conceiv'd more generous and disinterested than the GENERAL's entire Confidence in the Honour and Goodness of the King; nothing a greater Argument of Innocence, and a real and habitual Affection to the King's Service. Guilt is always distrustful; and if the GENERAL's own Conscience had accus'd him as much as some others have done, he would have been more careful, upon the Return to his Duty, to have secur'd the Pardon of his former Disloyalty, or at least, the Reward of his growing Services.

And for the Motive of Self-preservation; this Pretence, if possible, is still more unreasonable than the former, having indeed no manner of Foundation. For the GENERAL always had it in his Power to prevent the Restoration, without any Danger or Difficulty. When he modell'd his Army in Scotland, instead of giving Umbrage to their Jealousy of him, by putting in Persons, in their Language, disaffected, could he not as easily have found others of different Inclinations? When he was at Coldstream, and Lambert marching against him with a much superior Force, could he not have concluded a safe and Advantageous Peace, instead of running the Hazard of a total Defeat? And after he came to London, instead of dissolving the Juncto, and calling a new Parliament, the

Inclinations

Inclinations of which he could easily guess at, could he not have remov'd their Suspicions, and prevented their Attempts upon his Life, by joining with them, and the Forces commanded by Fleetwood? *The Difficulty and Danger of attempting the Restoration, is urged as an Argument against* GENERAL MONK'*s intending it, while they make the Restoration the safest thing he could think of. But how to make out the Necessity of doing a thing in order to our Preservation, which is attended with the greatest Difficulties, and the most imminent Dangers, does not, I confess, appear clear to my Apprehension, and cannot, I believe, be naturally accounted for by any other Person.*

There is one Imputation more, respecting the good Intentions of GENERAL MONK *towards the* King'*s Return, which a learned and worthy Person, Mr.* Echard, *has thought worth transcribing at large from Mr.* Lock *into his History. I wish he had thought it worth a particular Consideration, and not have* left *it wholly to the* Judgment of the Reader; *since every Reader is not attentive enough, nor otherwise qualified to make a true Judgment of a Matter of Fact, where so many Circumstances are to be compar'd, in order to judge with Certainty concerning the Probability, or Improbability of it. The same Justice and Tenderness are due to the Character of deceased Persons, which were owing to their Reputation when living; and if an Historian inserts any Relation, either upon the Credit of common Fame, or the Authority of any Writer, which obscures the Glory of a great and good Action; it should be mention'd with all its Circumstances of Credibili-*

ty

PREFACE. xxxvii

ty and Incredibility, for fear an indolent, an inaccurate, or ignorant Reader should believe and propagate it, upon the bare Credit of the Person by whom it is related; it being very natural for the World to conclude, that a judicious and candid Person would not relate any thing to the disadvantage of an eminent Character, especially without declaring his disbelief of it, if he thought it incredible. Nay, I cannot but consider this Rule as more particularly binding upon an Historian; because if he does an Injury, he does a more lasting and irreparable one, by transmitting it to distant Ages; and injures not only the Reputation of him who is immediately affected by it, but is an Enemy to the publick Good of Society, by weakening the Force of those Motives and Incitements to Virtue, whereof Mankind are generally most sensible. And I will venture to say further, that this Observation concerns an Historian whom I have lately mention'd, as much as any Historian, whose deserv'd Reputation for Diligence, Candor, Capacity, and Fidelity will be so likely to give Weight and Authority to the Facts he reports.

But there is one Circumstance which does not perfectly agree with the Neutrality Mr. Echard *professes in this Matter. Immediately after the Relation of it, he says,* This gave the great Turn to the Restoration of King *Charles. And in the* Index, *under* Ashley Cooper *I find this general Head,* The main Instrument of the Restoration; *referring, for the Particulars, to this Story of Mr.* Lock. *From whence I conclude, that Mr.* Echard *thought Sir* Anthony *the main Instrument of the Restoration, and that he grounded his Opinion upon the Evidence of this Story; which is not*

leaving

leaving it wholly to the Judgment of the Reader, *but giving his own Judgment, and declaring his Belief of it. If I have injur'd this worthy Gentleman's Meaning, I heartily ask his Pardon: But I can understand it in no other Sense.*

The Story which I am going to examine, may be seen in Mr. Lock's *Memoirs of Sir* Anthony Ashley Cooper, *afterwards created Lord* Shaftsbury, *or in Mr.* Echard's * *History. It is too long to be transcrib'd here, but the Substance of it is thus:*

" That General Monk's *Wife overheard him*
" *making an Agreement with the* French *Ambas-*
" *sador, to take the Government upon himself, up-*
" *on the Assurance of Assistance from* France;
" *that she sent Sir* Anthony Ashley Cooper *im-*
" *mediate Notice of it, who summoned the* Coun-
" cil of State, *whereof he was one; That Sir* An-
" thony *skilfully, and by distant Intimations,*
" *charg'd the General with it, who discover'd, by*
" *some Disorders and Confusion in his Looks, that*
" *he was guilty; and so disappointed him in his*
" *Design, by proposing such Alterations in the*
" *Army, as made it cease to be at his Devo-*
" *tion.*"

I only desire the following Circumstances to be considered; and then I shall be very willing, with Mr. Echard, *to leave the Determination of the Case to the* Judgment of the Reader.

In the first Place, Mr. Echard *observes, that* this Account is singular, *being taken Notice of by no other Writer but Mr.* Lock, *nor attested*

Page 758. Third Edition.

by

PREFACE.

by any other Evidence; which Circumstance alone seems very much to lessen the Credibility of the Fact. The GENERAL *is said to have been so confounded in the Council, when Sir* Anthony *charg'd him with it, that* all the Company were convinced some foul Play was intended, though they did not then particularly know what the Matter was; *that Sir* Anthony *laid hold of this Opportunity to propose, what the* GENERAL *under those Difficulties found himself oblig'd to consent to,* so great a Change of the Army, that it ceas'd to be at *Monk*'s Devotion, and was put into Hands that would not serve him in the Design. *Now it is at all probable that so remarkable a thing should happen, that such sudden and great Changes should be made in the Army, without any mention made of it in History? That none of the Council should afterwards enquire more particularly into the Occasion of them, when they saw, by the* GENERAL'*s Confusion, that it was some deep Design, at which he was then aiming? That among so many Enemies as the* GENERAL *then had, watching all Opportunities to asperse him, and so many more envious of his Glory and Power, none of them should know or publish the Fact wherewith he had been charged?*

Mr. *Echard observes further, that* Mr. Lock had this Account, probably, from the Fountain Head, *meaning my Lord* Shaftsbury. *Which, I think, is so far from being a probable Circumstance, that it carries another just Ground of Suspicion. That Lord was not absolutely free from Ambition and Opiniatrety; and this Story tended to gratify his Vanity, as it might be thought to afford a signal Proof of his Penetration and Address, in dis-*

discovering, and disconcerting the GENERAL'*s Project; which is professedly the Reason of Mr.* LOCK'*s mentioning this Story. And it likewise favour'd his Prospect of Interest at Court, as it gave him a Pretence to make a Demand upon the Crown, of some considerable Post of Honour or Profit, for so extraordinary a piece of Service.*

Much of the Probability of this Matter depends upon the Evidence of the GENERAL'*s Wife, and her Evidence in a good Measure upon her Zeal for the Restoration, which is not so clear as it ought to be, considering the Stress which is laid upon it. If I had the Liberty to use the Name of a great Man now living, I might convince the World, that she was not likely to oppose the Advancement of the* GENERAL, *when it was offer'd by the* French *Ambassador, having before shewn so much Resentment to Mr.* MORRICE *for endeavouring to persuade the* GENERAL *to refuse an Offer of the same Nature from the* Parliament.

But upon the Supposition of her violent Zeal, let us consider what her Evidence is, and how far it will go. She, from another Room, *hears the Particulars of the* Agreement *under Consideration. Now if her Affections were so warmly interested in this Matter, they must needs excite her Fears, and her Fears might naturally make her fansy she heard things which she did not, and improve some broken and imperfect Sentences in an express and positive Contract. Which is the more likely to be true, from the natural Caution of the* GENERAL, *who was not us'd to talk so loud upon such dangerous Subjects, that a Person in another Room might hear distinctly the Particulars of their Conversation; especially considering his own Quickness*

Preface. xli

of hearing, which was so exceeding perfect, that no-body could safely whisper a Secret in the same Room *.

But according to Mr. Lock's *Account the main Part of the Evidence is the Disorder and Confusion of the* General; *from whose Looks and Behaviour they argue more, than from the Authority of the Lady's Information. In answer to this, I shall only cite a Passage in* Ludlow's *Memoirs, relating to King* Charles I. *his Reception of the News of the Massacre in* Ireland. *I have it, says he, from good Hands, that the King was pleas'd with it. Now what did these good Hands found this horrid Calumny upon, but the* King's *Looks and Behaviour, observed by some who happen'd to be present at that Time? For it never was pretended, that he ever acknowledged so impious and inhuman a Pleasure: If then the Hatred of any Person or Persons towards that good Prince, whose natural Tenderness and Compassion, and whose habitual Piety render'd him so averse to Acts of Cruelty, could occasion so wide a Misconstruction of his Behaviour and Looks; may we not with more Reason allow something to the Vanity of Sir* Anthony Ashley Cooper, *or to some other Passion, or Prepossession in the rest of the Council, in the Construction of* General Monk's *Looks and Behaviour?*

In what Order of Time to place this memorable Conference, Mr. Lock *does not inform us. Mr.* Echard *relates it immediately after the Re-*

---

* *Skinner*, p. 418.

fusal

fusal of the Government *from the* Parliament. *But whether it was before or after (about that Time, no doubt, it happened, if at all) it was prior to* Sir John Greenvil's *Application to the* GENERAL, *when the* GENERAL *first own'd his Design of restoring the* King, *saving what he told* Dr. Price *privately at* Coldstream. *Now this Account of Mr.* Lock *supposes, that the* GENERAL *had given* Sir Anthony, *and the rest of the Council, Assurances of it before; which must be the Meaning of the following Words:* The General averring, that he stood firm to what he had professed to them. * *Here is an Inconsistency never to be reconcil'd, and which explains the whole Intent of this Piece of private History.* Sir Anthony *wanted to have it believ'd, that the Plan of the Restoration was laid by him, and that* GENERAL MONK, *was drawn into it by the Influence of his Councils.*

Besides these Inconsistencies, and Defects in the Evidence which is to support this Fact, the Fact itself is improbable. For though † *Mr.* Echard *calls this,* The General's greatest Temptation, *I can never believe, that a wise Man would accept of the Government from a* French *Interest, and refuse it from the* Parliament *of* England: *A People, to whom the Apprehension of a* King's *coming in, or governing by a* foreign *Power, was so dreadful, that an Attempt of that kind would have united all the several Interests in the Kingdom against the* GENERAL: *The* Republicans, *upon the Strength of their insuperable Aversion to* Monar-

---

* Page 758. † Pag. 757.

chy

PREFACE. lxiii

chy; *the* Royallifts, *in regard to their* Mafter's *Intereft. Even his own* Army *was not so united to him, or so absolutely devoted to his Intereft, but that a great Part of his Officers would have left him,* if he had taken such a Resolution; *much less was it* his Design to form an Army to an implicit Obedience to whatever Resolution he should think fit to take, *as my Lord* Clarendon * *represents it, but to a Compliance with his Measures for the* Restoration. *Otherwise how could his Regulations in the Army become, as undoubtedly they were, the avow'd Grounds of their Jealousy concerning him? How came they never to entertain the least Imagination of his having a Design to set up himself, but only from the Temper and Inclinations of his Army, which they knew to be towards another Person? Before he began his March from* Scotland, *the* Scots, *who, from their Esteem and Love for him, were the most likely to serve him in such a Design, offer'd to raise, and maintain at their own Charge, seven Thousand five hundred Men, which he refus'd to accept, tho' he was going with less than six Thousand against* Lambert, *whose Army consisted of twelve Thousand. The Reason of his refusing this seasonable Supply, in Appearance so necessary to his own Safety, and the Ends of his Ambition, if he had any such in view, can be resolved into nothing, but his extreme Caution, lest he should give Occasion to suspect, that he had any Design of employing a Foreign Assistance, whereby he might enslave the Nation, and is absolutely inconsistent*

---

* Pag. 715.

with

with the Supposition of his intending to set up himself.

Upon the whole Matter: Whatever political Reasons the GENERAL *might have for deliberating, as Mr. Echard says* * *he did, whether he should accept the Government as the Gift of the Parliament, or for seeming to comply with the same Proposal from the* French *Ambassador, according to Mr.* Lock, *(which indeed I do not believe) there is no Reason to think he intended either.*

There is another Reflection upon his Character, which is equally groundless with any of the foregoing ones, That he was in his Inclinations for Presbytery.

So far was he from being inclin'd to Presbytery, *that when he was offer'd the* Covenant, *to qualify himself for his first Commission under the Parliament, Dr.* Gumble *tells us, he consulted with many learned Men, before he could satisfy his Scruples about the Lawfulness of That Engagement, the principal Design of which was to abolish* Episcopacy. *What Encouragement he gave the* Presbyterians *a little before the* Restoration, *was wholly political, and for Reasons very obvious. The rest of his Carriage towards that People, especially in* Scotland, *where they had most Power, and thereby the best Opportunity of discovering their Principles and Temper, bespeak his Opinion of them; as also their avow'd Hatred towards him, (which my Lord* Clarendon *takes particular Notice of, in a Passage already cited in this Preface) is a Witness that they did not esteem him a Friend either to their Cause, or their Persons.*

---

* Page 757.

But

PREFACE. xlv

But in his Speech to the Juncto, *concerning the Settlement of the Kingdom, he says :* Moderate, not rigid Presbyterian Government seems best adapted to the Interest of *England.*

Occasional Arguments expressed in such loose and general Terms, are very uncertain Proofs of a Man's Sentiments. The GENERAL *was arguing upon this Occasion from* Republican *Principles ; and a* Common-wealth *in the Church, might agree well enough, perhaps, best with a* Common-Wealth *in the* State. *But a Parity of Orders in the one will not agree so well with a Subordination in the other ; nor the Discipline of a* Kirk, *with the Prerogative of a* KING. *Episcopacy, as it is most agreeable to Scripture and primitive Antiquity, so it has been, and ever will be found the best Friend to* Monarchy ; *Which is the true Reason of some Peoples dislike of it. How they mutually support and strengthen each other, and how unlikely it is, that either of them should long subsist, separately, in* England, *we learn unhappily from the Fate of* CHARLES I. *Like* Saul *and* Jonathan, *they were lovely in their Lives, and in their Deaths they were not divided.*

I shall detain the Reader no longer than while I give him a short Account of the Manuscript from whence the following Life was taken.

In the first Place, I must assure the Publick, That I have not alter'd the Sense or Expression in any one Instance throughout the History ; except that I have, in some few Places, added a Word where it was necessary to a Grammatical Construction ;

struction; and divided the Book into Chapters and Sections for the Reader's Conveniency..

The Copy was found in the Study of Mr. Owen, late Curate at Bockin in Essex. I had trac'd it up by a probable Tradition in that Neighbourhood, to Dr. Skinner, who liv'd at Colchester, and was Physician to the Duke of ALBEMARLE, when residing at New-hall in Essex. And I have since compar'd it with some of the Doctor's Bills from off the File at Colchester; and from the Similitude of Hands, I believe it to be the Doctor's own Hand-writing.

But after the greatest Part of my Copy was printed, Mr. Great, an eminent Apothecary in Colchester, was so kind as to send me another Copy, which agrees literally with mine, and was transcrib'd by Mr. Shelton, formerly Rector of St. James's in Colchester; after whose Death, it fell into the Hands of Mr. Great. I presume this Copy was transcrib'd, by the Author's own Direction, for the Press, because it has his Name, the Title, the Year, the Place, and Printer's Name to it, which mine had not. However it demonstrates, that this History was written by Dr. Skinner. The Reader also cannot but observe, that the Author of this History mentions his having wrote something of a like Nature, though in another Language; by which he certainly means his Motus Compositi.

Anthony Wood, in his Fasti Oxonienses, Vol. II. Pag. 189. gives the following Account of Dr. Skinner.

" *Thomas*

PREFACE. lxvii

"*Thomas Skinner* of St. *John*'s College, *Oxford*, was actually created Doctor of Physick, by Virtue of the Letters of the Chancellor of the University, which say, that he was for some Time bred at *Cambridge*; but was forc'd to leave that University in the Times of Usurpation, by Reason of the illegal Oaths, and other Impositions offered to him, whereby he was prevented taking his Degree. And this Doctor hath added a third *Latin* Part, which he calls *Motus Compositi*; afterwards translated into *English* by another Hand, with a Preface by a Person of Quality."

There is a Collection of Papers referred to at Pag. 333. which I never could get any Account of.

The Epitaph upon the Duke of ALBEMARLE *was printed by itself a little after his Death, and being out of Print, I have subjoyn'd it to his History, hoping it may be acceptable to the Reader.*

Feb. 13. 172$\frac{2}{3}$.
Hind-Court,
Fleetstreet.

William Webster.

THE

THE
AUTHOR's
PREFACE.

 HAVE heretofore published something of a like Nature with the following Sheets, (tho' in another Language) wherein several Things, thro' want of better Information, were imperfectly described; yet the fair and charitable Reception it met with from the Readers, has not only encouraged me to entertain them again with the ensuing Relation, but has equally oblig'd me to make them some Amends by a more correct and enlarg'd

enlarg'd Account of those things, concerning which I was then either mistaken or defective.

YET if any Man thinks he has Reason to admire at my Attempt in writing the Life and Actions of the late Duke of *Albemarle*, I shall meet him with a juster Wonder, that this Province had not been undertaken by some other Hand; and that whilst the Lives of several less considerable or subordinate Persons have been deservedly written, we find so little († except an hasty and loose Account published to serve a private Occasion) recorded of this great *Instaurator*. But whilst some (by the Benefit of his Prudence and Success) have had so great Leisure, and others so great Obligations, the History and Actions of this illustrious Person have (for ten Years since his Death) lain altogether neglected, and passed over in Silence.

THIS Disregard towards his Memory does loudly arraign the Ingratitude of this Age, and is a sort of new Fanaticism, successive to the former, which he had so fortunately suppress'd; by which we are become as much Enemies to his Glory, as the *Committee* of *Safety* or *Rump* Parliament were to his Designs, or *Scot* and *Cobbet* to his Person. Po-

---

† *The Life of General* Monk, *by Dr.* Gumble.

sterity

PREFACE.

sterity will blush and wonder, to find no other Monument of him than a stuff'd *Effigy* in a Press at *Westminster*, to whose Fame and Memory, in elder and more grateful Times, Temples and Altars would have been erected.

And now this Attempt of gathering a few rough Stones towards his Monument, being fallen to my Share, I am very sensible, that in describing the Fortune and Actions of the *Duke* of *Albemarle*, I must also encounter all his Enemies, and run over the whole Series of his Adventures again from *Colestream* to *London*: Yet whilst I am employed in this Service, I esteem my self still under the Protection of the Sword, and the wise and auspicious Conduct of that great *General*.

But that I have undertaken his History, who was never concern'd in any of his Actions, and had the Honour to know him only in the last Years of his Life; I reckon it a very little and unequal Exception against me, since I am sure no Histories have been worse written than by those who had some Share in the Actions they relate; nor better, than by others who were unconcern'd, and took their Aim at a Distance. For though the former may be presumed to have a more distinct and perfect Knowledge of things, yet such Writers have always had some body whom they fear'd to displease, and others whom they were oblig'd to dignify; besides an inseparable Humour of working in some little Actions of their own, which have scarce ever been so decently inserted, but that they have put some Shadow or Disadvantage upon the Lustre of the chief Actor. Upon this Account many are the trifling Passages of *Philip de Comines*, which would never have been mentioned by any Writer but himself, who had acted some Part in those times. And that I may not trouble the Reader with remoter Instances, the Accounts that are already extant of this great Person, whom we are now describing, and drawn by such as stood somewhat nearer to the Scene of his Actions, are (to say nothing harder) a very particular and convincing Argument, that such Persons are not always the fittest to relate them.

YET in Matters of this Nature the *Dictator Cæsar* must always be excepted, who was a very extraordinary Person at his Pen, as well as his Sword, and wrote his own Actions and Encounters as regularly as he fought them.

ON the other side, *Livy* has given us the History of the *Roman* Commonwealth and *Consulary* Times with the greater Exactness and Eloquence; and *Tacitus* has describ'd the *Imperial* Government with the deeper Judgment

PREFACE.

Judgment and Research; yet the first was coeval to the last Part of his own *Decad*, but died under the Empire: And the other was an Infant at the End of his own *Annals*, and but of Years fit to write about the Time which concludes his History: So that neither of them wrote from any particular Knowledge of their own, but both of them had a great Industry to collect Relations, an equal Judgment in chusing the best, and perhaps some particular and concealed Advantages for Information. The most steady and exemplary Writer of Lives, *Plutarch*, never saw the Faces of any of those brave *Greeks* and *Romans* whom he described, who were all in their Urns and Ashes many Years before his Time.

The History of the *Belgic* War is very justly esteemed one of the most absolute and compleat Draughts of modern Story; yet we find not, that the Author *Strada* was ever nearer *Flanders* than his College at *Rome*; but drew all those fair and exact Lines from the Letters, and Memorials, and other Informations of the Prince of *Parma*.

In which Advantage we pretend to some Parallel with that great Author, having had the Opportunity to peruse a great Part of those Papers rescued from the Fire in *London*, besides other Memorials and MSS. relating to the Time and Actions we describe. We have

have had also the Privilege of frequent and particular Discourse and Information from more Persons of Honour and Quality than were immediately concern'd or employ'd in the principal Affairs of that Age, so that the Reader may believe we have written with some convenient Light by us.

AND whereas several Passages are herein mentioned, that serve only to continue the Order and Connexion of our Story; I have not held my self oblig'd to describe them more particularly than was necessary for that End, reserving our principal Care and Exactness for those Affairs in which the Duke of *Albemarle* was most especially concern'd.

IN those Instances which the Wisdom of the State has thought fit to conceal, we have not presumed to make too near an Approach, or pry too inquisitively into the Art of Government; nor in doubtful Passages to amuse our Reader with bold and presumptuous Conjectures: But in all Particulars (reserving our Allegiance to the Supremacy of Truth) have endeavour'd to make the best of our own Age, being sure that the succeeding (when we have done all we can) will not fail to pay us home with Satire and Reflexion.

BUT though I have given my Reader some Account of such Advantages, as came in my Way for compiling this Work, and have made him privy to my Aim and Method in the
Manage-

PREFACE.

Management of it, yet I esteem my self oblig'd to acknowledge to him my many other particular Defects; and to ask Pardon of this Age, and of Posterity also, that being placed in the Vale of a low and private Life, I have adventured to draw the great Lines of a Person that stood so high; who, as he was singled out by the supreme Providence for great and extraordinary Performances; so he was certainly none of the ordinary Productions of God's Hand, but a very sublime and singular Person, fill'd with all those Qualities and Endowments, which were necessary to accomplish those great Things to which he was designed.

He had Prudence sufficient to discern or frustrate all the Arts and Contrivances of the Crafty; a Courage that was not to be encountred by the boldest Rebels, or Opposers of his Allegiance; a deliberate Patience in chusing the true Measures and Minutes of his Business; and an impregnable Silence, by which he kept himself and his Purposes in the dark to his Enemies, and left no Track behind him.

All, which, with the particular Actions of his Life, we have endeavour'd (with greater Faithfulness than Ability) to describe in the ensuing Story, that the Reader may first inform his Knowledge in the stupendous Contrivance of his Majesty's Restauration, and anew confirm his own Allegiance by so great an Example.

As to the Truth of Things, (especially in the main Point of this History) it shall be answer'd for by my self; but for my manifold Defects in the Method or Language, I must be enforc'd to lean somewhat hard upon the charitable Opinion and Indulgence of my Reader.

THE
LIFE
OF
General *MONK*.

CHAP. I.

I. *His Birth, and some Account concerning the Circumstances of his Family.* II. *The Occasion of a most base Indignity offer'd to his Father, Sir* Thomas Monk. III. *He resents it after a Manner that obliges his Father to send him sooner into* Spain *than he otherwise intended, under the Command of Sir* Richard Greenvill, *his Relation.*

tion. IV. *The next Year he goes in the Expedition to the Isle of* Rhee, *and is made an Ensign.* V. *Peace being concluded with* France, *he repairs, in the Earl of* Oxford's *Regiment, to serve in the Netherlands: Is afterwards removed under the Command of Lord* Goring, *and made Captain of his own Company.* VI. *His Conduct in that Service.* VII. *A memorable Act of Injustice done to him at* Dort; *upon which he generously throws up his Commission.* VIII. *His Return to* England *upon the first Beginning of the* Scotch *Rebellion, with the true Grounds of it.*

I. GEORGE, Duke of *Albemarle*, was born at *Potheridge* in *Devonshire* on *Tuesday* the 6th of *December*, in the Year 1608. In his Youth he was brought up at School in the Country, residing sometimes with his Father, sometimes with his Grandfather by the Mother's Side, Sir *George Smith*, who was also his *Godfather*. Being a younger Brother, and the Estate of the Family somewhat in Declension, he was designed to make his Fortune by the Sword, and to be sent to the Wars abroad, being not yet full seventeen Years of Age. To which Employment he was hasten'd somewhat sooner than his
Friends

Friends intended, by an Accident, which, though it be sufficiently known, yet, being the first publick Adventure of his Life, we will not omit the Relation of it.

KING *James* being newly dead, and the Business of the *Palatinate* growing now desperate, and the *Spanish* Match broken off, in such sort as seem'd to threaten a War with that Crown, and which was also voted in Parliament; His Majesty, *Charles* I. among other Instances of his Care, visits those Parts of his Kingdom which lay most directly opposite to *Spain*, to take a View of the Condition of his Navy, and upon that Account came as far as *Plimouth* in *Devonshire*, where the Gentry, according to their Duty, were making ready to attend him. Among the rest Sir *Thomas Monk* (who was always a very considerable Person in the publick Affairs of the County) resolv'd to be present. But knowing there were several Encumbrances left by his Father upon the Estate, and that he might be obnoxious to some Judgment or Statute against him, he first sent his Son *George* to the Under-Sheriff of the County, desiring that he might with Liberty and Freedom attend upon his Majesty, upon this publick Occasion, now entring the County: And for so great Respect shew'd him, that he would accept the Gratuity he had sent him

him by his Son. The Attorney acknowledg'd Sir *Thomas Monk*'s Desire to be at that Time very fair and reasonable, accepted the Present, and promis'd him Security. Yet, notwithstanding, afterwards he found it his Interest to arrest the Person of Sir *Thomas Monk* upon an Execution, in the most publick Place of the County where they were, at their Convenience, to receive his Majesty.

II. The Villany of this treacherous Action was not so deeply resented by Sir *Thomas* himself as by his Son *George*, insomuch that he sought out the next Opportunity to meet the Under-Sheriff at *Exeter*, where, having expostulated the Indignity of the Action, he effectually cudgel'd him for his Perfidy. The Courage of the Attorney was much at the Rate of his Honesty; but being a Retainer to the Law, he expected the Law should vindicate him; and to that End was making ready his working Tools, to reckon with the young Gentleman for the Battery.

III. This Accident led his Father to send him abroad somewhat sooner than he had intended. And the Voyage for *Cadiz* in *Spain* being then designed, he was committed to the Care of a near Relation, Sir *Richard Greenvill*, who had Command in that Expedition. This was the first Tryal he was to make of that Profession he intended to follow, and which prov'd so unlucky as might well have discourag'd a new Beginner. For the Expedition, through many Misadventures of Wind and Weather, and other unfortunate Accidents, besides a contagious Sickness in the Navy, proving unsuccesful, the Fleet return'd about the End of the Year home to *Plimouth*, and this our young Soldier with it.

IV. THE following Year began the War with *France*, upon Causes sufficiently known. And in the Expedition to the Isle of *Rhee* and *Rochel* he accompany'd Sir *John Burroughs*. In the Voyage to *Spain* he had served only as a private Soldier, but now he was made *Ensign* in this Voyage to the Isle of *Rhee*; it is not easy to say which were greater, the Misfortunes of the *English*, or their Courage. But in less than two Years time the *Rochellers*, for whose Sake the War was undertaken, submitting to their own King, and the Crowns of *England* and *France*, by the Mediation of the State of *Venice*, coming to an Agreement, he came back from *Rhee* 1628. and the next Year (being now 21 Years of Age) he went into the *Low-Countries*.

V. ENGLAND being now at Peace with her Neighbours, and having no Occasion for Men of the Sword, the Ensign *Monk* betook
himself

himself to the great Seminary of War and warlike Men, the *United Provinces*, where he was first entertained in the Regiment of the Earl of *Oxford:* And after some Years was remov'd into the Command of the Lord *Goring*, and made Captain of his own Company, not being yet arrived to the 30th Year of his Age.

VI. IN this Service he did not, like a young Captain, retain his Commission as a Warrant for Luxury and Extravagance, but in earnest minded the Business of a Soldier, informing himself duly in all the Methods and Arts of War, being present at most of the great Actions that happen'd, during his almost ten Years Continuance in that Employment.

VII. IN the last Year of his Service to that State (the Business of the Summer being over) he had his Winter Quarters assign'd him at *Dort:* Where there happen'd a Difference between him and the *Burghers*, upon this Occasion. Some of his Soldiers had committed Disorders in the Town, for which he was ready and severe enough to have punished them according to Martial Discipline. But the imperious *Burgher-Masters* would take the Business under their own Cognizance, pretending they could allow no Authority in their own Liberties equal to, or distinct from their own.

own. And this proceeded at last to so great a Quarrel, that the Matter was brought to the Hearing of the Prince of *Orange:* Who, though he had lately, in the same Instance, given his Judgment for Sir *Richard Cave,* yet was now so far prevail'd upon to favour rather the Authority of the *Burghers;* and Captain *Monk* was forc'd to exchange his Quarters at *Dort* for worse in a meaner Place. The Circumstances of this ill Usage so greatly disoblig'd him, who, under a plain and moderate Behaviour, carry'd great and generous Spirits; that he quickly after threw up his Commission, disdaining to expose himself any longer in the Service of an ingrateful Commonwealth.

VIII. From *Holland* he return'd back to *England* about the 30th Year of his Age, about the Time that the first *Scotch* War began. A War never to be remembred without Horror and Detestation, as being the Prelude, by the Success and Advantage of it, to the Rebellion in *Ireland,* and to the long and bloody Civil War that presently after followed in *England.* This Rebellion in *Scotland* was fomented by some of the *Nobility* of the Kingdom, to avoid refunding back to the Church the Lands they had in the Minority of King *James* alienated; by the insolent *Clergy,* to withdraw themselves from Subjection to their *Bishops;* and by the *People,*
through

16 *The LIFE of*

through a certain Sottishness of Nature, and a deprav'd Education. From *France* it was supported by the Cardinal *Richlieu*, who sent private Emissaries over, to advise and encourage them, and thereby was revenged on King *Charles* I. for aiding the *Rochellers*. From *England* it had the Approbation and good Wishes of all the *Puritans* and *Nonconformists*, who abetted the Dissensions of *Scotland*, as a Support to the Common Cause, or a Place, if there might be Occasion, of Retreat.

CHAP. II.

I. *He is made Lieutenant-Colonel in the Expedition against the Rebels in* Scotland; *his Conduct and Bravery in that Expedition.* II. *A Treaty at* Rippon *with the* Scots, *too favourable and advantageous to those Rebels.* III. *Earl of* Leicester *made Lord Lieutenant of* Ireland. IV. *Lieutenant-Colonel* Monk *attends him thither, and is made Colonel of his own Regiment.* V. *His Services against the Rebels about* Dublin, *recommend him to the Government of that City.* VI. *The Incursion of the* Scots *into* England. VII. *Which caused a Cessation with the*
Irish

Irish *Rebels, and obliged the King to recall the* English *Army to his Assistance.* VIII. *Colonel* Monk *returns with them, but is suspected, as being the Earl of* Leicester's *Colonel, to favour the Parliament; and, upon that Suspicion, ordered to be secured at* Bristol: *Lord* Hawley, *Governor of that Place, permits him to go upon his Parole to the King at* Oxford, *to whom he is introduc'd by Lord* Digby. IX. *The King, in regard to the great Reputation which he had acquired in the Army, admits him to a private Conference with his Majesty.* X. *His Opinion concerning the State of the King's Army there, which he declares to the King, who makes him Major General to the* Irish *Brigade. He is taken Prisoner by Sir* Thomas Fairfax. *A Character of Sir* Thomas. *And of how great Importance Major General* Monk *was thought by the Parliament, who remove him from* Hull *to the Tower of* London. XI. *His Father, Sir* Thomas Monk, *dies, and leaves him an Annuity. Obstacles to his Release from his Imprisonment.* XII. *The King privately sends him a* 100l. XIII. *The Parliament proposed, by his long Imprisonment, to gain him over to their Side. A favourable Occasion for his Enlargement.* XIV. *The Motives upon which he accepted a*

C *Commission*

Commission to serve against the Rebels in Ireland, *under the Lord* Lisle, *with whom he return'd to* England.

I. CAPTAIN *Monk* had, by his long Stay in the *Netherland*'s War, brought home the Reputation of a good Soldier; and at the Recommendation of the Earl of *Leicester*, to whom he was ally'd, was placed Lieutenant Colonel to the Regiment of the Earl of *Newport*, who was then General of the Ordnance. Both those Northern Expeditions had but little Action in them. But at *Newborn*, after the *Scots* pressed hard upon his Quarters, with very few Men, and less Ammunition, he so lined the Hedges with his Firelocks, and brought off the Ordnance with that Bravery and Conduct, that none of all the *Scotch* Regiments had the Courage or Confidence to impede his Retreat. And when the Earl of *Strafford*, General of the Army, moved the King, instead of treating further with such insolent Rebels, to give him Leave to charge them: Lieutenant Colonel *Monk* was one of those few that earnestly urged a Battel, and gave very good Reasons for the Security of the Event: And was many times afterwards heard to discourse it with a particular Indignation, that so brave a Force of Horse and Foot, able to have reduced a better Army than the Covenanters could raise,

and

General Monk.

and another kind of Kingdom than *Scotland*, should be so basely betrayed and baffled by those, who had their Influence upon, or betrayed the Counsels of the late King.

II. But this War ending at last in a Treaty begun at *Rippon*, with so much Advantage to the Covenanters; who, for this their *Scotch* Rebellion, were paid with *English* Money, pardon'd and caress'd by the King and Generals, thank'd by their Party in *England*; the great Success thereof gave new Encouragement to the long-design'd Rebellion in *Ireland* to break out, *October* 23, 1641. Which was the more confidently attempted by the Death of the great Earl of *Strafford*, then seasonably destroy'd by the Malice of a Faction, whose Power and Policy was only dreadful to the *Irish*.

III. To obviate these growing Evils in *Ireland*, the Earl of *Leicester* was both by King and Parliament (then sitting) agreed upon as a fit Person to succeed in the Lieutenancy of that Kingdom, after the Death of the late Earl of *Strafford*: And Forces also were voted to be rais'd in *England* for the War.

IV. In this Service Lieutenant Colonel *Monk* was appointed by the Earl of *Leicester* to be Colonel of his own Regiment, which, with the other Forces, was not sent
into

into *Ireland* for some while after. All those Supplies were much retarded, through those Jealousies which then began to arise between the King and his (then long and fatal) Parliament: So that much of the Money rais'd here for carrying on the War against the Rebels in *Ireland* was, by the Parliament, employ'd in their own Civil War in *England*. And many of the Soldiers, at first listed for *Irish* Service, were engaged in the Army of the Earl of *Essex*. But though the *English* Forces were at last sent over, yet the Earl of *Leicester* never went to his Government, discouraged either by the Fate of the Earl of *Strafford*, or the ill Condition of the *Irish* Affairs; which the War in *England*, then in Prospect, was like to make worse. The Earl of *Ormond* was in the interim appointed by him Lieutenant General of the *English* Army in his Absence, and his Commission was also confirm'd by the King.

V. AGAINST this Rebellion, which was so far advanc'd before the March of the *English* Aids, Colonel *Monk* did very good Service in and about *Dublin*: Insomuch as the Lords Justices thought him to be the fittest Man to be Governor of that City.

VI. BUT whilst Colonel *Monk*, and those other Forces in *Ireland*, were strenuously
carrying

carrying on the War against the Rebels there, the Civil War in *England* between the King and Parliament began, and had so far prevailed with some Advantage on the King's Side, that the Parliament began to think of calling in the Aid of the *Scots*, who, some while after, very readily trussed up their Trinkets and Covenant, and in Shoals came marching into *England*, zealous for their Common Cause and Plunder. To balance in 1643 some Measure this foreign Aid from *Scotland*, his Majesty was enforced, by the Counsel of Necessity, to assent to a Cessation with the *Irish* Rebels, and recall the *English* Army to his own Assistance at home, some whereof were landed at *West-Chester*, others at *Bristol*.

VII. WITH these Officers and Regiments Colonel *Monk*, according to his Duty, returned also into *England*. But at the Return of these Regiments the more loyal Party in the Kingdom had some Distrust of the Earl's Officers, and particularly of Colonel *Monk*, being his own Colonel, so that it was suspected at his Return into *England*, he would rather serve the Parliament than the King. At his Arrival therefore at *Bristol*, there were Orders sent from the Marquiss of *Ormond*, and from the Lord *Digby*, then Secretary of State at *Oxford*, directed to the Lord *Hawley*,

ley, who was then Governor of *Bristol*, to secure Colonel *Monk* till further Order. Upon his Arrival the Lord *Hawley* acquainted Colonel *Monk* with the Order he had receiv'd. Colonel *Monk* represented to him the unjust and malicious Suspicion that had been upon him; that he was return'd into *England* with no other Resolution but to serve his Majesty.

VIII. The Lord *Hawley* was so well acquainted with Colonel *Monk*, that he knew him to be a Person not only of Courage, but of Integrity and Honesty, and that would not falsify his Word: So that instead of securing him at *Bristol*, his Lordship took his Parole to go directly to the King at *Oxford*, and sent Letters by him to the Lord *Digby*, Secretary of State; who was so well satisfy'd concerning him, that he introduced him to his Majesty in the Lodgings at *Christ-Church*.

IX. By this time Colonel *Monk*, through his long Service in the *Netherland*'s War, and his Action upon the *Scots*, and now of late against the *Irish*, brought with him to *Oxford* the Reputation of an extraordinary Courage and Conduct: Insomuch as his Majesty then thought it worth the Time to have some private Conference with him, in order to the Prosecution of the War.

X. Colo-

X. Colonel *Monk*, in his short Stay at *Oxford*, had quickly observed the Condition of the King's Army there, that they were Men of Courage and Bravery enough, but the Discipline was much more remiss than he had observed in the Armies abroad. Thereupon he took the Boldness to tell his Majesty, that a less Army under greater Discipline, would be sufficient to manage the War, and that the only Way to make his Army superior to his Enemies was, to equal them in military Discipline. His Majesty could better discern the Defects in his Forces than amend them at present; but there was so much Reason and Truth in what Colonel *Monk* had discours'd, that it pleas'd his *Majesty* to command him into *Chester*. And because upon the former Suspicion of him, his Regiment was already given to Colonel *Warren* that had been his Major; his Majesty was pleas'd to entrust him with a Commission to be Major General to the *Irish* Brigade. At his Arrival there he found the Lord *Byron*, who commanded in Chief over the *Irish* Regiments, had besieged *Nantwitch*, then garrison'd for the Parliament. To whose Relief Sir *Thomas Fairfax*, who, for his Courage and Experience, was certainly the best Man at Arms in the Parliament's Service, made such haste out of *Yorkshire*, as he wholly surpriz'd the *Irish* Brigades, raised the

the Siege, and, among other Officers, took Colonel *Monk* Prisoner, and for the present secured him in *Hull*. The Value of this Person could no more be conceal'd from the Parliament than it had been from the King. His Courage against the *Scots*, and how roundly he had gone to work with the Rebels in *Ireland*, were too late Actions to be presently forgot. And besides, Sir *Thomas Fairfax*, who had the Fortune to surprize him, and several other *Low-Country* Officers in the Parliament Service, had known him very well abroad, and made their Masters quickly understand that Colonel *Monk* was a Man worth the making. The Parliament therefore (who had resolved not hastily to exchange him) commanded his removal from *Hull*, and secured him in the Tower of *London*.

XI. AND here begins the passive Scene of this Gentleman's Life, without which Ingredient, no eminent Virtue was ever raised in the World. He had brought little with him into *England*, except his Sword and his Liberty, and now he has lost both. The Parliament had provided him House-room, which he would have thank'd them to have kept for themselves; but for his other Accommodations, he was enforc'd to be his own Steward. Some while before his Confinement, and to make his Prison the more easy to him, his Father, the good old Knight, Sir *Thomas Monk*

General Monk.

Monk, died, 1643. leaving him, a younger Brother, (according to the Custom of *England* in the best Families) a small Annuity for his Life, which, in the Commotions of that County, at so great a Distance, was ill paid him; his elder Brother, who had the Estate, being on the King's Side engaged in the War, which before this Time had reach'd as far as the remoter Counties of *Devon* and *Cornwall*. By these Accidents he was prevented of seasonable Supplies from his Relations. And his Interest at *Oxfotd* (where he made a short Stay) was not such that he could expect to be suddenly enlarged by an Exchange; there being so many other Officers and Persons of Quality in the same Condition with himself, who had powerful Friends at Court, that expected to be released before him. Nor was it easy to offer such a Person in Exchange for him as the Parliament would be willing to accept.

XII. But the Character that was receiv'd of him, and those small Conferences he had with the King at *Oxford*, had left so fair an Impression of him in his Majesty's Mind, that when he could not procure Colonel *Monk's* Liberty, he was careful to provide for his Support; and to that purpose there was secretly convey'd to him an hundred Pounds in Gold, at a Time when such a Sum was a

greater

greater Matter in his Majesty's Coffers, than in many of his meaner Subjects. And this so seasonable and indulgent Bounty of the King towards him, he has been often heard to mention with a very tender and sensible Gratitude.

XIII. DURING his Imprisonment in the Tower, most of the great Actions of the Civil War were over, and their greater Battles fought, as at *Marston-Moor*, *Newbery*, and *Naseby*, which made Colonel *Monk*'s Confinement so much the more uneasy to him, who was in the Flower of his Age, and thirsty after Glory. But it pleased God, who had design'd him for another Purpose, to rescue him from those Services. Yet whilst he was a Prisoner in the Tower he wanted not many and good Offers for his Enlargement, upon Acceptance of a Commission to serve the Parliament; which was the Design of driving a Bargain with him, by so long and close a Confinement, who yet kept up Hopes of procuring his Liberty upon better Terms, continuing still to solicit his Exchange, by the small Interest he had at *Oxford*. But having at last spent almost four Years Time in a long and tedious Confinement, through many Wants and Destitution of things necessary to his Person and Quality, and the impairing of his Health; and having no Hopes or Prospect of returning again to *Oxford*, there fell out a very seasonable Opportunity for his Enlargement, upon this Occasion.

XIV. THE Marquiss of *Ormond*, (who at first was appointed Lieutenant General in the Absence of the Earl of *Leicester*) declaring wholly for the King in *Ireland*, without any Regard to the Parliament at *Westminster*, so far displeas'd them, that they voted the Lord *Lisle*, eldest Son to the Earl of *Leicester*, to take the Government of that Kingdom. His Lordship presently thinks upon his Kinsman, Colonel *Monk*, in the Tower, and offers him a Commission under him. He had been (as we related before) Colonel to the Earl of *Leicester*'s own Regiment in *Ireland*, and therefore was the more willing to take the same Commission from his Son. Besides, he had been particularly oblig'd to that Family, for some seasonable Kindness and Supply, during his late Imprisonment in the Tower. In this War he had been engaged before, and it was very agreeable to his Principles and Conscience. The King also and Parliament, who at this time could agree in nothing else, did jointly vote the *Irish* then in Arms, to be Rebels. And Colonel *Monk* having receiv'd his Liberty for this Service, was too generous to employ it to any other Use. But before he quitted the Tower, he took Leave of several of his Fellow-Prisoners, with whom he was acquainted, and, among the rest, of the Bishop of *Ely*, Dr. *Wren*, from whom he requested his episcopal Blessing; telling him, he was now going to do the King the best Service he could against the Rebels in *Ireland*, and hoped he should one Day do him further Service in *England*. All which, with the Circumstances of it, has been several times attested by that Reverend and Pious Prelate, in the hearing of many great and illustrious Persons. Upon this he readily attended the Lord *Lisle*, who on the 28th of *January* set out from *London* towards *Ireland*. His Lordship was ordered to land at *Dublin*, but the Marquiss of *Ormond* having received no Command from his Majesty, to deliver up the City to him, could not give him Admission. Thereupon the Lord *Lisle* and his Forces made their Way into *Munster*, and landed near *Cork*. Very little was done by this Voyage of the Lord *Lisle* into *Ireland*. So that after two Months Stay in the Country, his Commission being expired, he set Sail *April* 17, and returned again into *England*, and Colonel *Monk* with him, who

1647 then was above 38 Years of Age.

CHAP.

CHAP. III.

I. *He is commission'd to go again into the North of* Ireland, *against those Rebels. The Difficulties he surmounted in this Province.* II. *A remarkable Instance of his Frugality, and provident Care towards the Support of his Soldiers.* III. *Upon what Reasons he concluded a Peace with* O Neal; *after which he returned into* England. IV. *It was suspected that he had express Commands from* England *to conclude that Peace.* V. *The Murther of the King.* VI. *The General, in his Return to* England, *meets* Cromwel *then going Lord Lieutenant to* Ireland. VII. *His elder Brother dies.* VIII. *He is out of all Employment.* IX. *A new Occasion of his entring upon Action.* X. Cromwel, *upon the Lord* Fairfax's *Refusal of that Employment, is made Commander in Chief against the* Scots; *who makes* Monk *Lieutenant General of the Ordnance.* XI. *The great Confidence that* Cromwel *reposed in him, and upon what Grounds.* XII. *Animadversions on the* Scotch *Clergy, and the Death of the Marquifs of* Montrofs. XIII. *A Misconduct of* Cromwel, *and the Error of it retrieved by General* Monk, *by which Means the* Scots *were defeated at* Dunbar. XIV. *The good Effects of this Victory, tho'*

in

in some Measure obstructed by the Remonstrators. XV. *The King with the* Scotch Army *goes to* Worcester, *and is pursued by* Cromwel, *who had left General* Monk *to reduce* Scotland. *His great Success there.* XVI. *He returns sick into* England. XVII. *An Act of Coalition to unite* England *and* Scotland *into one Commonwealth.* XVIII. *An Union of this kind had been projected by King* James, *at which the* Scots *were much discontented, and for what Reasons.* XIX. *General* Monk *appointed one of the Commissioners for concluding this Coalition.*

I. AT his Return Colonel *Monk* having discovered his Inclination rather to serve the Parliament in *Ireland*, than in any other Employment, some of the Members of Parliament knowing his Averseness to be employed in the Civil Wars at home, and all knowing him for his Courage and exact Discipline, a most fit Person for the *Irish* Service, they offered him a Commission to command the *British* Forces in the North of *Ireland*, which he accepts; and now takes his third Voyage into that Kingdom. In this Command he had a very nice and difficult Province: For the *Scotch* under *Monroe*, and the *English*, though conjoin'd together, did not perfectly agree or trust each other; yet

he

he kept them both in so good Order, as he effectually prosecuted the War. Much of his Business was against *Owen Roe O Neal*, a bold and restless Rebel, and accounted the best Soldier among them, having many Years served the King of *Spain*, and who had trained up the Forces under his Command, to a Courage and Resolution beyond the usual Temper of the *Irish*: Yet Colonel *Monk* look'd so narrowly after all his Goings, and kept him so short of Provision as made him weary of the War.

II. This was but a dry and barren Employment, and the Parliament at *Westminster* had too many Irons in the Fire, to take any Care of Money or Provision for an Army in the North of *Ireland*. But Colonel *Monk*, who was not only a good Soldier, but a good Husband also, so ordered the Tillage and Improvement of the Country, and providently disposed of all Booties taken from the Enemy, that he made the War support it self without much Relief from *England*.

III. All Things, through his Industry and Conduct, had succeeded so well in the North of *Ireland*, that the Parliament thought the *Scotch* Forces unnecessary in *Ulster*, and voted their Discharge home, which gave Occasion to some Jealousies and Discontents between the *English* and *Scotch* Soldiers, insomuch that Colonel *Monk* suspected *Monroe*, and the other *Scotch* Officers, to have some Design upon his Person and Liberty. At the same Time the Marquiss of *Ormond*, the Lord *Inchequin*, and divers others, coming to an Agreement, a great Part of Colonel *Monk*'s Forces revolted from him at *Dundalke*; so that he was beset with so many Difficulties, as enforced him to close up an hasty Pacification with *O Neal*, and to return into *England*.

1649

IV. But this Action, being of so transcendent a Nature, gave Occasion to many considering Persons to believe that Colonel *Monk*, being a Person of so much Honour and Courage, would not, by any Necessity whatsoever, have been brought to such an Agreement, if he had not been particularly commanded to it by his Superiors in *England*, who, being resolv'd to fall upon the Royal Party in *Ireland*, made no Scruple to clap up a Peace with the Rebels.

V. Somewhat before this, during Colonel *Monk*'s Employment in *Ireland*, was committed the execrable Murder upon the Person of the late King; an Action of so great Impudence and Villany, as can find no Parallel in past Ages, and the succeeding will as

hardly

hardly believe it. And here let me arrest my Reader with the Contemplation of the divine Wisdom, which had designed this Colonel *Monk* to be the Restorer of Monarchy, and his present Majesty; that he should at this Time, though he served the Party, be disposed of in an Employment of so much Distance and Privacy, as he could hardly know, much less be concern'd in, so great a Guilt, as was the Murther of that excellent King.

VI. In his Return home he met Lieutenant General *Cromwel*, then hastening to consummate the *Irish* War, with five Regiments of Horse, and seven of Foot. This Cessation with *O Neal* did greatly facilitate *Cromwel*'s Business, who, in less than a Year's Time, finished that War, and then hasten'd back into *England* to prosecute the other high Designs of his Ambition.

VII. About this Time his elder Brother *Thomas Monk*, Esq; dy'd by a Fall from his Horse, leaving only two Daughters behind him; and the Estate being settled upon the Issue-Male, it came to Colonel *Monk* as now Heir in Tail: who, as he had raised his Name and Family to the higher State of Nobility and Honour, so he accordingly repaired the Ruins of the Family, and advanced it to a Condition suitable to support the Greatness of its Quality.

VIII. Colonel *Monk*, after his Return out of *Ireland*, was now out of all Employment, and very well contented to have continued so; but a new War at hand brought him again into Action.

IX. After the Death of the late King, the *Scots* had enter'd into a Treaty with his present Majesty, for restoring him to his Kingdom of *Scotland*, which this Year came to a Conclusion; but upon such Terms as *Goths* and *Vandals* would have been ashamed to offer to an hereditary Prince. There was then in *Scotland* a very honest and loyal Party, that were desirous to restore him upon Conditions agreeable to their Allegiance and Duty. But the Covenanters, who were much the greater Number, having formerly made so good a Bargain by the Sale of his Father, were now driving another, almost as advantagious to them, with the Son. His landing and Reception in *Scotland* gave a smart Alarm to the Parliament at *Westminster*. They easily foresaw a War would ensue, and therefore thought it most agreeable to their Gallantry and Puissance to be the Aggressors. Whereupon they voted their Army to march Northward, and invade *Scotland*.

1650

land. And Lieutenant General *Cromwel*, having done his Business in reducing *Ireland*, was return'd to *London* as seasonably as if he had contrived it. Both he and his Party were desirous, that he might command as General in this Northern Expedition, and so consummate the Circle of his Glories, by the Conquest of *Scotland*. The Noise of a Brush with the *Scots* alarm'd all the *Presbyterian* Party, and their Clergy, in *England*, who own'd themselves obliged, by their solemn League, not to enter into War with their covenanted Brethren. And some of them, who had a great Ascendant over the Lord *Fairfax*, and also on his Lady, had so practised upon both their Consciences, that he willingly disabled himself for this Service. This Advantage was quickly discern'd, if not at first contriv'd, by *Cromwel* and his Party, who laugh'd in their Sleeves at the conscientious Qualms of the Presbyterians. And this Scruple of the Lord *Fairfax* was farther promoted in him, by the Fineness of some of the demure Independents in the House of Commons, that were in *Cromwel*'s Interest. So that in the Conclusion the Matter was so decently carry'd, that *Cromwel* was voted to the sole Command against the *Scots*.

X. Having gain'd the Authority he so long affected, his next Care was for modelling his

his Army, which indeed was made up of the Flower of the *English* Forces. About this time he had taken a particular Notice of Colonel *Monk*; and obferving how with fmall Force he had managed his Bufinefs upon the Rebels in *Ireland*, he found him an abler Officer for the *Scotch* War, than many of his own infpired Colonels. And becaufe he would by no means want his Company, he furnifhed him with an extempore Regiment drawn out of feveral others, and afterwards made him Lieutenant General of the Ordnance. Befides the Importunities of *Cromwel*, which could not fafely be deny'd, there are two things which feem the more to have inclined Colonel *Monk* to this War: One was a kind of Indignation and Prejudice fettled in him againft the Nation, ever fince their Rebellion and Infolencies againft *Charles* the Firft, in which War he had been employed. The other was the Perfidy and ill Ufage he had met with from the *Scots*, when he commanded them lately in the North of *Ireland*.

XI. To this *Scotch* Expedition he feem'd to be defign'd by the fecret Fate that governed him. For by his extraordinary Conduct and Prudence in this War, he gain'd fo upon *Cromwel*, as to be thought the only fit Perfon to be trufted with the fole Command of the Country. By which Station he became

GENERAL MONK.

at last capable of doing those great and happy things which we are afterwards to relate.

XII. The *Scots* might very well have expected this Invasion from *England*, where a great Army was always in Readiness: But their Counsels were chiefly governed by their loud and bellowing Clergy, with some other Male-contents, obtruding every Day new and insolent Conditions upon his Majesty, accusing and distinguishing Malignants, and an infinite Number of wild and endless Babble about their Covenant; so that *Cromwel* was very far advanc'd towards them, before they had brought their Army into any good Readiness. And to fill up the Measure of their Villanies with the Slavery of the Nation, the Year before they had maliciously made away the great and valiant Marquiss of *Montross*, who was accounted the best Man of Arms their Nation ever bred; whose Courage and Conduct, had he been alive and entrusted, was more than *Cromwel*'s Match, and might have sav'd their Nation.

XIII. General *Cromwel* being advanced as far as *Berwick*, kept on his Way towards *Edenburgh*, and finding the *Scots* not willing to come to a Fight, traversed his Ground back again towards *Dunbar*, the *Scotch* Army pressing somewhat hard upon his Rear.

Here he had run himself into such a Noose, for all the Cantings and *Magnificats* of his Party, as did greatly blemish his Discretion. The *Scots* were Masters of the Hill, and had coop'd the *English* Army into a narrow Neck of Land, the Sea behind them, and no Way for Retreat but by the Pass at *Coppesmyth*, then strongly possessed by the *Scots*. Now would *Cromwel* have willingly exchang'd his Command with *Fairfax*, to have been safe in his Room at *London*. But here the Experience and Conduct of Lieutenant General *Monk* help'd him at the dead Lift. For at a Council of War he moved, to make a present Assault upon the Enemy, when never an Officer there had the Courage to think of it; and undertook the Charge himself, with such Success, as ended in an entire Victory. Unless *Cromwel* had secretly corrupted the Officers of the *Scotch* Army, or those Covenanters had been the arrantest Cowards in Nature, they could not have been so shamefully routed, being almost double in Number to their Enemies, and possessed of such great Advantages upon them. But by the Fortune of this Day, the Covenant was most miserably batter'd by the *Lord of Hosts*, which was the Word given in the several Armies before the Fight began.

XIV. The

XIV. The loyal Party in *Scotland* was not greatly concern'd for this Defeat at *Dunbar*, which had chiefly cut off so many of the violent Kirk Party, that might well be spared. But it had also a farther Effect upon the rest; for it took down the Heat of the Covenanters, that they came at last to a calm Resolution of admitting all Parties, and that since they had been brought to those Streights by the Loss of *Dunbar*, it was necessary, for Defence of the Cause of God and the Kirk, to take in the Assistance of such as had serv'd the late King, and such also as had been in Duke *Hamilton*'s Army. This was the Resolution of the greater Part of the *Scots*; but was remonstrated against, as a betraying the Interest of *Jesus Christ*, and his Kirk, by a more refined sort of whining Hypocrites: And these were called the *Remonstrators*. Which Schism of the Resolutioners and Remonstrators became as natural and malicious among them, as between the *Jew* and *Samaritan* of old, or the late *Guelfs* and *Gibellins*.

XV. But by this Resolution, and that which succeeded it, his Majesty came the next Year to have an Army which he could better govern, and were more obedient to the Methods he had designed. Which, taking

1651

Advantage of *Cromwel*'s Army being pass'd over the *Frith* into *Fife*, he gave them the Go-by, and slipt into *England* by the Way of *Carlisle*, and was pursued to *Worcester* by the Body of *Cromwel*'s Army, who had left Lieutenant General *Monk* with six thousand Men, to perfect the Reduction of *Scotland*. Whether Lieutenant General *Monk* had desired this Province, of following the War in that Country, or his usual good Fortune had so far befriended him, as to rescue him from an Employment he so much disliked, *viz.* of fighting in *England*, we cannot absolutely determine. But after that *Cromwel* was marched after the King into *England*, he so warmly prosecuted the *Scots*, that after the taking of *Edenburgh* Castle, the Surrender of *Tantallon* Castle, the Rendition of *Sterling*, and the surprizing of *Dundee*, with several other considerable Places, yielding presently to the Fortune of the Victor: Such was Lieutenant General *Monk*'s Dispatch, that he had gain'd a great Part of *Scotland*, by that Time *Cromwel* had fully done his Business at *Worcester*.

XVI. But in this Summer's Expedition, Lieutenant General *Monk*, (either as an Allay to his Success, or as a Chastisement upon him for serving under such Confederates) fell into a violent Sickness, which held him all the Winter,

GENERAL MONK.   41

Winter, and reduc'd him to that Weakness, that he was enforc'd to return'd into *England* for Repair of his Health; and the following Summer he recover'd it at the *Bath*.

XVII. AND at his Return thence to *Lon-* 1652 *don*, he found the Parliament, having now conquered *Scotland*, resolved to extirpate Monarchy among the *Scots*; and, to secure their Subjection, they had framed an Act of Coalition, whereby both Nations should be united into one Commonwealth.

XVIII. A Design at which King *James* was aiming, when he altered the Royal Style, and proclaimed himself King of *Great Britain*. Great were the Discontents in *Scotland* about this Union. The loyal Party utterly declined it, in Hopes of some more fortunate Season ro restore Monarchy. And the covenanting Presbyterians equally railed against it. They had already observed the Declension of their Presbyterian Government here in *England*, and were greatly afraid, as Independency had already conquered their Country, so it would extirpate their Religion.

XIX. To settle this Union of both Nations, Commissioners were sent down, that were cunning old Grandees of the Party, and
of

of the Independent Interest. To whom Lieutenant General *Monk*, being thought to have better Knowledge of them, and Interest among them, by his late Command there, was also added: Who, though he had conquered the Nation, yet had been so fair and so honourable an Enemy, as they were persuaded to an Union by him, more than by all the Tricks and Artifices of the rest. And having at last settled the Coalition according to their Instructions, both he and they return'd to *London*.

CHAP. IV.

I. *The Power and Pride of the Parliament incline them to a War with the* Dutch. II. Blake *made Admiral, who gains some Advantages over them.* III. *The next Year* Dean *and* Monk *are made Admirals, equal in Commission.* IV. *The Zeal of the Parliament in prosecuting this War; whom, notwithstanding,* Cromwel *dissolves, and erects a Council of State, to which the Direction of military Affairs was committed.* V. *An Engagement between the two Fleets on the Coast of* Flanders, *wherein* Dean *is killed. The Presence of Mind, Bravery, and Conduct of* Monk

Monk *in that Action. He pursues the Dutch, and the next Day sinks six, and takes eleven of their Ships.* VI. *The Dutch repair their Fleet, and the next Month the* English *Fleet engaged them a third time; in which Engagement thirty of their Ships were sunk, their Vice-Admiral* Everston, *and their Admiral* Van Trump, *killed by a small Shot.* VII. *The surprising Success of this Action; upon which the States found themselves obliged to sue for Peace, with the Conditions to which they were forced to submit.*

I. NOW was the Juncto Parliament at *Westminster* come to the Meridian of their Power and Usurpation, from which they quickly after declined. They had reduc'd *Ireland*, conquer'd *Scotland*, and utterly baffled the King's Interest in *England*; which rais'd them to that Height of Pride and Confidence, that now they were resolved to reckon with their Neighbours, the States of *Holland*, for certain Insolencies they had sustained from them. Hitherto they had dissembled their Resentments for the Death of *Dorislaus*, who went to complement the *Dutch* to an Alliance to their new Commonwealth; and also the Affronts that were put upon their extraordinary Ambassadors, *Saint-John*

John and *Strickland*. Neither wanted there Complaints about Trade, which they designed to reduce by an Act for Encouragement of Navigation; succeeded with such high Demands upon the *Dutch* for Reparation of Injuries, and of settling a free Trade, &c. as the States were resolved to enter into a War, rather than make so hard a Bargain for their Peace. The Honour and Esteem of the *English* Nation was at this Time utterly lost abroad, by the bold and insolent Actions of the Commonwealth Parliament, and the astonishing Murther of the late King; so that the *Dutch* somewhat scorn'd to be first in making Alliance with so infamous a People, and did also equally despise them. Nor did they greatly like, that a Revolt from their natural Prince should thrive in other Hands, so much as it had done in their own. The *Dutch* very well remember'd, the Kings of *England*, looking on them as a trading People, had never severely inspected or stated things with them, in Matters of Profit. But now they were to deal with a coarse and scraping sort of People, that would upon occasion be quarrelling with them for their Penny, and look to their Trade with as much Concern as themselves. After a great deal of religious Tampering on both Sides, they fell at last to Blows.

II. O*n*

II. On the first Year of this War, it was managed on the Juncto's Side by their Admiral *Blake*, who, in a Fight near the *Goodwin* Sands, and afterwards near *Portland*, worsted the *Dutch* Fleet. 1652

III. Against the next Year, they had ordered General *Monk* and General *Dean*, being join'd in equal Commission, to carry on the War. This was something an odd Province for General *Monk*, who had all his Life commanded in Land Service, now in the 45th Year of his Age, to take up a new kind of Warfare at Sea. But as all Countries are alike to a wise Man, so are all Elements to the valiant. 1653

IV. The Parliament was very busy in hastening their Preparations for this War; and were so intent upon their Enemies abroad, that they overlook'd greater at home. For on *April* 23. *Oliver Cromwel*, whose Ambition could hold no longer, enter'd the House of Commons, accompanied with some of his Officers, and dissolv'd the Parliament, after their twelve Years Continuance in the Practice of such Mischiefs and Depredations, as are not easy to be recounted. But though the Parliament was at an End, the *Dutch* War went on, being managed for the present by by a Council of State, made up of some principal Officers in the Army, and some Members of the late Juncto, that were *Cromwel's* Confederates.

V. The first Engagement this Year was *June* the 2ᵈ, on the Coast of *Flanders*; the *Dutch* Fleet commanded by *Van Trump*, the Vice-Admiral *Van de Ruyter*, the two *E-vertsons*, and *De Witt*; and their Number of Ships much the greater. The *English* was led by General *Monk* and *Dean*, having *Jordan, Lawson, Goodson* with them. The Fight began very early in the Morning. At the first Shot from the *Dutch* Fleet *Dean* was kill'd, walking by the Side of General *Monk*; who at his Fall (nothing discomposed in his Mind or Looks) cast his Cloak over him, and afterwards ordered him to be carried into his Cabbin, commanding the Soldiers and Seamen to look to the Ship, and follow their Business. By ten of the Clock the Fight grew very sharp, especially between the Squadron commanded by *de Ruyter* and the Blue Squadron led by *Lawson*. To the Relief of the first *Van Trump* came in, and General *Monk* in excellent Order sailed to reinforce the other, so that now the Fight became very hot on both Sides, till three in the Afternoon, about which Time the Wind favouring the *Dutch*, they bore away before it, it, being pursued till Night by General *Monk*: Who, the next Morning, found himself nearer than he imagined to the Enemy's Fleet. Yet he could not get up to them till towards Noon, and then both Fleets engaged till ten at Night: The Wind being fresh and Westerly, General *Monk* pressed hard upon them, and sunk six of their best Ships, and two more of the *Dutch* were, through Misfortune, blown up by their own Fleet. Eleven Ships were taken that Day from the Enemy, the rest were secured, by *Van Trump*, running upon the Flats at *Dunkirk*.

VI. After this Fight General *Monk* lay upon the *Dutch* Coasts, surprising several of their Ships, and disturbing their Trade, till foul Weather drave him off their Shoars. In less than two Months time the *Dutch* had got together a very great Fleet of about one hundred twenty five Sail, which was the last Effort of their Strength and Courage. And *July* 29. both Fleets came in View of each other. General *Monk* had not above ninety odd Sail of Ships, which were all a Stern, so that till towards Evening they could not get up to come to any Engagement, which began with some of the lighter Frigats, and encreased to about thirty, and fought till the Night parted them. This was but the Prelude to the next Day's Work: For on the next

Morning

Morning early General *Monk* tack'd upon the Enemy, and a most fierce and bloody Fight began on all Hands, which continued till about three in the Afternoon. In this Battel the General, being much inferior to the Enemy in Number, had commanded the Captains to attempt to destroy or sink what Ships they could, without taking of any, whereby he should be oblig'd to weaken his Fleet, through the Absence of those that must go off with them. In this Fight were sunk of the *Dutch* Fleet near thirty Ships, among which was Vice-Admiral *Evertson*, with the Loss only of one *English* Frigat. And to consummate the Fortune and Glory of this new Admiral, in this Fight fell the brave and aged Seaman *Van Trump*, famous for many Victories, and accounted one of the best Seamen of this Age: He was kill'd by a small Shot, and dy'd like an Admiral, with his Sword in his Hand, as he was standing on the Deck of his Ship, encouraging his Men to the Fight. The Loss of so many Ships, with the Fall of their chief Commander, so discouraged the *Dutch* Fleet, that they presently made all the Sail they could, and run into the *Texel*.

VII. THEY who were at Leisure to consider the Circumstances of this Fight, have wondered at the Success of it. The *Dutch* had

had much the Odds in Number, their Ships and Men fresh; the Fight upon their Coasts; they had also Fire-Ships with them, and the *English* none. The Loss of their best Commander, and of so great a Part of their Fleet, put the States of *Holland* into such Apprehensions, and their common People into such Disorders, as they hasten'd back their Ambassadors, who were newly return'd home for further Instructions, to make such a Peace with the *English* as they could get. But the Council of State held them to hard Meat. They would abate nothing of their last Demands, made for the Common-wealth Parliament. Nothing would do except, beside striking the Flag, they made a Recognition of the *English* Sovereignty to the Narrow Seas, a Rent to be paid for the Fishery, the Trade in the *Indies* to be free, and Satisfaction for all Merchants Losses, and Reparation for the Charge of the War, and a Coalition of both Nations, to the excluding the Prince of *Orange* from any Place of Government. Great was the religious Knavery and Falshood on both Sides, and the *Dutch* had already learnt to cant and wheadle in the Gibberish of the *English* Sectaries.

CHAP. V.

I. *The little Parliament at* Westminster, *and their fanatical Projects of incorporating the seven Provinces.* II. *The Dutch Commissioners at a Loss how to treat with Men, whose Schemes and Principles appeared so very chimerical. The Design which* Cromwel *had to serve by them.* III. *Having laid them aside, he takes the Government upon himself, with the Title of* Protector; *makes several Condescensions to the* Dutch *Commissioners, towards the more effectual Seclusion of the House of* Orange *from the Power and Dignity of Stadholder.* IV. *The Articles on both Sides in Reference to this Point.* V. *The States General ashamed of it, yet, by the Advice of* De Witt, *they at last agree to it, as a secret Article, but without the Consent of the other Provinces. Upon which a Peace is concluded between* England *and* Holland, *wherein* Cromwel *sacrifices the publick Interest to the private End of his Malice and Ambition.* VI. *This Agreement opposed by General* Monk, *but to no Effect.* VII. *An Army raised in* Scotland *for the Service of the King, and by what Means their Design was frustrated.* VIII. *Yet* Cromwel, *anxious for the Success of it, and suspecting* Lilbourn's *Courage,*

who

GENERAL MONK. 51

who commanded the English *Forces there, recals General* Monk *for the* Scottish *Expedition.* IX. *General* Monk *envied. His cautious and prudent Behaviour. His great Affection for his Country.* X. *A special Reason of* Cromwel's *employing him in this Expedition, from whence he returns no more, till he is made the happy Instrument of the Restoration.* XI. *The State of* Scotland *upon his Arrival there. The Use he made of their extravagant Disputes and Disorders about Religion.*

I. WHILST this *Dutch* War and Treaty were carrying on, that pretty Machine, called the *Little Parliament,* was sitting at *Westminster.* A sort of little insipid Fops, whom *Cromwel* had set up, to make his last Step into the Government the easier. Many of these were settling a Kingdom only for *Jesus Christ* in the World, but yet so as to make themselves his Vicegerents. They look'd upon the *Dutch* as a Company of cheating, covetous Worldlings, and Enemies to the Kingdom of *Christ,* as well as that of *England,* so that nothing would satisfy them less than a Coalition, whereby the Seven Provinces should be incorporated into this their *Fifth Monarchy.*

E 2   II. The

II. The solemn and formal Ambassadors were at some Loss how to deal with this frantick Sort of People, whom they thought a Society fitter for *Bedlam*, than a Conclave of Senators; and had look'd so far into the State of Things, and the ambitious Inclinations of *Cromwel*, that they cunningly insinuated, if he would assume the Government himself, they should be more ready to a Compliance with him. These People were certainly call'd together by *Cromwel* only for a while, to shew Tricks to the People, and play the Fool with the Government, that thereby the Nation might be as willing as himself to have the Reins taken into a more steady Hand.

III. The Resignation of this Parliament's Power was quickly after contrived; and on *December* 16. he usurp'd the Government, with the Title of *Protector*. Being now more concern'd to provide for his own Settlement, by looking after his Enemies at home, than to prosecute a War abroad; and that he might gain entirely the Article for Seclusion of the House of *Orange* from Stadholder-General, or Admiral, and no Entertainment to be given to any of his Enemies in their Dominions; he was willing to deal very indulgently with them in the rest of the Particulars. And therefore he accepted the Article for

striking

striking the Flag, without a Recognition of the Title. Inſtead of a Coalition, a defenſive Alliance ſerved the Turn. The Fiſhing paſs'd without either Leaſe or Rent; and the Merchants, for their free Trade, and Satisfaction for Damages, were wholly left in the Lurch.

IV. It were tedious to relate all the Tricks and Artifices that paſſed between the Protector and theſe Ambaſſadors, about the Article of Secluſion.

V. There was ſo much Baſeneſs and Ingratitude in the Thing it ſelf, that both the States General and their Agents were utterly aſhamed of it: Inſomuch that the Protector at laſt was contented to accept it in the Quality of a ſecret Article, but without it refuſed to exchange the Ratifications. At laſt the States of the Province of *Holland* and *Weſt-Freezland*, guided by the Counſels of the late Penſioner *De Witt*, and without the Concurrence of the other Provinces, ſigned this ſecret Article: That they would never elect his preſent Highneſs, nor any of his Lineage, to be Stadholder or Admiral of their Province: Neither ſhould their Province give their Suffrage or Conſent, that he, or any of his Family, ſhould be Captain General of the Forces of the *United Provinces*. This being ſent over to the Ambaſſadors, and by them

them delivered to *Cromwel*, the Peace was presently and finally concluded, and the three hundred thousand Pounds, which they offer'd the Year before to the Commonwealth Parliament, was also thought to have been cast into the Scales, being a seasonable Present to *Cromwel*, wherewith to support himself in the Infancy of his Power and Greatness. And thus (as an Essay of his future Government) he abandon'd the Concerns of the Nation, and all the Advantages of this War, to the Interest of his own secret Malice and Ambition.

VI. GENERAL *Monk* (whose History we have been forc'd to interrupt by this necessary Digression) was, during this Treaty, lying upon the *Dutch* Coasts, blocking up their Havens, and interrupting their Trade, and did all he could to hinder this Agreement. He exclaim'd against it, as a thing infamous and dishonourable to the Nation. He represented to them, that the *Dutch* could not be able to fight another Battle; and that they had never an Ally in the World, that would be concern'd for them. But all he could do was only to remonstrate against it. The time was not yet come for General *Monk*, by his own Authority, to govern the great Concerns of the Nation, nor to put an End to Usurpation and Tyranny.

VII. THE

VII. The Protector *Cromwel* had no sooner concluded the *Dutch* War, but another begun to be formed against him in *Scotland*. The Marquiss of *Athol*, the Earl of *Glencarn*, and several of the Nobility, having declared for the King, had raised an Army in *Sotland*, consisting of about eight or nine thousand Men, headed and commanded by Officers of the principal of the Nobility and Gentry of the Nation, to which some Force out of *Holland*, by *Middleton*, was to be added: Who, though he came from his Majesty with a Commission to be General of the Army which the Nobility had raised, did yet disoblige them, and afterwards the withdrawing and dividing the Forces, did frustrate the greater Part of the Attempt.

VIII. This Insurrection in *Scotland* being in the Morning of his Usurpation, did greatly disquiet his Protectorship (who could better dissemble his Hatred than his Fears) not knowing how far it might suddenly prevail in a Nation restless and dissatisfied at the late Coalition, and that were watching upon all Occasions, to recover again the Loss of their Reputation, with the Liberty of their Country. Since the Removal of General *Monk* out of *Scotland*, Colonel *Dean* commanded in Chief there; and being afterwards called off

off by the Juncto to be the Admiral in the *Dutch* War, Colonel *Lilbourn* was entrusted with the Government of the Country, and the *English* Forces there. Him *Cromwel* thought a Person of too little Courage to be trusted at this time with so strong and tough an Employment. Besides, he had already discovered his own Weakness and Fears, by representing the Business to the Protector worse than indeed it was: And was so at his Wit's End, that he dared not look out of his Quarters. This made *Cromwel* more solicitous, not only about the Design it self, but the Choice of a Person fit to be employed. And the Command of so large and considerable a Country was not to be disposed of at Adventures. By his assuming the Government in the Quality of a single Person, he had displeas'd several of his stoutest Officers, that were for a free Commonwealth, and therefore was resolv'd not to employ them further. Among his own Relations (whom he could best have trusted) there was not a Person fit for this Service. Some of his Council propos'd his Brother in-Law, *Desborow*; but *Cromwel* better understood the Man, and knew him to be a coarse and boisterous Clown, that wanted Sense and Discretion. *Fleetwood* was as unfit as the rest of them. And for *Lambert*, he resolv'd not to trust him so far out of his Sight. The only suitable

General Monk. 57

able Person for this *Scotch* Expedition, was General *Monk*, who had reduc'd the Country before, and who best knew how to handle the *Scots*.

IX. His Reputation at Arms was grown equal with any of the rest of the *English* Commanders, and by his Success in the last *Dutch* War was become their Superior: So that several of them began to emulate and suspect his Greatness. He was unluckily cast among these People, rather by his ill Fate, than any Choice of his own; but was still especially careful to keep himself from their greater Guilts and Hypocrisy. He would never be concern'd in any of their more secret Intrigues or Cabals, never pretended to their Frenzies of Preaching or Praying, nor to any of their Revelations or Impulses. But as a stout and valiant *Englishman*, he loved his Country, and still hoped for some better Season to express it.

X. Whatever was suggested, so soon as the Protector found, by Conference with General *Monk*, that he was no ways dissatisfy'd with his dissolving the late Commonwealth Parliament, and that he had no Concern for that Interest, he presently entrusted him with the Command of *Scotland*. And because all things then run into greater Disorder, he was
hasten'd

hasten'd away to his Province, taking his Leave of *Cromwel*, whom he never saw more, nor set his Foot again in *England*, till he brought back with him the Redemption and Deliverance of his Country.

XI. At his Arrival in *Scotland*, about the 23ᵈ of *April*, he found all things in Disorder; a querulous, discontented People: an ungovern'd Army, fill'd with all Sorts of violent Fanaticks and Anabaptists, which was the Religion of Colonel *Lilbourn*, their Governor; and they had crouded and justled the Presbyterian Clergy out of their Kirks and Pulpits, and expos'd their Discipline to Ridicule. But General *Monk*, who was too wary to be concern'd in any of their religious Disputes and Extravagancies, quickly found them some other kind of Employment for their Diversion. And having settled some necessary Affairs in *Edenburgh*, he presently draws out his Army, and marches them up into the Highlands, where he kept them so close to their Work as abated some of their religious Madness.

CHAP.

CHAP. VI.

I. *The Earl of* Middleton *under great Difficulties in the* Highlands; *whither General* Monk, *with Major General* Morgan, *marches after him.* II. *The Earl holds a Council of War, and determines not to engage the General's Forces.* III. Cromwel *secretly promises the* Scotch *Nobility and Gentry their Pardon, upon their Submission, which they seem willing to make.* IV. *Some of General* Monk's *Officers are for compelling them to a Battle, but the General is against it.* V. *Major General* Morgan *defeats a Party of the* Scotch *at* Loughgerry; *upon which the Earl of* Middleton *escapes to* Holland, *and his Forces lay down their Arms.* VI. *General* Monk *hires* Dalkeith *House, where he keeps his Head Quarters, during his Stay in that Country.* VII. *He Regulates the Civil and Religious Affairs of* Scotland, *and restrains the Power of the Kirk.*

I. THE Citadel, Forts, and Castles, and all Places of Strength in *Scotland*, being already possessed by the *English* Forces; the Earl of *Middleton*, having no Garrison or Retreat for his Army, defended himself in the open Country of the *Highlands*, where, besides other Difficulties, he was much distresfed with the Want of Provision. General *Monk*, before his March up into the Country, had already laid up Provision of Bisket and Cheese in three several convenient Places, at *Leith*, *St. Johnston*'s, and *Inverness*; for other Supplies, they were to find them in the Country as they could. And having left a Party of Horse and Foot to range about the *Lowlands*, and prevent the raising of more Forces, he, with General *Morgan*, marched up into the *Highlands* in two distinct Bodies, having about two thousand five hundred Foot, and about six hundred Horse, in each Party; with which Force he pursued the *Scotch* Army, retreating still before him. And as he took in any Castles or Places of Strength, he had them presently supply'd with Provisions from his former Stores at *St. Johnston*'s or *Leith*, by which Means his Army was never very distant from some Place of Supply. And at any Stage the Soldiers took with them in their Knapsacks such Provision of Cheese and Bisket, as served them for six or seven Days; it being otherwise impossible for his Soldiers to have Courage to attend the Enemy through a Country so desolate and full of Bogs. As he marched through the Countries or Lands of such as were wholly in Arms, he destroyed almost all before him; so that he knew at length they would be forc'd to submit or starve.

II. T*he*

II. The Earl of *Middleton*, obferving daily the Decay of his Forces, and the Ruin of the Country, was very earneft to have come to a Battle with General *Monk*, or with Major General *Morgan*, who kept on their Way in two diftinct Bodies, and within four Days March one of another. But this Refolution was laid afide at a Council of War, upon the Confideration, that if they fhould have the good Fortune to engage one Party with Succefs, the other, being frefh, might advance upon them, before they could be in Condition to receive them, to the Hazard or Lofs of their whole Army.

III. But there was alfo another fecret Contrivance on Foot, that did moft of all take off the *Scotch* Nobility and Gentry from coming to an Engagement. For the Ufurper *Cromwel*, being not yet warm in his Seat, and knowing how many Enemies he had, both to his Perfon and Fortune, had greatly apprehended their rifing in *Scotland* as a Prelude to a farther Infurrection in *England:* And having greater and more neceffary Affairs upon him, than profecuting a War in the *Highlands*, had, by his fecret Agents, attempted fome of the *Scotch* Nobility and Gentry in the Army, and let them know, that, for this their hafty Rifing, he was content

to

to accept their Submission, and, upon laying down their Arms, and returning quietly to their Houses, they should be restored to their Estates and Fortunes. Which being offered to them in the midst of so many Straits, besides the Decay of their Forces, and the ill Posture of their Affairs, induced them not to put all to Hazard upon so great Disadvantage, but rather to submit for the present, in Expectation of some more fortunate Opportunity for recovering their Liberty, and restoring their King.

IV. SOME of the more eager and zealous Officers in the *English* Army were frequently importunate with him, to come close up to the Enemy, and enforce them to a Battle. But General *Monk* better understood the Nature of this War than his inferior Commanders; and, having continual Account of the *Scotch* Army by some *Highlanders*, he assured his Officers, that the Enemy's Army was in such Difficulties, and so daily decreasing, that the Business would be certainly done without a Battle: Nor did they afterwards find him deceiv'd in his Prognosticks.

V. BUT in the Interim Major General *Morgan*, with that Party of the *English* Forces under his Command, surpriz'd some *Scotch* Forces at *Loughgerry*, and utterly defeated them.

them. Upon which the Earl of *Middleton* retreated to an Island, from whence afterwards he got back again into *Holland*. Others of the Nobility and Officers making their Submission, General *Monk* settled convenient Garrisons in the Country. And having perform'd such a March thro' the Country of the *Highlands*, where no Force of the *English* had ever left a Footstep behind them, and which the Inhabitants accounted inaccessible to any but themselves, by the End of *August* he return'd to *Edenburgh*, which, being the capital City of the Nation, was the most proper Place of Residence for the Prefect, or chief Governor.

VI. But General *Monk*, who always affected the Privacy and Retirement of the Country, and taking a particular Fancy to the Situation of *Dalkeith-House*, became a Tenant to it: Where he continu'd his Head-Quarters, during his more than five Years Command of that Country. It was pleasantly seated in the midst of a Park, and at the commodious Distance of five Miles from *Edenburgh*. Here, in the Intervals of publick Business, he diverted himself with the Pleasures of Planting and Husbandry; resembling therein some of the Consuls and Dictators of the ancient *Rome*; who, after they had subdued Nations, and led Kings in Triumph, return'd turn'd again to their Tillage, and with their own Hands dressed their Trees and Vineyards.

1655   VII. Upon the Reduction of the *Highlands*, there being now no Enemy in Arms in *Scotland*, General *Monk* found himself at Liberty to inspect the Civil Affairs of the Country. And because the Covenanting Clergy were grown so insolent in their Power and Influence over the Government and People, a particular Care was used to abate their Rigour. They had indeed the undisturbed Use of their Kirks and Preaching, during General *Monk*'s Command; but were not permitted the Liberty of making Reflexions upon their Superiors, or the Government, unto which, by the Complexion of their Religion, or the pragmatical Spirit of the Clergy, they are greatly inclined. The Power of Excommunication, and the Consequents upon it, which was the Palladium of Presbyterianism, was wholly taken from them. Their Presbyteries were indeed connived at, but their general Assemblies disturbed and forbidden: So that they who some Years before, in the Height and Ruffle of their religious Zeal, being abetted by their Party in *England*, had the Confidence to outlaw the late King, when he forbad their Assemblies, were now so reduced and baffled by the *English* Army, that they would

would have diflolved any of their Conventions at the Command of a Corporal. Nor were the Nobility and Gentry permitted to wear Swords, to ride on a Horfe of Value, to profecute their old Animofities among themfelves, nor to exercife any arbitrary and violent Practices towards their Inferiors and Servants.

CHAP. VII.

I. Cromwel *appoints a Council of State, confifting of Seven, whereof General* Monk *was one*. II. *Three of the Council afterwards concur with General* Monk. III. *Colonel* Overton *endeavours to corrupt the Army, and defigns the Affaffination of the General, but is detected, and fent Prifoner to* London. IV. Scotland *enjoys great Peace and Plenty under the General's Adminiftration*. V. Cromwel *jealous of him*. VI. *He is under great Affliction for the Death of his fecond Son*. VII. *A friendly Correfpondence between the General and the* Scotch *Nobility and Gentry*. VIII. *Which was improved by his Enemies to the Confirmation of* Cromwel's *Jealoufy of him; whereupon* Cromwel *writes to him*. IX. Cromwel's *artful Manner of Writing*. X. *At the fame Time*

Time he was very weak in trusting a Person whom he suspected, with a Place of such Command.

I. AND now the Protector having fully secured the Subjection of *Scotland*, there was appointed by the Usurper a Council of State, for the better Administration of the Civil Government. *viz.* The Lord *Broghil*, President of the Council, General *George Monk*, Colonel *Howard*, Colonel *William Lockhart*, Colonel *Adrian Scroop*, Colonel *John Wetham*, and Major General *Desborow*. To this Employment they were authorized by a Commission under *Cromwel*'s Broad Seal, dated *June* 1655, though they came not down to exercise their Commission in that Nation till about the middle of *September* following. By which they were enabled to order and dispose of the Revenues in *Scotland*, to appoint the Officers of the Exchequer, the Commissioners of Excise and Customs, and of the Sequestrations, and all subordinate Officers under them. They had also the Nomination of all Justices of the Peace, of Sheriffs and Commissaries in the several Counties; which Commissaries kept their Courts for Probate of Wills, and granting Administrations in their respective Limits. And by an additional Power from *Cromwel*, they were afterwards authoriz'd to approve

and

GENERAL MONK. 67

and allow of all Incumbents that were to be admitted into any Ecclesiastical Benefice.

II. This Council was continued in *Scotland* during the Usurpation of *Cromwel* and his Son. But three of those Commissioners, namely, the Lord *Broghil* Earl of *Orrery*, Colonel *Howard* Earl of *Carlisle*, and Colonel *Whetham*, who was Governor of *Portsmouth*, did afterwards very effectually co-operate with General *Monk* in those great and happy Alterations, which at last introduced the King.

III. About this Time the Commonwealth Party in the Army, who secretly maligned the Protector's Government, were framing Designs against him, which were to take Effect in the Armies of all the three Nations. Among whom Colonel *Overton* was one, who had so far dissembled his Discontents, as to obtain the Command of Major General of the Infantry, in General *Monk's* Army; where he quickly fell to practising upon the discontented Party of the Soldiers, and had set up Agitators to corrupt the particular Regiments; so that under the old Pretence of *seeking the Lord*, a considerable Number of Male-contents met in order to this Defection at *Aberdeen*. He had held several

veral secret Meetings, and framed a smart Declaration against *Cromwel* and the Government; proceeding so far as to design to himself the chief Command of the *English* Army in *Scotland*, which could not be effected but by the Death of General *Monk*, whom they had resolv'd to surprize on *New-Years* Day in the Morning, and *Miles Sindercomb* (afterwards more famous for designing upon the Life of the Protector *Cromwel*) was one of the Assassins. All this Practice was not so secretly carry'd, but the wary General had Notice of it. And having taken Care for his own Security, he suffered *Overton* and his Accomplices to proceed, till he had sufficient Matter against them, and then imprison'd them all in their several Quarters. *Overton* he sent up to *London*, to be reckon'd with by the Protector himself, who laid him fast in the Tower, having before secured many other Officers of the Faction in several Goals and Castles. *Overton*'s Regiment was given to Major General *Morgan*, and for the rest of the Confederates, General *Monk* imprisoned or cashired them.

1656 IV. AFTER this little Mutiny in *Scotland*, we find no more Disorders in the Country, during the General's Command there; but an universal Peace among them; and (the Effect of Peace) an universal Plenty and Trade.

For the General was always very careful in providing the Pay for his Army, both by the Tax in *Scotland*, the sixty thousand Pounds *per Mensem*, and what was further assigned from *England*. So that the Soldiers, being well paid, were enabled to discharge their Quarters duly, and the Money did so universally circulate thro' the Country, that there was never known so much ready Coin in *Scotland*, as during General *Monk*'s Command there. He had formed his Army to a very exact Discipline, so that nothing was more rare than to hear of any Mutinies among themselves, or Depredations on the People: Insomuch that tho' General *Monk* continued among them to secure their Subjection, yet they had a great Opinion of his Generosity and Justice; and so much Kindness for his Soldiers, during a long and peaceable Neighbourhood together, that they looked upon them no otherwise than as Natives of the Place, or a Part of their Country; and as Guardians rather of their Safety and Liberty, than Instruments of their Servitude and Subjection.

V. HITHERTO the Protector had wanted Leisure, or Pretence, to remove General *Monk* from his so long Command in *Scotland*: Yet his Jealousy found out other Ways to prevent him from having too much Influence over his Army, by removing often some Regiments which he most trusted, and sending down to him all those restless and violent Parties, which he could least govern in *England*. And these furious and hair-brain'd Sectaries gave him frequently a great deal of Trouble, before he could take down their Mettle, and bring them to live quietly in their Quarters, and to know Discipline.

VI. About this Time, as an Allay to his Felicities, General *Monk* lost his second Son, *George*, who, in his Infancy, dy'd of a Feaver, attended with Convulsion Fits, and was buried in the Chapel of *Dalkeith House*. The Death of this Child affected the General with so unusual and deep a Sorrow, as was greatly admired by those, who know not that, in the highest Courage, there is a Mixture of the greatest Tenderness; or have not read, how that the brave *Æmylius* * was so concern'd for the Death of his two Children, that it took from him the chief Satisfaction of his late Victories, and withered the Laurels of his Triumph.

VII. Since the Insurrection of the *Highlanders*, there had been for some Years no

---

* *Plutarch*'s Life of *Æmylius*.

considerable Hostility in *Scotland*. And Time, that overcomes all Things, had worn out in a great Measure the Memory of all past Animosities. So that the Nobility and Gentry of *Scotland* came to a better Understanding of their General, whom they frequently visited; and there were among them several worthy and honourable Persons, for whom General *Monk* had a very particular Estimation, insomuch as he frequently desired their Conversation, and did advise with them in the Management of several publick Affairs in their Country. Even the brave and valiant Party of the *Montrossians*, had a Place in his Estimation and Kindness, so far as the Condition of Affairs then, and the jealous Temper of the Age, would admit. And tho' General *Monk* abated nothing of his Discipline, yet by his other Methods of Moderation and Prudence, he had so far obliged all Parties, that whilst the Protector, with all his Arts of terrifying or informing, could not keep himself a Year round from Designs or Insurrections against him in *England*, General *Monk* continued the Government in *Scotland* without any further Plot or Practice upon him.

VIII. But this his quiet and peaceful Government of *Scotland*, and the general Estimation that waited on him there, was, by his Enemies in the Country, and others about 1658 the Protector, represented as a jealous Instance. And *Cromwel*, whose Humours towards his Declension, grew like other Liquors near their Bottom, sharp and turbid, had entertain'd some Apprehension of him. The Discontents between him and his late Parliament, and the Discovery of another new Plot upon him, led him to other Thoughts: Only some while before his Death, he wrote to him a Letter with his own Hand, containing only general Matters relating to the Government; but in his Postscript he subjoins:

There be that tell me, that there is a certain cunning Fellow in Scotland, *called* George Monk, *who is said to lye in wait there to introduce* Charles Stuart; *I pray use your Diligence to apprehend him, and send him up to me.*

IX. This was a kind of Grimace in the Protector, to wrap up his Suspicions in Drollery: And it was another Part of his Cunning, to place that in a Postscript which in Reality was the main Occasion of the Letter.

X. And here I desire my Reader to observe, that the Suspicion upon General *Monk* of restoring King *Charles*, did not first arise from his wary Reservedness, and studied Concealments of himself, in his celebrated March

from

from *Colstream*; but it was an Apprehension that did long before distress the Minds of those, who had been guilty of excluding his Majesty from his Dominions, and whose Interest therefore it was to hinder his Return.

It was certainly a great Oversight in *Cromwel* to continue so great a Command, as the Government of *Scotland*, in the Hands of General *Monk*, of whom he could have no great Security from his Principles, nor as partaking with him in mutual Guilts. But whatever his secret Resentments were, they proceeded no further, being prevented by his own Death, which quickly after ensued on *September* 3, 1658. a Day which in his Lifetime he had kept as an anniversary Festival, and now by his Death made it truly such to the Commonwealth. And now having five Years followed Providence in doing all the Mischief he was able, he left the Usurpation with so little Content to himself, or Hopes of its Continuance, that he had taken no Care of the Succession, if he had not been put upon it by the Importunities of those about him.

CHAP.

CHAP. VIII.

I. Cromwel *dies, and his Son* Richard *is proclaimed at* Edenburgh, *who sends Letters of Compliment to General* Monk. II. *The State of* England *at that Time. A Parliament called. Some of the Members cabal against the young Protector. The Commons resent it; while the Protector, by the Advice of* Thurloe, *displaces some of the Officers of the Army; the House of Lords, on the contrary, favouring them.* III. *The Parliament dissolved; by which Means the Officers recover their Places and Interest.* IV. *And are for restoring the* Rump *Parliament.* V. Fleetwood *and* Desborow *desert the Interest of the Protector, and fall into* Lambert's *Measures.* VI. *The Protector turned out.* VII. *And the Rump Parliament restored; with the Reasons of that Resolution.* VIII. *The Rump Parliament, to secure themselves, empower their Speaker to grant Commissions in the Army, appointing a Committee of Seven for the Nomination of Officers.* IX. *General* Monk's *Conduct upon these Alterations.* X. *The Loyalists in* England *take Advantage from them.* XI. *How the King's Affairs had been managed since the Death of his Father.* XII. *The Presbyterians join with the Royalists; their Reasons for so doing.* I. THE

I. THE Death of the Protector, and the Orders for proclaiming his Son, came to General *Monk* to *Dalkeith* much at the same Time. And presently after *Richard Cromwel* was proclaimed at *Edenburgh*, but with so cold and indifferent Ceremony, both in the People and *English* Army, that it seem'd rather an Act of Obedience, than Affection. But to settle a better Understanding with General *Monk*, the Protector *Richard* sent presently Commissary *Clarges* with Letters to him, both to compliment his farther Service, and to desire his Advice. They who conversed with General *Monk* in those Times, have reported it as his Opinion, that if *Oliver Cromwel* had lived, he could not have held the Government much longer: And therefore for his easy Son, he presently foresaw, he would not be able to continue his Station many Months. Yet he return'd him very civil and wary Answers to his Letters, and carefully securing his own Command, he was resolved not to concern himself with the Affairs of *England*; but to leave the young Protector to the Conduct of those about him, and his own hasty Destiny.

II. THE last Protector had left his Son many Enemies against his Government, and those he could trust were rather Friends to
his

his Fortune than himself. He had left the Government in such a miserable Condition, with so many Debts and Arrears to his Army, that his Son was not able to keep open Doors any longer, without the Help of a Parliament, which was convened to sit down, *January* the 17th, consisting of an House of Commons, and another they call'd in those Times, the *Other House*. In this Assembly there were so many return'd of different Humours and Principles, that against the opening of the Parliament, many of the Officers of the Army hasten'd up to *London*, where, meeting several others formerly disoblig'd by the late Protector, they fell presently to caballing with other Male-contents, how to wrest the Government from his Son. Of this Party one of the leading Persons was Colonel *Lambert*, whose conceal'd Ambition began now to discover it self. They had held several Meetings in order to these Ends, with so much Ceremony, as if they had been the hereditary Princes of the Nation; and had so fool'd *Fleetwood* and *Desborow*, and other half-witted People of *Cromwel*'s Alliance, who had no true Notion of their own and *Cromwel*'s Interest, that they saw not their Error till it was too late to retrieve it. These bold and open Assemblies of the Officers gave some Alarm to the Commons then sitting, who discover'd their Jealousy and Displeasure

against

1596

against these Conventions, by their voting against them, and favouring rather the Interest of the young Protector, while the other House abetted the Assembly of the Army-Officers against him; who at last ran into such high and insolent Resolves, as the Protector *Richard* was prudently advis'd to secure their Persons, then assembled in Sir *Henry Vane*, or Sir *Arthur Hazlerig*'s House, and dispose of their Commands. But his Secretary *Thurloe* persuaded him to recall their Commissions, yet to leave their Persons at Liberty. By which timorous and middle Counsel, he had no way oblig'd them to continue his Master's Friends, nor disabl'd them from becoming his Enemies.

III. The Officers of the Army did hitherto greatly fear the Influence and Displeasure of the House of Commons, as they despis'd the Weakness and Incapacity of their Protector *Richard*, and therefore insolently compelling him to dissolve their Session, they then presently seiz'd the Army wholly into their own Hands, displacing all Officers that most favoured the Protectorate, by which Alteration Colonel *Lambert*, and the rest of those discarded Commanders, recover'd again their Stations in the Army.

IV. The

IV. The Protector's Relations were all this while so stupid and senseless, that they did not yet discern they had ruined themselves and him, by this Breach upon his Power: But being still fooled with a Bell and a Rattle, they had the Vanity to persuade him, all should be very well with him, and tho' he had lost his Authority, yet he should continue his Government. But at the next Meeting of those Officers they quickly found their Error, when it was past Remedy. For tho' these People, who had magnify'd the *Cromwels*, as the *Moses* that had led them out of the House of Bondage, yet now they are resolved to set up *Fleetwood* their Captain, and to return again into *Ægypt*. For now nothing would please them, but to restore the late Tail of a Parliament, to whose Dissolution, five Years ago, most of them had been consenting; and some of them had actually assisted *Cromwel* in pulling them out of the House, and exposing them to the World as a Pack of Knaves and Villains, who had spent more than ten Years Time there in cheating the Nation. Notwithstanding their former Contempt of them, when it served their Ambition or Interest, the religious Hypocrites were not ashamed, by their Declaration, *May* 6. to proclaim the same People, the

eminent

General Monk. 79

eminent Afferters of the good old Caufe, and fuch as had a fpecial Prefence of God with them, and were fignally bleffed in the Work.

V. Fleetwood and *Desborow* did eafily difcern, that the Difcourfe among them for reftoring the late Parliament, muft prove the certain Ruin of the Protectorate. And when they had found, that, by their own ill Management or Credulity, they had utterly loft *Richard*'s Game, they took Care to fave their own Stake, and to fecure their high Commands in the Army, by complying with *Lambert* and the other Officers, leaving their young Kinfman friendlefs and defencelefs to the Contempt and Revenge of his Enemies.

VI. And thus ended the Ufurpation of the *Cromwels*, begun by the Villanies and Falfhoods of the Father, and concluding in the Follies of the Son; and the fame People that had been the Afcent to the one, became the Precipice to the other. They who had fo officioufly lent *Oliver* their Hand to raife him up, were now as bufy with their Feet to kick down *Richard*.

VII. The Officers of the Army, who had thus thrown down the Protectorate, had no other Authority to which they could retreat, but reftoring the old Commonwealth Parliament.

ment. They could not support the Government by a military Council of their own, because that Constitution could raise no Money, which was then extremely wanted. And the great ones were grown to such an Height of Self-opinion and Jealousy of each other, that they could never agree to submit to any single Person chosen from among themselves; nor could they trust a new Parliament, which was likely enough to declare them Rebels. There was therefore no other Way but to mount their good old Cause again upon this Rump of the late Long-Parliament, and to ride till some of them (having ripen'd their Designs) could find an higher Ground to alight at.

VIII. The Members of the late Long-Parliament gave good Words to them that had restored them, now a second Time, to a Capacity of doing further Mischief. Yet they were resolv'd first to secure their own Station, by fixing the Army in a more certain Dependance upon themselves. And to that End, tho' they granted to *Fleetwood* a Commission to command as General, yet they allow'd him no Power to sign Commissions to others, but reserv'd that Trust for the Speaker of their House; from whose Hands only all Commissions should pass. And at the same Time appointed a Committee of seven Persons, *viz.*

Lieutenant

Lieutenant General *Fleetwood*, Sir *Henry Vane*, Sir *Arthur Hazlerig*, Colonel *Lambert*, *Desborow*, *Ludlow*, and *Berry*, with Authority to model the Army, and difplace all fuch Officers in the three Nations as they thought fit.

IX. GENERAL *Monk* fat all this while filent in *Scotland*, keeping a very fteady Eye upon all thefe feveral Scenes and Alterations in *London*. And knowing himfelf to be in a Station fo confiderable, as they would be enforc'd to make Applications to him, he was refolv'd to keep himfelf at a Diftance, and fecure his own Command, leaving them a while to manage their Game at their own Rate.

X. NOR did the loyal Party in *England* ftand as idle and unconcern'd Spectators upon this great Change of Affairs. They had indeed unfortunately loft the Field in the Civil War; but yet contriv'd the Continuance of feveral Infurrections and Parties, in order to reftore the Monarchy; which hitherto, by the Vigilance of their Enemies, or the Treachery of fome among themfelves, had been fruftrated. Yet fupporting themfelves with the Affurance and Confcience of fo good a Caufe, they kept up their Hopes and Endeavours, and, with a very fingular Attention, obferv'd thofe wild Alterations and Inconftancies of their Enemies, hoping this their Giddiness, by so many turnings round, would enforce their Fall at the last.

XI. His Majesty's Affairs in *England*, since the Death of his Father, had been managed by a secret Conclave chosen out of the loyal Nobility, and other Persons of Honour and Quality, that had surviv'd the late War on the King's Side, and were authorized to this Employment by a Commission under his Majesty's Hand; as the Earl of *Oxford*, Earl of *Northampton*, Sir *John Greenvil*, now Earl of *Bath*, the Lord Viscount *Mordant*, the Lord *Bellasis*, Colonel *John Russel*, Colonel of his Majesty's Guards, Sir *William Compton*, late General of the Ordnance, Sir *Orlando Bridgman*, late Lord Keeper of the Great Seal, Sir *Jeffrey Palmer*, late Attorney General, Colonel *William Legg*, one of the Gentlemen of his Majesty's Bedchamber, Colonel *Edward Villers*, of the Bedchamber to his Royal Highness, Mr. *Newport*, Brother to the Lord *Newport*, Dr. *Hewit*; and to these was unfortunately added Sir *Richard Willis*, who afterwards fell into Suspicion, and was not entrusted. Some of these secret Commissioners were always residing in *London*, both to hold Intelligence with several Persons of Worth and Loyalty, that were engag'd for his Majesty's Service in every

GENERAL MONK. 83

County of *England*, and also to transmit to his Majesty an Account of Things according to any new Emergency.

XII. About this Time several of the Royal Party found a fair Opportunity to inlarge their Interest, by the Accession of several among the more moderate of the Presbyterians. The restoring again the Tail of the late Parliament, had greatly disobliged that Party; and the rather because all the Presbyterian Members (who had as much Right to sit as the other) were kept out by the Insolence of the Juncto, being abetted by the Power of their Army. These Resentments run at last so high in the whole Body of the Presbyterians, that, disdaining to submit again to a Juncto of Knaves that had fool'd and cozen'd them, and to their boisterous Army of Fanaticks, they chose rather to join themselves to their old Enemy the Royal Party, for the Recovery of their common Liberty.

CHAP. IX.

I. *An universal Insurrection in every County agreed upon, and a Declaration for the Freedom of Parliaments, without mentioning*

tioning King or Monarchy. Sir George Booth *the first that appeared in it.* II. *A farther Design to attempt the bringing over some of the Officers. General* Monk *esteemed the most likely to be prevail'd upon, and Sir* John Greenvile *the most proper Person to be sent to him for that purpose.* III. *An Account of Sir* John Greenvil. *His Descent, with some Account of his Father. His several Advancements and Conduct in the Army.* IV. *Compounds for his Estate, and lives retired upon the Seat of the Family at* Kelkhampton. V. *Presents Mr.* Nicholas Monk, *Brother to the General, to the Living of* Kelkhampton. VI. *Whose Presentation is admitted by the Committee of Tryers.* VII. *Sir* John *leaves the Country, and resides in* London, *for the Discharge of a Commission from the King. He recommends Mr.* Nicholas Monk *to the King, as a fit Person to be sent to the General in* Scotland. VIII. *The King's Letter to Sir* John *for that purpose.* IX. *The King's Letter to the General.* X. *Sir* John *acquaints Mr.* Nicholas Monk, *then in* Cornwal, *with the King's Pleasure, who readily accepts the Trust, and immediately repairs to* London *to Sir* John, *and from thence to* Scotland. XI. *Mr.* Monk *arrives in* Scotland, *and communicates his Business to Dr.*

Price,

Price, *the General's Chaplain, who gives him some Instructions about the Management of it.* XII. *Mr.* Monk's *Interview with, and Reception from, the General.* XIII. *The Committee makes several Alterations in the General's Army, which he refuses to comply with, but improves them to the Service of that Resolution which he had taken upon the King's Message to him.* XIV. *An Oath of Secrecy.* XV. *And a Declaration to the Juncto, signed by the General and his Officers; wherein the Juncto was commanded to fill up their Members, and to provide for frequent Parliaments. A remarkable Expression of the General's to Dr.* Price. XVI. *Sir* George Booth *defeated.* XVII. *Upon which the General burns the Declaration.* XVIII. *The Juncto and their Army in* England *disagree.* XIX. *The Army sends to their Brethren in* Ireland, *and to General* Monk *in* Scotland, *for their Concurrence against the Parliament; whereupon General* Monk *declares for the Parliament.*

I. THE King's Commissioners very well understood how to deal with these People, and to make use of their Interest; and therefore having first agreed, that an universal Insurrection should be made in every County

County of *England*, and every one upon the same Day (for which several Persons of Quality had undertaken) they consented that the first Appearance should be of such Persons only as had not been engag'd on the King's Side in the late War; thereby both to prevent the greater Jealousy of the Army against them, and with Hopes to have drawn over the more moderate Party among the Soldiers. They agreed also to a Declaration, which should not mention the King, nor monarchical Government, but only for the Freedom of Parliaments, according to the known Laws, and for Liberty and Property of the People. And in this Insurrection the first and only Person that appear'd was Sir *George Booth*.

II. But besides this Design of an universal Insurrection, (which, if it had succeeded right, had given the Juncto and their Army Trouble enough) it was resolv'd by his Majesty and his Privy-Council at *Brussels*, to attempt the Allegiance of some principal Commanders in the *English* Army. And that since it had not been possible to deal with them while united, to see what good might be done by engaging one Party against the other, which was an Experiment that could never yet be made: Upon an exact Consideration of several great Officers among them all, there was no Person of whom they could
entertain

entertain any probable Hope but General *Monk* in *Scotland*, who, being a Gentleman born, and of better Quality than most among them, and having formerly been in the Service of the late King, and no way concern'd in their Principles and deeper Guilts, might be thought, by the Condition of the Command he held, to be a Person very proper for such a Service as this: Nor were there wanting certain Conceits and Forebodings in the Minds of Men concerning him. Having therefore resolved to make some Attempt upon him, the next Care was in the Choice of a Person fit to undertake it: When it was seasonably remember'd, that there was a very near Relation between General *Monk* and Sir *John Greenvil*, one of the secret Commissioners above-mentioned. And therefore there was dispatched to him a particular Commission, to find out some Way of treating privately with General *Monk*, in order to his Majesty's Service.

AND because we are here fallen upon the mention of a Person, that was so principally concern'd in the great Affair we have undertaken to relate; and made so considerable a Figure in it, I must lead the Reader a few Steps backward, for the giving him a clear Prospect into the following Relation.

III. SIR *John Greenvil* was the eldest Son

of the valiant and loyal Sir *Bevil Greenvil* of *Kelkhampton* in *Cornwal*, who, at his own Charge in the Year 1638. rais'd a Troop of Horse to attend his late Majesty, in his first Expedition against the *Scots*; and, being afterwards return'd Knight of the Shire for *Cornwal* in the late Long Parliament, was sent down by the King to settle the Commission of Array in that County. After which he led on the *Cornish* Forces against the Rebels in *Devonshire*, and the Western Counties, where he obtain'd several considerable Victories both at *Bodmin* and *Launceston*, &c. and afterwards in the Battle of *Lansdown* lost his Life, valiantly fighting in the midst of his Enemies, by whom he was kill'd with many Wounds. This Gentleman, his Son, Sir *John Greenvil*, now Earl of *Bath*, at fifteen Years of Age commanded his Father's Regiment, and afterwards was entrusted with five Regiments added to it, with which Force he successfully served the King in the Western Parts of *England*; from whence marching afterwards, at the second Battle of *Newberry*, exposing himself very far, he was dangerously wounded. At eighteen Years of Age he was made Gentleman of the Bedchamber to the Prince, his present Majesty, whom (after all was lost in *England*) he attended in his Exile abroad. And whilst his Majesty stay'd at the *Hague*, the Garrison and

Islanders

Islanders of *Scilly* revolted from the Parliament, and, having seiz'd their Governo they sent their Submission to his Majesty, desiring him to send them a Governor, and some more Forces. Whereupon the King, knowing the Courage and Resolution of Sir *John Greenvil*, besides the Interest which his Name and Family had in those Western Parts, thought him the fittest Person for this Service; and immediately sent him to command the Island, with Directions also for the Marquiss of *Ormond*, to send him three hundred Soldiers out of *Ireland*, which were accordingly dispatched over to *Scilly*. But the Parliament at *Westminster*, having brought all *England* into Subjection, having lately reduc'd *Ireland*, and being in a fair Way for conquering *Scotland*, disdain'd to be out-brav'd by two or three little Islands, and therefore, 1651, they order'd their Admiral *Blake* and *Aiscough*, with a good Force of Men of War and Soldiers, to attack the Island. He came before *Scilly* with so considerable a Force, that Sir *John Greenvil*, and those Officers with him, presently found they should not be long able to hold the Island against him: But putting a good Face upon an ill Business, they slighted his Summons, and prepared themselves for Defence. Yet afterwards, coming to a Treaty, the Island was surrender'd upon Articles so honourable and advantagious to the Besieg'd, that the Parliament

ment refus'd to confirm them. But General *Blake*, who was a Person of Honour and Generosity, telling his Masters how little he car'd to keep his Commission otherwise than by keeping his Word, they were at last contented, that this Agreement should be allow'd.

IV. By the Benefit of these Articles, Sir *John Greenvil* came into a Condition to compound for his Estate, and to live quietly in his own Country. And retiring himself to his Seat at *Kelkhampton* in *Cornwal*, upon the Borders of *Devonshire*, he found not only his Estate, but also the Parsonage, under Sequestration. The Incumbent Mr. *Rowse*, being turn'd out of his Living for Disaffection to the Parliament, the Sequestrator had introduc'd his Son. But some while after Sir *John Greenvil*'s Return thither, by the Death of Mr. *Rowse*, the Living came again into Sir *John*'s Gift. The Sequestrator was very earnest with him, to confirm his Son-in-Law, by granting him the Presentation; and the Value was considerable, with the very best of the Country, being worth three hundred Pounds *per Ann*. In those villainous Times the sequestred loyal Party found it their Interest to gratify and oblige those Publicans and Sequestrators; but Sir *John Greenvil* had a greater Design in his Eye than his own private

vate Advantage. For both himself, and some other of his Relations, were not without Hopes, but that, at one Time or other, their Cousin *Monk* in *Scotland* might become an useful Man for his Majesty's Service; and though he wanted Opportunity of obliging the General himself, yet he resolved to come as near it as he could, in being kind to his Brother, Mr. *Nicholas Monk*, who was already settled in the Country, about twelve Miles from *Kelkhampton*, in a moderate Living, where he had married a Widow, with some Accession of Fortune; and, in those dangerous and unquiet Times, possessed a sweet and comfortable Privacy.

V. To this Gentleman, who was also his Cousin-German, Sir *John Greenvil* was resolv'd to give the Living of *Kelkhampton*, and thereupon sent for him to his House; when, after other Discourse, and some Conference relating to General *Monk* in *Scotland*, he very freely gave him the Presentation, upon no other Condition or Reserve, but that if he should afterwards have Occasion to use or employ him, he would be assured of his Readiness therein; which was very willingly promis'd by Mr. *Nicholas Monk*, and it was afterwards as faithfully perform'd. Mr. *Monk* had in those Times the Character of a very honest and worthy Person, and was generally
look'd

look'd upon as a Man firmly devoted to the King and Church of *England*; yet by his moderate and silent Behaviour, he had escaped with less Observation than many others of that Party and Principles.

VI. But though he had received the Presentation from his Patron, yet, before he could be legally admitted into this Living, he was to run the Gantlet at *London*, through a Contrivance, call'd in those Times *the Committee of Tryers*, which was made up chiefly of Camp-Chaplains, and other Incendiaries of the Pulpit; where, if any Man came for Approbation, with a Title to a Living of Value, they had a thousand Tricks and Rogueries in Readiness to frustrate the Presentation, and dispose of it among themselves, or their Party. Mr. *Monk*, very well knowing the Character that was upon him, had some Distrust of these Tryers; but though they lik'd the Living better than the Man, yet understanding his Relation to General *Monk* in *Scotland*, they were afraid to put any of their Tricks upon him, but dismiss'd him and his Title with Allowance.

VII. About a Year after Mr. *Nicholas Monk* was settled in this Parsonage at *Kelkhampton*, Sir *John Greenvil* was oblig'd to leave the Country, and to reside in *London*, in order to the Discharge of that secret Trust, of which we have given an Account before. Where, receiving the Instructions before mentioned, to pursue some Means of treating with General *Monk*; he dispatch'd a Messenger, with a Letter in Cypher, to the Lord Chancellor *Hyde* at *Brussels*, giving an Account of what had passed between him and Mr. *Nicholas Monk*, and propos'd him as the fittest Person to be sent to his Brother the General in *Scotland*. The Chancellor communicated this Letter to his Majesty, who so far approv'd the Design and Method, that Letters were presently dispatch'd back to him to proceed therein accordingly. That to Sir *John Greenvil* was as follows:

VIII. *I Am confident General* Monk *can have no Malice in his Heart against me, nor has he done any thing in Opposition to me which I cannot easily pardon, and it is in his Power to do me so great Service as I cannot fully reward; but I will do all I can. And I do hereby authorize you to treat with him, and not only to assure him of my Kindness, but that I will very liberally reward him with such an Estate in Land, and such a Title of Honour as himself shall desire, if he will declare for me, and adhere to my Interest: And whatever you shall promise to him on my Behalf, or whatever he,*

or

or you by his Advice, shall promise to any of his Officers, or the Army under his Command (which Command he shall still continue) I will make good upon the Word of a King.

C. R.

IX. But by his secret Instructions he was confin'd to the Proposal of one hundred thousand Pounds *per Ann.* for ever to be distributed, at General *Monk*'s Discretion, to such Officers in his Army, and others, as should comply with him. And in the same Packet there was inclos'd this following Letter, to be convey'd to General *Monk*.

Sir,

I Cannot think you wish me ill, nor have you Reason to do so: And the good I expect from you will bring so great a Benefit to your Country, and to your self, that I cannot think you will decline my Interest. The Person who gives, or sends this to you, has Authority to say much more to you from me. And if you once resolve to take my Interest to Heart, I will leave the Way and Manner of declaring it entirely to your Judgment, and will comply with the Advice you shall give me. The rest I refer to the Person that conveys this to you. It is in your Power to make

make me as kind to you as you can desire, and to have me always,

Your affectionate Friend,
July 21, 1659.
C. R.

X. Upon the Receipt of these Letters, Sir *John Greenvil* presently dispatch'd a Letter down to Mr. *Nicholas Monk* in *Cornwal*, to hasten his Journey up to him; and at his Arrival acquainted him privately with the whole Business; and that he was resolv'd to send him to General *Monk* in *Scotland*, shewing him his Commission from the King to treat with his Brother, and withal his Majesty's Letter to the General. And having fully instructed him in the Nature of his Employment, the next Care was, to oblige him to entire Secrecy. Both during his Stay in *London*, and when he was arrived in *Scotland*, he was engag'd not to discover his Message to any other Person but the General himself. And because all things were in Tumult and Disorder, upon Sir *George Booth*'s Insurrection, and the Roads full of Soldiers upon their March; it was thought most safe to go by Sea. Mr. *Monk* very willingly accepted the Employment, not only as an Instance of his Duty to the King, but also of his Gratitude to his Patron; yet feared to be entrusted with so dangerous a Charge as his Majesty's Letter, which therefore was, for the present, left still

in

in Sir *John Greenvil*'s Hands. But before Mr. *Monk* left the Town, he thought it necessary to find out Commissary *Clarges*, who was Brother to General *Monk*'s Lady, and a Person very particularly intrusted by him, through all his greatest Concerns in *England*. He acquainted him therefore, that he was going into *Scotland* to fetch home his eldest Daughter, who was then residing with her Uncle at *Dalkeith*, and to advise with him about a Match propos'd for her with a Gentleman of their own Country. All which was also really true, and had been very lately before treated of by Letters between the two Brothers. And here Commissary *Clarges* did him a very seasonable Kindness, in procuring for him the Convenience of a Vessel going off for *Scotland*, which landed him safely at *Leith* in three or four Days after. From thence he found Convenience for his Passage five Miles further to the Head-Quarters at *Dalkeith*.

XI. AT his Arrival there, he found General *Monk* very busy in Dispatches (as there is seldom much Vacancy in the Head-Quarters of an Army) and therefore, till the Evening, was entertain'd by Dr. *Price*, who was domestick Chaplain to the General. Of this Person's Integrity and Allegiance to the King, Mr. *Monk* had receiv'd so clear and undoubted a Character, that though he was expressly charged by Sir *John Greenvil*, not to communicate his Business to any Person but his Brother, yet he adventur'd the same Day that he came to *Dalkeith*, to intrust the Doctor with the Knowledge of this great Secret: Who was as much surpriz'd with the Strangeness of the Relation, as he was pleased with the Design: But advis'd him not to acquaint any other Person with this Message; and that there were not many about the General, who were fit to be trusted with a Secret of this Nature. And knowing the General's Temper and Condition better than his Brother did, (who had not seen him for many Years) he gave him several wary Instructions, how to manage his Discourse with him.

XII. By this time they had talk'd themselves into the Evening, and both of them went to attend upon the General, it being then the usual Season for him to be at Leisure. But coming into the Dining-Room they found some Officers of *Leith* and *Edenburgh*, that were not yet dispatch'd. Afterwards, late at Night, Mr. *Monk* and the General being alone, he took the Opportunity to reveal his Message to him: That he was sent to him from their Kinsman Sir *John Greenvil*, who had shew'd him a Commission under the King's Hand, to treat with General *Monk* in order to his Restauration; but the Manner of doing it, and the Reward of his Service, should be wholly left to his own Choice. Only in the general he propos'd to him one hundred thousand Pounds, to be annually secured to him, and to such of his Officers, as should adhere to him therein. Then he inform'd him, that he had seen a Letter directed to him from his Majesty, which he was afraid to be entrusted with, and was still remaining in Sir *John Greenvil*'s Hand. Next he represented to him, the Seasonableness of the Attempt at this Time, there being an universal Insurrection form'd against the Rump-Parliament to take Effect over all *England*. That his Countrymen and Relations in *Devonshire* and *Cornwal* were engag'd in it, mentioning Mr. *Morrice*, Sir *Hugh Pollard*, Sir *Thomas Stukely*, and others. That Sir *George Booth*, and several Persons of Honour and Quality, were actually in Arms in *Cheshire*, when he came out of *London*, the Copy of whose Declaration he had brought with him, and shewed the General. And that the Lord *Fairfax* had undertaken to rise in *Yorkshire*, and those Counties. The General ask'd him several wary Questions about the Business, and what other Persons were intrusted with the Knowledge of it. Mr. *Monk* assured him, that no other Person in *England* was privy to it beside Sir *John Greenvil*; and that since it had

been

GENERAL MONK. 99

been revealed to himself, he had acquainted only Dr. *Price* with the Knowledge of it. The thinking silent General said no great Matter at present to his Brother upon all this Discourse, and so they parted for that Night; and all things were kept so secret, that, during Mr. *Monk*'s continuance for above two Months at *Dalkeith*, it was never apprehended he had any other Business there, but to advise with the General about the matching of his Daughter, and to carry her home with him.

XIII. DURING this Intrigue at *Dalkeith*, the Septem-virate of Commissioners, which we mentioned before, had made vile Work among the Officers of his Army, having displac'd many of the bravest and stoutest Commanders: And though he reflected upon these Impositions upon him with some Resentment, and interceded with the Parliament for the Continuance of his Officers, yet he could not fully stop these Alterations. But these Proceedings, as they greatly enrag'd the cashiered Officers, and formed an universal Jealousy in several of the rest, who expected the same Measure, so they mov'd a deeper Indignation in the General himself, who, though he carry'd always the Appearance of a silent and steady temper, yet was implacable to Affronts; and very well known that these Alterations,

terations, which, no doubt, they made with that View, would at last make his own Station uneasy or precarious, he was resolved, when all was done, not to part with his Commanders. But by the Resentments among them, General *Monk* (who very well knew how to make use of other Men's Passions) came to a better Understanding of those about him, and the Inclinations of his Army, insomuch as he entered into a private Consultation with some whom he could best trust, where it was agreed to frame a declaratory Letter to the Juncto at *Westminster*: The Substance of which was, to represent to them their own and the Nation's Dissatisfaction at the long and continued Session of this Parliament, desiring them to fill up their Members, and to proceed in establishing such Rules for future Elections, that the Common-wealth Government might be secured by frequent and successive Parliaments. This Letter was drawn up by Dr. *Price*, at the Direction of the General, and Dr. *Gumble*; and the next Sunday following, after Evening Sermon, General *Monk* and his Brother, together with Dr. *Barrow*, Principal Physician to the Army, Dr. *Gumble*, Preacher to the Council at *Edenburgh*, and Adjutant *Smith*, met all at Dr. *Price*'s Chamber, who gave the General, and all of them successively, an Oath of Secrecy in these Words:

XIV. *You*

XIV. *YOU shall truly swear, that you will not reveal any thing that shall be dicoursed of by us, or read unto you, without the Consent of all us here present.*

XV. NEXT they proceeded to the Perusal of their Letter, which being sign'd by the General, and the rest of them in their Order, they agreed severally to procure Subscriptions to it from such other Officers in the Army, as were most likely to comply with their Design. The General then commanded Adjutant *Smith* to hasten to *Edenburgh*, and to treat with Captain *Clifton*, Governor, about the Security of the Castle. From thence he was to pass to *Leith*, to ensure Captain *Hughes* and Captain *Miller*, who commanded the Citadel there; which being the Sum of what was resolv'd on that Night, the General left them, and went down Stairs, being always accustomed to advise privately with his own Thoughts, as well as with those about him. But before Adjutant *Smith* was ready to take Horse, he return'd into the Chamber again, and told them, that, upon better Consideration, he thought it most secure for them, to arrest their further Proceedings till the Return of the next Post, which would give them a clearer Prospect of the Affairs of *England*, and thereby they might

might shape their own Way the better. That by the next Letters they should know more perfectly, how near *Lambert* was advanced, what Force was join'd to Sir *George Booth*, and whether any other Parties were risen in *England* to give Diversion. This was so advisedly propos'd by the General, that they all consented to it, and so parted for that Night; only Dr. *Price*, who had a particular Zeal for any Enterprize that might determine in the King's Service, presently after sought out the General, whom he found discoursing with *Gradeen Ker*, a valiant *Scot*, that had formerly serv'd under the Marquiss of *Montross*, and was also an expert Greyhound Master, which being a Diversion the General much delighted in, it led him often both to his Acquaintance and Favour. Having ended his Conference with him, Dr. *Price* approach'd the General with some Earnestness; telling him, they had enter'd upon their Design somewhat too late already, and that he fear'd all farther Delay would make it worse. To whom the General reply'd with some Passion: *Our Business can receive no Prejudice by attending till the Arrival of the next Post, and would you needs be so hasty, as to bring my Neck to the Block for the King, and ruin the whole Design, by a too forward and unseasonable declaring.* Which being only an accidental *Remora*, we have thought fit to mention

mention it in this Place, that the Reader may observe in what Dialect General *Monk* could talk, (even in those early Days) when he was secure of those that heard him.

XVI. The next Morning the Post from *London* arrived early at *Edenburgh*, and brought the News of the utter Defeat of Sir *George Booth*, and his Party; who, with greater Faithfulness than good Fortune, had adventur'd to appear alone in that universal Insurrection which was design'd.

XVII. Upon this News from *London*, General *Monk* was inwardly pleas'd with his own deliberate and wary Method of proceeding; being assur'd his expostulating with the Juncto, at the same time that Insurrections were form'd against them in *England*, would have given them Cause to suspect him as a Confederate in the Contrivance; and very well knowing this Defeat of Sir *George Booth* would raise, both in the Juncto and their Army, an extraordinary Confidence and Presumption, he was resolv'd for the present to put all his Passions in his Pocket, and wisely dissemble his Resentment, till some better Opportunity for producing them should offer it self. Therefore the same Day he call'd for the Paper, which had been subscrib'd the Evening before, and convening those who were

were privy to it, he burnt the Letter before them, conjuring them all to be faithful to their Oath of Secrecy.

XVIII. Now, could they have trusted each other, the Juncto and their Army might have carried all before them, and most Persons of Estate and Fortune in *England* being concern'd in the late Insurrection, had they made them away, (as was once propos'd among them) and seiz'd their Estates, it would shrewdly have weaken'd, if not extinguish'd the Royal Interest, and raised so vast a Sum of Money for the Payment of Debts, and the Continuance of their Army, as might have perpetuated the Usurpation. But instead of this, the Juncto at *Westminster* sat towring themselves in the high Imagination of their continued Power, after the Defeat of the designed Insurrection against them, their Army the mean while wantonly pluming and trimming their Feathers at *Derby*, whither they were advanced after their Defeat of Sir *George Booth*. And having routed a Company of new rais'd Soldiers, and unarmed *Welshmen*; they were as much transported with Pride and Vanity, as if they had fought the great Battle at *Arbela*, or utterly vanquish'd *Hannibal* and his Party in the Overthrow at *Metaurus*. But instead of pursuing the true Ends of their desperate Interest, they fell to quarrelling

relling among themfelves. The Juncto and their Army knew fo much Falfhood and Villany in each other, as it was not poffible for them to hold long together. Their late Actions in difabling their chief Officers from granting Commiffions, had fo leffen'd their Power and Influence on the Army, as they were refolv'd to take the firft Opportunity to reftore their military Authority to its former Grandeur. And becaufe *Lambert*'s conceal'd Ambition was moft concern'd to obviate thefe Practices, and his Brigade, by this War of half an Hour, were moft fpiritted with Sournefs and Arrogance againft their Mafters at *Weftminfter*; they were thought fitteft to begin the Contrivance, which was prefently after abetted by the other Regiments remaining in and about *London*, under the Command of Lieutenant General *Fleetwood*, with fuch bold and infolent Demands upon the Juncto, and fuch pert Expoftulations with them, together with a moft unmannerly Oftentation of their own Merits and Services, as muft needs either leffen the Authority of their Mafters, or end in a Rupture.

XIX. The Juncto, that wanted not Cunning to introfpect thefe Defigns of the Officers, were refolv'd to make fome further Alterations in the Government of the Army. And, on the other Side, the Commanders, both

both to strengthen their Interest, and that the Juncto might have no other Force to retreat unto for Support, had dispatched Letters to the Armies in *Scotland* and *Ireland*, to gain Subscriptions to their Representation and Petition. They had design'd, in this their new Model, to wheadle General *Monk* with the Place of General of the Infantry; who yet look'd so far into their Reach and Designs, that, upon Receipt of these Letters and Papers, he forbad all under his Command to subscribe to them, and return'd Answer to the Officers in *London*, that the House having already declar'd their Dislike of their Representation, he was resolv'd to keep his own Army in Obedience to the Authority of Parliament, and that several of his Officers were dissatisfy'd with this their Way of Proceeding.

C H A P. X.

I. *Upon a thorough Consideration within himself of the State of the King's Affairs, the General determines, for the present, to conceal his Design of serving him.* II. *He advises his Brother and Sir* John Greenvil *to concern themselves no more in the*

the Affair; III. *Though he was not inwardly displeas'd with the Proposal.* IV. *He receives Intelligence of a Rupture likely to ensue between the Parliament and the Army.* V. *Mr.* Monk *returns to* London, *and acquaints Sir* John Greenvil *with what had passed between him and the General, which is likewise communicated to the King by Sir* John. VI. *Delivers a Message from the General to Commissary* Clarges, *that he would support the Parliament.* VII. *Whereupon the Parliament voted, that no Taxes should be rais'd without Consent of Parliament, disbanded several Officers, and appointed Commissioners for the Government of the Army.* VIII. Lambert *immediately sets a Guard upon the Parliament, to exclude the Juncto.* IX. *And appoints a Committee of Safety.* X. *The General prepares to take Advantage of these Alterations in* England. XI. *And uses the Authority of the Juncto only as a Pretext.* XII. *The General's main Scheme supported by two Principles, that the Military must be subject to the Civil Power, and the present Form of Civil Authority must be Parliamentary.*

I. THE Interveniency of so many new Occurrences in *England*, had hitherto put a Stop to Mr. *Monk*'s Message to the General;

General; who yet, all this while, gave that dangerous Affair a particular Place in his Thoughts and Retirement. He considered the King's Interest was now so very low, that he could receive no Accession of Power from his Party; and by the Defeat of Sir *George Booth*, and of those other design'd Insurrections, all things were grown worse. That to enter into a Treaty at this Time with the King would be as dangerous, as to declare for him; since there have never wanted false or needy Men about his Majesty, by whom his Secrets had been hitherto betray'd. He forgat not how much he had been oblig'd by his Relations, the Family of the *Greenvils*; but being removed out of his Country, and from the Conversation of his Kindred, when he was very young; and himself and Sir *John Greenvil* having been engag'd on different Sides, and wholly Strangers to each other, he could not yet satisfy himself, whether he were a Person of Abilities and Secrecy enough to transact with in so difficult an Affair. And for his own Brother, he look'd upon an Employment of this Nature and Intricacy, as altogether foreign and unsuitable to a private Clergyman, that had been bred up among his Books and in Retirement. The Designs of restoring the King by Plots and Insurrections, he had always esteemed but as so many Toys that would come to nothing, where

where raw and unexperienc'd Soldiers were to encounter with Regiments, that had been so long used to Arms and Victory. He was resolv'd therefore at present, not to discover his Inclinations to the King's Service, till he could first see himself in such a Station as would be able to support him alone, and justify his Proceedings, without depending upon the accessory and contingent Assistances of others. The revealing also of this dangerous Message to others beside himself, was some Prejudice to the Success of it. For though General *Monk* trusted Dr. *Price* as much as most of those about him, yet he cared not to stand at any Man's Mercy or Discretion for the concealing his Secrets. And having nothing but a Message by Word of Mouth, and the King's Letter being left behind, it made him have the colder Aspect upon the whole Business; which may easily be believ'd by those that shall consider, what Effects these Letters had seven Months after, when they came to be delivered in better Circumstances.

II. But this Affair being for the present wholly laid aside, that which puzzled the General's Thoughts most, was, the Care of concealing it. To that End he took the next Opportunity of discoursing privately with his Brother, advising him to follow his Studies, and the Care of his Living, and no more to concern

concern himself in publick Business; and that he should carry this Advice to his Cousin *Greenvil*, not to meddle any more in such dangerous Adventures; and conjuring them both to an entire Secrecy, he told his Brother with some Passion: *That if ever this Business were discovered by him, or Sir* John Greenvil, *he would do the best he could to ruin them both.*

III. By all these Passages the considerate Reader will easily discern, that General *Monk* was not so really displeas'd with the Proposal made to him, as that it surpriz'd him in the midst of so many unseasonable Circumstances; so that his principal Care was, first to conceal his own Intentions from others, and next to oblige the Secrecy of those that had been dealing with him.

IV. THE General had all this while a particular Account, by Letters from *London*, of the Discontents risen between the Parliament and the Army, which were likely to determine in a downright Quarrel. And being resolved to make his Advantage of them both, he directed his Brother, now preparing for his Return into *England*, to find out Commissary *Clarges* so soon as he came to *London*, and deliver his Message to him. And having given Mr. *Monk* such Advice and Assistance

tance as was necessary for the bestowing of his Daughter, he dismiss'd them both with a very particular Kindness.

V. Mr. NICHOLAS MONK took his Leave at *Dalkeith* about the 8th of *October*, intending to return the same Way he came, and Dr. *Price*, who, by this long Conversation with him, had a particular Esteem for his Person, as well as his Message, accompanied him and his Daughter to the Shore at *Leith*, where he took shipping for *London*, and arrived there about four Days after. He first found out Sir *John Greenvil*, and acquainted him with the whole Account of his Voyage to his Brother, and of all that pass'd between them; assuring him that, at least for the present, nothing could be expected from General *Monk*, with whom he had taken an Oath of Secrecy, about which he was not to be examin'd, but hoped good Effects of it would in due Time appear, and he was resolv'd now to hasten home to his Family. Sir *John Greenvil* took the first Opportunity to acquaint his Majesty and the Lord Chancellor *Hyde* at *Brussels* with this Account; which, coming to no farther Period, was laid aside for the present, till we find it resumed again in the Sequel of our Story.

VI. THE

VI. The same Evening Mr. *Monk* coming to Commissary *Clarges*, he acquainted him with the General's Message; by which he was directed to inform the Members of the Parliament, that if the Army in *London* continued in their Disobedience towards them, he would assist them therein, and if things should run into farther Extremity, he would be in Readiness to march his Army into *England* in Defence of them.

VII. The next Morning early Commissary *Clarges* acquainted some of the leading Members with the Message from General *Monk*; which being communicated to the rest, had a present Effect both upon their Spirits and Counsels. They were dogged and angry enough before at the Insolence of their Servants; but now something of Bravery and Disdain began to sparkle in their Displeasure. Insomuch that the old Senators adventured now to ruffle with their Colonels; being resolv'd that if they must leave their soft Seats, they would first empty out the Feathers. They had already discharg'd the Commonwealth from all Taxes, otherwise than by Consent in Parliament: Now they pass'd a brisk Vote, to strike eight or nine of the most daring Colonels off the Tally, and vacated their Commissions, (*viz. Lambert, Desborow,*

Desborow, Berry, Kelsey, Ashfield, Cobbet, Packer, Creed and *Barrow*) And then dissolving the present Constitution of the Army, they pass'd an Act for the appointing seven Commissioners to take the Charge of it, (*viz. Fleetwood, Monk, Hazlerig, Ludlow, Morley, Walton,* and *Overton,*) who were to enter upon their Trust from the 7th of this present *October*, and to continue till the 22d of *February* following.

VIII. These nimble Proceedings of the Juncto put the discarded Officers and their Party into some Disorder; who thereupon resolv'd to venture at all, before these new Commissioners should have any Time to settle their Interest or Authority over the Soldiers. The next Morning therefore very early, *Lambert*, having gotten together such Force as he had at Hand, possess'd himself of all the Avenues to the Parliament House, and excluded the eminent Assertors of the good old Cause from further meeting there. In whose Room a Combination of the Army-Officers had presently in Readiness another new Device to succeed, which they call'd a *Committee of Safety*.

Oct. 13.

IX. They who soberly observed the Falshood and Hypocrisy, the Folly and Madness, of these boisterous Colonels, did believe them

I possess'd

possess'd with more Devils than one, having, in six Months Time, shifted three Governments, and set up another Idol and Scheme of Government, that was not likely to outlast two Moons.

X. EVER since the Death of *Oliver Cromwel*, General *Monk* expected nothing else than a successive Series of extravagant Alterations in *England*, which he hoped might give him Opportunity of obliging his Country; and therefore more narrowly inspected the Temper and Inclinations of his Officers and Army. And though he was a Person naturally provident, yet of late Years he was more careful than before, in taking the Accounts of the Treasury of War, and in keeping good Store of Money in *Bank*, of which he had seventy thousand Pounds, besides what was in other Hands. The Magazines also of Arms and Ammunition in *Scotland* were very well supply'd.

XI. THE General very well knew this Juncto which the Army had disturbed, were People neither to be endured nor trusted; therefore he was resolved to make use of them, and their Interest, no further than as a Pretext to oppress the insolent Designs of the *English* Army, and afterwards to lay aside our Juncto also.

XII. AND

XII. And here we will seasonably acquaint the Reader, with the two declared Principles of General *Monk*, which he had framed with that popular Appearance and plausible Aspect, as they became the Basis of all his Proceedings. And though he was sometimes forc'd to sail by different Winds, yet he still kept himself steady to these two Points. One was, *That the Government could not be supported but by an entire Subjection of the Military Power in Obedience to the Civil:* The other, *That the present Constitution of the Commonwealth was to be administer'd by Parliaments.*

With these two Principles, prudently managed, he was sure to have always a Game to play in all publick Alterations. By the first he had contriv'd to awe or oppose the Extravagancies of the Army in *England*. And by improving the other to successive Elections, he was not without Hope, but that at one Time or other such a Parliament might happen to be chosen, as would be willing to restore the Monarchy. And that he was still aiming at this Contrivance, will appear both by his Letter to the Parliament at *Westminster*, and by his Instructions given to his Commissioners at the following Treaty; by his Design of dissolving the Juncto, and by Admission of the secluded Members, in order to to a new and full Parliament. Besides, the usual Emulation and Jealousies which so frequently happen among those that command Armies; the Temper and Principle of General *Monk*, and the chief Officers in *England*, was wholly incompatible. Nor is it easy to say, whether he did more hate or despise them, knowing himself superior to them in all the Arts of War and Conduct. And tho' he abhorr'd the Thought of assuming the Government himself; yet he greatly disdain'd that *Lambert*, or any other, should dare to attempt it, whilst himself had a Sword in his Hand.

CHAP. XI.

I. *General* Monk *receives Intelligence of the Proceedings of* Lambert *and his Party*. II. *Begins his March into* England, *having first made a Speech to his Army*. III. *Sends Captain* Johnson *to secure* Berwick, *Captains* Berry *and* Hall *to* Edenburgh, *whither he himself follows, taking up all disaffected Officers in those, and other remoter Garrisons*. V. *Marches to* Leith *and* Linlithgow, *from whence, after having made some Regulations, he returns to*

Eden-

Edenburgh. VI. *A Character of Dr.* Gumble. VII. *Colonel* Cobbet *is sent to* Scotland *by the Committee of Officers, to cause Division in General* Monk's *Army; but Captain* Johnson *carries him Prisoner to* Edenburgh. VIII. *A more particular Account of* Cobbet's *Designs, with some other Indignities from the* English *Army, which the General resents.* IX. *The General publishes a Declaration: The Substance of it.* X. *Writes to* Fleetwood *and* Lambert; *to* Lenthall *the Speaker, and to the Independent Churches.* XI. *As also to the Forces in* Ireland, *desiring their Assistance.* XII. *And to the Fleet, both which refuse to join with him.* XIII. *The General's Resolution.*

I. THE News of interrupting the pretended Parliament by *Lambert* and his Party, came to *Dalkeith* by the next Post, and was no Surprizal upon General *Monk*, who expected no less; and therefore was before-hand resolv'd how to go to work with them. For the same Minute he receiv'd the Intelligence, he communicated his Resolution to such Officers as were then about him, and presently dispatch'd away Adjutant *Smith* to *Edenburgh* and *Leith*, commanding the Officers of both those Garrisons, which were within five Miles of him, to attend him presently

Oct. 17.

sently at *Dalkeith*; where he acquainted them with his Resolution of marching into *England*, to restore the Parliament: Unto all which they unanimously assented. And the same Night he commanded, that no Post should pass for *England*, to give Account of his Preparation, till he were further advanced. The Citadels of *St. Johnstons* and *Ayr* were both important Places; but at a considerable Distance from *Dalkeith*. And General *Monk* had no great Opinion of the Persons that commanded them in chief: He had therefore sent for Captain *Witter* of the one, and Captain *Robinson* of the other, being Officers he had some Confidence in, who were both of them with him at *Dalkeith*, when the News came of the Interruption upon the Parliament. The next Morning therefore he dispatch'd them both with Instructions to secure those two Citadels, with Authority also to imprison such Officers or others as should dissent or oppose them therein: Which was some Days after effectually perform'd by Captain *Robinson* at *Ayr*, and Captain *Witter* at *St. Johnstons*.

Oct. 18.

II. In the Afternoon General *Monk*, being attended with his Guards at *Dalkeith*, marched to *Edenburgh*; where were quarter'd only two Regiments of Foot, one whereof was his own, the other Colonel *Talbot's*, who was
then

General Monk. 119

then abfent at *London*. And having fecured or difcarded fuch Officers as he diftrufted, and placed others in their Room, he told them at the Head of the Regiments then drawn up, *That the Army in* England *had broken up the Parliament, out of a reftlefs and ambitious Humour to govern all themfelves, and to hinder the Settlement of the Nation. That their next Practice would be to impofe their infolent Extravagancies upon the Army in* Scotland, *that was neither inferior nor fubordinate to them. For his own Part, he thought himfelf obliged, by the Duty of his Place, to keep the Military Power in Obedience to the Civil; and that fince they had receiv'd their Pay and Commiffion from the Parliament, it was their Duty to defend them; in which he expected the ready Obedience of them all: But if any did declare their Diffent to his Refolution, they fhould have Liberty to leave the Service, and might take Paffes to be gone.*

III. This was fpoken with the Authority and Spirit of a General, and without Difguife or Artifice, but was receiv'd with the univerfal Shout and Submiffion of the Regiments. The fame Evening retiring to his Quarters, it was deliberated by the General, and Officers about him, of how much Importance it would be to fecure *Berwick*. He was well enough

I 4   affur'd

assur'd of the Fidelity of Colonel *Meers*, who commanded the Garrison. But the rest of the Officers were Anabaptists, in whom he could have no Confidence, and which were a sort of Vermin, which he was now resolv'd to worm out of his Army. The same Night therefore he dispatch'd away Captain *Johnson* with a Party of Horse, to assist the Governor in securing the Place, with Orders also to bring off with him all unquiet and disaffected Officers.

IV. At the same Time there were attending at *Edenburgh*, Captain *Derry* and Captain *Hall*, who commanded in Colonel *Cobbet*'s Regiment at *Glascow*, and had receiv'd Orders to march the Regiment to *Edenburgh*, and secure the Officers that dissented. The Colonel was then at *London*, and the two Captains perform'd their Instructions. And before General *Monk* left *Edenburgh*, he sent for several suspected Officers, who commanded in remoter Garrisons, to attend him there, who, at their Arrival, were secured in the Castle of *Edenburgh*, and their Commissions granted to such as he could better trust. The Regiments at *Aberdeen* were secured by Colonel *Fairfax* the Governor. And Colonel *Rhead* was made Governor of *Inverness*, and ordered to send three of his best Companies to the General at *Edenburgh*. And having

GENERAL MONK. 121

ing thus settled the remoter Garrisons by such Officers as he esteem'd most faithful to him, the nearer were disposed of by himself.

V. HAVING stay'd two Days at *Eden-* Oct. 20. *burgh*, he march'd to the Citadel of *Leith*, where was lodg'd a considerable Part of the Stores; and having displaced most of the Anabaptist Officers, he intrusted Mr. *Hughes* with the Command of that Place. The next 21. Day he passed to *Linlithgow*; and having satisfy'd himself in the Settlement of that Garrison, he return'd again to *Edenburgh*.

VI. WHERE he had much Conference with D[r]. *Gumble*, who was Preacher to the Council of State, and by that Employment, and his continual Residence at the capital City, (besides his own forward Inclination) he had a very intimate Acquaintance with, and some Influence upon, most of the Officers; so that General *Monk*, who very well knew how to chuse his Instruments, had of late admitted him to several of his Counsels. He had formerly been Vicar of *Wickham* in *Buckinghamshire*, in which Town Mr. *Scot* had lived, and was Burgess for that Place. By Mr. *Scot*'s Interest he was thought to have been preferr'd to this Employment in *Scotland*, where he kept always an exact Correspondence with him, and others of the Party, being

ing a very zealous Commonwealth's Man, insomuch as he could not conceal his Discontents against the Usurpation of *Cromwel*, and his Son, in setting up the Government of a single Person. The General having resolved (as the best Expedient at present) to justify his quarrelling with the *English* Army, by declaring to restore the Commonwealth Parliament, made very great Use of Dr. *Gumble*, to represent his Designs advantagiously to Mr. *Scot*, who was a leading Man among them, and a President to their Council of State; and also to inspirit the Officers and Soldiers of *Scotland* to a Compliance with the Resolution of their General. In both which Particulars he did him very great Service; and in this Affair of restoring the Parliament, Dr. *Gumble* was so intent and earnest in all Discourse with the General and others, that some of the Officers thought him the first Promoter of the Design against the Army in *England*. And others, that dissented, wrote in their Letters to their Party in *London*, that *Gumble* was the grand Incendiary, in provoking General *Monk* to this Resolution. The General, who knew the Suspicions that were upon him, was very well pleas'd with this Apprehension they had taken up among them, being willing they should believe any thing the Cause of these Proceedings rather than the true one.

VII. A-

VII. About this Time Captain *Johnson* (whom we mention'd before) returned to the General from *Berwick*, where he had assisted Colonel *Meers* in settling the Garrison, and imprisoning the dissenting Officers. But before they had fully done their Business, Colonel *Cobbet* arrived from *London* thither, in his Way to *Glascow*, where his Regiment was quarter'd. He was hasten'd down by the Committee of Officers in *London*, to dispose the Army under General *Monk* to a Compliance with their Designs, and to oppose or secure such Persons as dissented; being a stout and active Man, and of very great Interest in the Army. So soon as he came to *Berwick*, he began to be very busy in declaring against General *Monk*'s Proceedings, and to remonstrate against them: So that the Officers there (notwithstanding all his bustling) took the Boldness to lay him fast; and Captain *Johnson* had now brought him Prisoner (with the other Malecontents of that Garrison) to *Edenburgh*, where they were all secur'd in the Castle.

VIII. General *Monk* was well pleas'd with this Service of Major *Johnson*, in preserving a Place so important to his further Designs, and in securing so dangerous a Person as Colonel *Cobbet*; having before receiv'd,

from

from his Intelligencer at *London,* the Advice of his coming, and the Instructions he had from *Wallingford-House,* to make Disturbances and Parties in the *Scotch* Army, and to improve his Interest so far amongst the Soldiers, as to seize the General himself if he did not comply with their Actions. This Design upon him, before they could possibly know any thing of his dissenting, did greatly provoke the General, both against them and their Officers at *London,* and their Instrument *Cobbet:* Besides some other of their little Affronts which they had put upon him, in their last Letters, when they desired Subscription in the *Scotch* Army to their Representation. They had cajol'd General *Monk* with the Offer of General of the Infantry over all the Forces in the Army; but in their new Model, since their Interruption of the Juncto, they had taken no Notice of him. Though he was not desirous to receive any new Obligation of Kindness from those he was resolv'd to quarrel with, yet he resented the Indignity, being as dextrous in dissembling Affronts that were put upon him, as he was sure to remember and requite them.

IX. The General being by this Time gotten somewhat before-hand in his Business, by settling and securing so many of the nearer Garrisons and Regiments; it was next deliberated

rated by him and his Council of Officers, to give the Nation an Account of this their Proceeding, by a publick Declaration. The Substance whereof was: *That they had now taken Arms only to defend the Freedom and Privilege of Parliaments, and to vindicate the Rights and Liberties of the People against all Opposition whatsoever.* This was accordingly printed at *Edenburgh*, and dispersed through *Scotland* and *England*.

X. But at the same Time some of those that had consented to follow their General in these Proceedings, began to be afraid of making so wide a Breach between the two Armies; and therefore propos'd to the General, that he would endeavour to rectify these Mistakes and Prejudices between both the Armies, by writing first to the principal Officers in *London*. They who best understood the Interest of the Army in *Scotland*, did greatly dislike the Proposal; but, in their present State of Affairs it was not safe to decline that Method, so much to the Discontent or Suspicion of those who were Authors of it. Letters therefore were agreed to be drawn up to *Fleetwood* and *Lambert*, in which the General, expostulating their Violence to the Parliament, declar'd his own, and the unanimous Resolution of the Army under his Command, to assert their Authority. At the same Time
other

other Letters were also written to Mr. *Lenthall*, the Speaker of the late Parliament, to acquaint him, that if the Interruption did continue, he should be ready with his Army to restore them to their Session, according to the Duty of his Place. And because several of his Officers that adher'd to him, were Members of Independent Congregations in *England*, it was thought fit by the same Messenger, to satisfy that Interest in the Justice of their Quarrel; assuring them by a Letter: *That they had no Contention with the Army in* England *relating to Religion, or any religious Persuasion; that their spiritual Liberties should not be violated by him, or his Army; but that he was in Duty obliged to support the Authority of Parliaments, against the ambitious Practices of the Army in* England. A Copy of the Letter to the Speaker, and of those also to *Fleetwood* and *Lambert*, were presently after put to the Press at *Edenburgh*. But the other to the Independent Churches, being against the Grain of the Presbyterian Methods in *Scotland*, was ordered to be printed at *London*.

XI. GENERAL *Monk* having dispatch'd away a Messenger with these Letters to *London*, was in the Interim careful to strengthen his Interest, by the Accession of other remote Correspondencies. To that End he wrote
Letters

Letters to the Forces in *Ireland*, representing the Justness and Necessity of his Proceedings against the *English* Army, and desiring their Assistance with him in restoring the Parliament; from whom he receiv'd a very cold and dissenting Answer.

XII. At the same Time there was a good Fleet riding in the *Downs*, commanded by Vice-Admiral *Lawson*, from whom he might, with much Confidence, expect a Compliance; having been, some Years since, their Admiral in the fortunate War against the *Dutch*, and had left them with an extraordinary Memory and high Estimation of his Bravery and Courage. But the Officers at *London* had beforehand, by their Agents, done his Business so effectually, by misrepresenting his Intentions, that the Fleet was resolv'd to stand off, till they were further satisfy'd in the Clearness of his Designs. The like Answers he receiv'd from Colonel *Overton*, then Governor of *Hull*, and some other Garrisons in *England*, who were content to become Intercessors between him and the *English* Officers for an Agreement; but would not otherwise be concern'd in the Quarrel.

XIII. No Man, except General *Monk*, could happily have kept his Thoughts steady and resolute in the midst of so many cross Accidents,

Accidents, which took him in the very Beginning of his Designs. But being only to form his own Army into an exact Obedience to himself; he was very much assur'd, if he could not be in a Capacity to invade *England*, yet his Enemies should never be able to force him out of *Scotland:* Having resolv'd to raise the Kingdom in Arms, and to entrust the Nobility and Gentry of that Nation, before he would take a Baffle from them.

CHAP. XII.

I. *The Effect of his Letters, the Army in* England *under a great Consternation.* II. *They send Commissary* Clarges *and Colonel* Talbot *to treat with General* Monk. III. Newcastle *secured for the Committee of Safety, by Colonel* Lilburn. IV. *Which proved an Advantage to the General.* V. *Commissary* Clarges *and Colonel* Talbot *arrive at* Edenburgh. VI. *Commissary* Clarges *privately informs the General, of the ill Condition of those who sent him; however, to gain Time for bringing together his distant Forces,* VII. *The General consents to a Treaty between the two Armies, and appoints Commissioners.* VIII. *Gives his Commis.*

Commissioners some private Instructions. IX. *The Council of Officers at* London *prepare for a War.* X. Lambert *marches into the North.* XI. *Meets with General* Monk's *Commissioners at* York, *and treats with them, but without coming to any Agreement.* XII. Lambert *sends a Message to General* Monk *by Major General* Morgan. XIII. *Who, at the same time, privately delivers a Message from the Lord* Fairfax *to the General.* XIV. Fleetwood *also writes privately a civil Letter to the General.* XV. *A Letter of Thanks from the independent Congregations in* London *to the General,* XVI. *Carried by two of their Pastors, and two Colonels: Their Behaviour and Reception.* XVII. *Fresh Endeavours to raise Sedition among the General's Soldiers.* XVIII. *The General's great Care to prevent it.* XIX. *He appoints a special Committee of Officers for the receiving and dispatching Messengers.*

I. ABOUT *October* 28. his Messenger arrived with the Letters at *London*, which had all of them the very same Effect that General *Monk* expected. For the Juncto were thereupon contriving to make Parties in the Army that might distract their Councils. But *Fleetwood* and *Lambert*, and their Committee

Oct. 28.

mittee of Safety, were greatly surpriz'd at the Receipt of these Letters. And being farther inform'd by his Messenger, (who was ill chosen for that Employment) how far General *Monk* had proceeded in modelling his Army and Officers to a Compliance with his Designs, and the Influences he had over them; that he had clapt up Colonel *Cobbet* so soon as he arriv'd, and secur'd or cashier'd one hundred and forty of his distrusted Officers; they began to think they had taken wrong Measures with him, and were merely impos'd upon by the foolish Persuasion of those who assur'd them, that the *Scotch* Army would not be brought to engage against their Brethren in *England*; and that, though it were believ'd General *Monk* would not comply with the Officers at *London*, yet he wanted Interest enough in his Army to lead them his own Way. And they knew him so well, that if he could fix his Army to a Submission and Dependance upon him, he had Courage and Conduct enough to give them more Trouble than all the Enemies they had yet met with.

II. They had therefore no mind to enter into a down-right War with General *Monk*; but, upon farther Consultation, it was resolv'd to attempt him by a Treaty; in Hopes to bring off the General himself, or at least

GENERAL MONK. 131

some of his Officers, to unite with them. Very late therefore the same Evening they *Oct. 28.* sent for Commissary *Clarges*, and Colonel *Talbot*, who had a Foot Regiment then quarter'd in *Edenburgh*, to attend them presently at the Council, then sitting in *White-Hall*. Where they inform'd them, that they had receiv'd Letters from General *Monk*; by which it did appear, their Proceedings in *London* had been misrepresented to him; that there were some evil Instruments about him, which had endeavoured to create Jealousies between the chief Officers in the two Armies, and (against the Interest of both) to engage them in a War, or Distrust of each other. And having given them farther Instructions how to manage their Message with the General, and his Officers, they commanded them both to hasten their Journey to him; being so nettled with the Business, that they allow'd them but three Hours Time to make ready for so long a Voyage. But if General *Monk* had chosen an ill Messenger to carry his Letter to *London*, these Officers had more grossly mistaken themselves, in sending these two Persons, especially the Commissary, on their Errand into *Scotland*.

III. But leaving these Gentlemen in procinct of their hasty Journey, we will pass before them again into the North, where we shall find General *Monk* busied in the farther modelling of his Army. And because he would have Passes enough for his own Motions, or for the Accession of such Parties as he hop'd might rise for him in *England*, he was resolv'd to secure the two grand Avenues into *Scotland*. To that End he had before sent Major *Dean* with a Party of Horse to secure *Carlisle*, who fail'd in the Attempt: And had now commanded Colonel *Knight* with four Troops of Horse, and Major *Miller* with six Foot Companies, to surprize *Newcastle*. But having marched as far as *Morpeth*, they receiv'd Intelligence, that Colonel *Lilburn* had prevented their Design upon *Newcastle*; and had already entered the Town with a Party, resolving to keep it for the Committee of Safety. This Person was quartered at *York*, and so soon as he heard of General *Monk*'s Proceedings in *Scotland*, was very busy in the North to contrive against him. For besides the Contradiction of their different Aims and Principles, *Lilburn* had an old Grudge against General *Monk*, ever since he was thought the abler Man to succeed him in the Command of *Scotland*, of which we have given an Account before. But so soon as General *Monk* had received Advice, that *Lilburn* had possess'd *Newcastle*, he dispatch'd Orders to Colonel *Knight* and Major

jor *Miller*, to proceed no farther; but, for the present, to retreat to *Alnwick*.

IV. Not long after, General *Monk* found his own good Fortune, in missing this Place: Which, being a Frontier Town, would happly have been besieg'd by *Lambert*, before the General could have been in Readiness to have march'd for the Relief of it: so that either he would have been enforc'd to enter upon Action before he had been prepared, or to have expos'd those Troops and Companies, which were some of the choicest Men of his Army, and greatly devoted to his Service; and the Officers, such as had given the most early Experiment of their Fidelity.

V. About the 2d of *November*, the fore- *Nov. 2.* mentioned Messengers from the Council of Officers, Commissary *Clarges* and Colonel *Talbot*, arrived at *Edenburgh*; and upon Delivery of their Message, General *Monk* presently perceiv'd the Officers in *London* did rather fear than despise him; since they had taken the Trouble of sending Agents on purpose so far, to compliment him into a better Opinion of their Proceedings, and to procure a Treaty.

VI. The General had much secret Discourse with Commissary *Clarges*, whose coming was

very

very seasonable to him, being able to give him a very good Account of the Condition of those who sent him. By whom he was assured, that they were jealous of each other, and in such want of Money, as they could not take up a few Weeks Pay for the setting forth the Army, which they were preparing to send down into the North. General *Monk* very well knew he had already proceeded farther, than was possible to be made up by a Treaty; that the Officers in *England* would never trust him, and he was resolv'd to have no farther Confidence in them: So that a Treaty could produce no good, nor did he intend it should. But because his own Officers might be better satisfied with the Equity and Temper of his Proceedings; and especially in regard a great Part of his Army was not yet fix'd and settled to his mind, and some of them were more than two hundred Miles apart; which would take Time both to inform the Officers, and to march those far distant Parties to a Rendezvous; he found it his own Interest and Convenience (for the gaining farther Leisure) to consent to a Treaty.

VII. THE next Morning therefore, at a Council of Officers, the General acquainted them with the Message he had receiv'd from *London*: That the Officers there were desirous of a Treaty, to adjust the Apprehensions and

General Monk. 135

and Jealousies between the two Armies, which was readily assented to by the Council of Officers; and that three Persons should be chosen among them for this Employment. But they were so civil towards their General, and confident in his Prudence, that they would refer the Nomination to himself; who therefore propos'd Colonel *Knight* and Colonel *Clobery*, and, in Requital of their Respect, left it to the Officers to appoint a third Person, who then chose Colonel *Wilks*.

VIII. These Commissioners were dispatched away with all convenient Speed, having receiv'd their publick Instructions from the Council of Officers. But before they took Leave of the General, he gave them also private Directions of his own, which they were particularly oblig'd to pursue, *viz.* besides treating with the Officers in *London*, they were to use all the Art they could, to inspect the different Aims and Interests that were among them, not to oblige themselves to the set Time, to which they were confin'd by the Council of Officers, but rather to protract it, if they found Cause. But in a most particular Manner they were charged not to consent to any Agreement, otherwise than by restoring the late Parliament; but if that Point could not possibly be gain'd, then that a new one should

should be chosen by the People. For General *Monk* very well knew, there was no dealing with them, if he could not bring the *English* Army to acknowledge some Authority superior to themselves: And if they could be brought to submit to a Parliament freely chosen, which would be sure to oppose them, he should then never want Opportunity or Interest to make himself their Match. He was now growing old in Armour, having turn'd the Shadow of his fiftieth Year, being in the Maturity of his Judgment and Experience, and was as much their Superior in the Methods of War, as in the Justness of his Cause.

IX. But the General Council of Officers in *London*, though they had sent down their Messengers, Commissary *Clarges* and Colonel *Talbot*, to procure a Treaty, yet, being doubtful of the Event, were resolv'd to second the Design for Peace, with Preparation to a War, in Case General *Monk* should prove restive or incomplaisant.

X. To this End Major General *Lambert* (who had contriv'd this Expedition in the last Stage of his Ambition) was order'd to march toward the North, with such Forces as could be spar'd out of the City, which were to be complcated with the Addition of those Regiments,

ments, that, after the Defeat of Sir *George Booth*, were quarter'd toward the Northern Counties. Their Success in *Cheshire* four Months before, had rais'd in them such an extraordinary Vanity and Confidence, that they did not consider they were now to encounter another Sort of Warfare, and another kind of General.

XI. Major General *Lambert* advanc'd presently with his Forces towards the North, and at *York* met the Commissioners of the Treaty in their Way to *London*; and was willing to have spar'd them the Trouble of a longer Journey, assuring them, that he had brought with him Powers from the Committee of Safety, and the Council of Officers, to treat with them, and to compose the Differences. But when they came to enter upon the Business, the Commissioners would assent to nothing, till it was first agreed, that the late Parliament should be restored. This was a Point which *Lambert* (who had dissolv'd the Juncto) could least of all assent to, and was resolv'd against; and therefore pretending he had no instructions to treat of it, the Commissioners were permitted to go on their Journey. Only it was here agreed, that, during the Treaty, neither of their Armies should advance from their several Quarters, and that no Act of Hostility should pass between them,

nor

nor any Interruption upon Letters or Messengers.

XII. In this Place Major General *Lambert* found Major General *Morgan*, then recovering from a long Fit of the Gout, by which he had been some Time disabled from returning to his Command in *Scotland*. But now having in good Measure got off from the Arrest of his Gout, he was afraid of a worse Confinement; and therefore prudently dissembled his Opinion of General *Monk*'s Proceedings; insomuch as *Lambert*, upon Conference with him, thought him a very fit Person to promote his Design in *Scotland*, where he was Major General to the Army; and of so particular a Credit with General *Monk*, and Interest among the Soldiers, that it was hop'd he would be able, either to incline the General to an Agreement, or to draw off a good Part of his Army from him. The next Day therefore he began his Journey to *Edenburgh*, where he attended the General about the 8th of *November*, being some few Days after the Arrival of Commissary *Clarges*, and Colonel *Talbot*. So soon as he came, he publickly gave General *Monk* an Account of his Message from *Lambert*, desiring his Compliance with the Army in *England*. To which it was answered, that if the Parliament were restored again, he had no farther Quarrel;

Nov. 8.

Quarrel: but without it there could be no Agreement.

XIII. In the Evening *Morgan* found Opportunity of private Discourse with the General, and deliver'd to him a Letter from Mr. *Bowles*, a Preacher in *York*, and a particular Agent intrusted by the Lord *Fairfax*, assuring him, his Lordship, and other Persons of Quality in the Country, would be willing to join with him against the Army in *England*, if, instead of restoring that Piece of a Parliament, (which was interupted the 13th of *October* last) he would consent to the Admission also of the formerly secluded Members, or to the calling of a new Representative. The General said little hereunto; but then resolv'd that Commissary *Clarges* should, in his Return to *London*, visit Mr. *Bowles*, and satisfy him a little in those Particulars. And upon farther Discourse together, Major General *Morgan* was so fully satisfy'd in the Justice of the General's Proceedings, that, though he had taken the Pains to bring *Lambert*'s Message, yet did not think himself oblig'd to carry back the Answer, being presently commanded by the General, together with Adjutant *Smith*, to march to the several Horse-Quarters, and to model those Troops according to Instruction.

The

The Presence and Usefulness of Major General *Morgan* was now so seasonable, that he look'd on this single Person as a Balance against those one hundred and forty Officers, that had left his Service, or had been cashier'd.

XIV. About this Time Lieutenant General *Fleetwood*, though he had dispatch'd away Commissary *Clarges*, and Colonel *Talbot*, by Consent of the Council of Officers, to procure a Treaty and Agreement; yet some few Days after, he thought fit to send Letters to General *Monk* by a private Messenger of his own. Before this Time he had entertain'd some Apprehension of *Lambert*'s Ambition, and therefore was resolv'd to procure (if possible) a good Understanding with General *Monk*, by whose Friendship or Conjunction he should be always able to obviate or balance the Designs of the other. To this End he sent down Mr. *Dean*, who was one of the Treasurers of the Army, with a very kind Letter and Proposals to General *Monk*, which though they came to no Effect, yet the General easily discern'd all was not right among themselves. This Messenger's Demeanour and Action in *Scotland*, was very much resented in the Army: For in his Way through their Quarters, he was still distributing Tickets to seduce the Soldiers from their Obedience.

ence. He was very well received by the General at the Head Quarters; yet had the Insolence to talk indecently to him at his own Table, charging him with Designs of introducing *Charles Stuart*; or if he did not design it, yet the Division he had already made between the two Armies, would certainly bring him in. Dr. *Price* was one Morning standing at the Head of a Foot-Company in *Edenburgh*, where this Mr. *Dean* pass'd by, and told them: *My Lord* Lambert *is coming upon you with such a Force, as all General* Monk's *Army will scarce make one Breakfast for him.* But a stout Soldier return'd this surly answer: *That the cold Weather had gotten* Lambert *a very good Stomach, if he could eat their Swords and Pikes, and swallow their Bullets.* But the General presently after gave him Answer, and dismiss'd him, not without some Reflection upon the Insolence of his Carriage and Deportment.

XV. And now the Messengers that procured the Treaty, Commissary *Clarges* and Colonel *Talbot*, having receiv'd their Instructions, return'd back for *London*. But the one fell into *Lambert*'s Army, and continued there; the other went on towards *York*, having Direction from the General to treat farther with Mr. *Bowles*, and to leave with him the General's Letter directed to the Lord *Fairfax*;
and

and had also Orders to settle other Correspondencies in his Way to *London*. We have before given Account of the Letter which General *Monk*, (in Compliance with such Officers of his Army, as were of that Persuasion) had sent to the Independent Congregations in *London*; some whereof were so sensible of his Respect towards them, in giving them the Account of his Actions, and declaring for their Liberty, that they thought themselves oblig'd to return him Thanks by Messengers of their own. Others of them that were more crafty and designing, had a farther Reach in this Contrivance. They were most concern'd for the Power and Interest of the *English* Army; and therefore were resolv'd, by this Opportunity of sending into *Scotland*, if General *Monk* and the rest should prove immoveable, to draw off their own Party there to a Compliance with the Army in *London*.

XVI. To this Employment were chosen two Pastors of their Churches, Mr. *Caryl*, a Person of Learning and Gravity, and Mr. *Barker*. There were also join'd with them, two Colonels of that Communion, *Whalley* and *Goff*; and when they came to *Newcastle*, their Company was increased by the Addition of Mr. *Hammond*, Preacher to a Congregation there, a severe Zealot of the same Way. The two Ministers were to effect an Agreement

ment betwen the two Armies; whilst the two Colonels, being upon this Occasion admitted into the Head-Quarters, should practise upon the inferior Officers, who, together with Mr. *Hammond*, were much accus'd for several very ill Contrivances during their Residence there. But after several Conferences, which did rather incense the General, than persuade him; General *Monk* gave them such Reasons for his Resolution to oppose the *English* Army, that the Messengers of Independency took their Leave of him, hoping his own Commissioners would be more fortunate in concluding the Agreement in *London*, which themselves could not begin at *Edenburgh*.

XVII. GENERAL *Monk* had no sooner dismiss'd these Importunities upon him from abroad, but he was encounter'd with new Disturbances at home. For though he had imprison'd some of those Officers whom he had displac'd, or who had deserted him; yet the most of them were set at Liberty, to settle the Accounts of their Companies, and to take Care of their other Affairs, before they left the Country. These Officers, having thus lost their Commission and Employment, grew very mutinous in *Edenburgh*, accusing the General for the Methods he had taken with them, contriving to raise Seditions and Parties among

among their own Soldiers againſt him: So that the General was enforc'd to command their Departure out of *Scotland* preſently, where they were neither to ſtay nor to return again at the Peril of their Heads. But for their Arrears, they were to ſtate them with their new Maſters whither they were going, being reſolv'd they ſhould not be enabled to fight againſt him with his own Money, to the Prejudice of the other Part of his Army, that continued faithful.

XVIII. But to fix the Reſolution of his Soldiers for farther Practices upon them, and to ſpirit them againſt the Army in *England*, there was particular Care taken in the placing ſuch Serjeants and Corporals over them, as were People of ſome Diſcretion and Truſt; who, converſing more with the common Soldiers than the ſuperior Officers did, had continual Opportunity of making better Impreſſions upon them. And to the ſame Ends there were frequently publiſh'd Pamphlets and Paſquils, with ſharp Reflections upon the Practice of the Army in *England*, and Dialogues printed, ſtating the Caſe of the Quarrel, between a Soldier of the *Scotch* Army and another of the *Engliſh*. All which were uſually read among them upon the Guards, and paraphras'd upon by the Serjeants or Corporals;

and

and every Week a *Gazette* of the same Purport was printed at *Edenburgh*.

XIX. The General was about this Time besieg'd with so many Letters and continual Messages to him from the general Council of Officers in *London*, and another general Council at *Dublin*, and a third at *Newcastle*, that, besides the standing general Council of all Commission Officers in the Army, he constituted a Committee of principal Commanders, to which were added some Persons of especial Prudence and Trust, who were to peruse all Letters, and to draw up Answers to them; to entertain such Messengers as were sent; to examine the Pacquets, and to stop such Letters as they thought fit; and to prepare all Business ready for the General's Dispatch, against such Time as he was at Leisure to come to Council.

CHAP. XIII.

I. *General* Monk's *Commissioners arrive in* London, *and come to an Agreement with those of the* English *Army, with the Articles of Agreement.* II. *The General is surpriz'd with the News of this Agreement.* III. *And refuses to confirm it, after*

ter having called a Council of Officers, who declare their Dislike of it: Upon which a Letter was sent to Fleetwood, *desiring an Explanation of some of the Articles.* IV. *Then he marches back from* Edenburgh *to* Haddington; *thence to* Dunbar, *and takes up his Quarters at* Berwick. VI. *Some of the General's Horse desert to* Lambert, *who was quartered at* Newcastle. VII. *The General's Letters arrive at* London. *The various Effects of them upon the several Parties there. The Council of State write a Letter of Thanks to him, and make him Generalissimo; though with the Restraint of five Commissioners join'd with him.* VIII. *His Commissioners return to* Scotland. IX. *Discontents in* Lambert's *Army.* X. Lambert *writes to General* Monk, *to resume the Treaty.* XI. *Intercedes for the Release of Colonel* Cobbet, *which the General refuses.* XII. Chillingham *Castle surpriz'd by* Lambert's *Forces, contrary to Agreement, upon which General* Monk *confines Colonel* Zanchy, Lambert's *Messenger.* XIII. *The Arrival of General* Monk's *Commissioners from* London, *and their Excuse. Colonel* Wilks *confin'd.*

I. WE left the Commissioners of the Treaty on their Way to *London,*
where

where they arrived *November* 12. and, with *Nov.* 12.
more Ceremony than Kindness, were receiv'd
at *Wallingford-House* by such Officers as
were appointed by Lieutenant General *Fleetwood* to confer with them. Here they were
so continually caress'd with the Attendance
and Respect of the Officers, that they had
no Opportunity to pursue their secret Instructions, in procuring Intelligence from the City, or the late excluded Members; nor scarce
Freedom enough to deliberate privately a-
mong themselves upon the Articles propos'd
to them. And every Day there were shewed
to them Letters of Intelligence from the North,
(most of which were framed in *London*) informing them of the continual and daily Revolt of General *Monk*'s Forces from him;
and so alarm'd his Commissioners, that
they were afraid at this Rate, within a little
Time, their General would not be worth a
treating with. And therefore instead of pursuing their private Instructions by artificial
Delays, within three Days after their Arrival,
they consented to an Agreement, signed by
them *November* 15. (the same Evening Com- *Nov.* 15.
missary *Clarges*, whom we left at *York*, returned to *London*) which was comprehended
in nine such wild and extravagant Articles,
as any one of them had been sufficient to
have ruined all General *Monk*'s Designs.

1. In the first, they fortify'd their *Conspiracy against the Family of the late King, and all Descendants from him.*

2. By the second, they *precluded the Pretence of any other single Person*; which was contriv'd by that Party of the Commissioners, who were for a Commonwealth, and whereby they might not only shut the Door against the Return of *Richard Cromwel*, but were resolv'd to keep it fast against the later Ambition of *Lambert*.

3. In the third, the Matter was so carried, *that the supreme Power of settling the Commonwealth should remain in the Hands of the general Council of Officers*; only now the Officers of the Army in *Scotland* and *Ireland* should come in for a Share of the Tyranny.

4. And because the late Juncto was not further to be trusted, the fourth *provided for the Election of a new Parliament*; but under such Qualifications as must needs let in only the greatest Villains in the Nation.

5. The fifth took Care for the *paying to the* Scotch *Army the Arrears of their Proportion formerly settled out of the Assessment in* England.

6. The sixth Article was the luckiest of them all, *constituting a Committee of fourteen Officers, half whereof were to be chosen*

General Monk.

sen out of the Army in England, *and the other half out of the Army in* Scotland, *who were to determine the Case of all such Officers as had been displac'd, or given up their Commissions since the* 7th *of* October *last past; and those Commissioners on both Sides were to meet at* Newcastle *in* December *next ensuing*.

7. And because they knew, that, by their manifold Guilts and lawful Practices, they stood in need thereof, the seventh *provided for their Indemnity*.

8. In the eighth; they design'd to render the Pulpit only a Kind of an idle Country Wheadle upon the Clergy of the three Nations, *for their better Support and Encouragement*.

9. And in the ninth was order'd the *Retreat of the several Forces in* England *and* Scotland, *to their former respective Quarters before the Quarrel began*.

II. The Officers at *Wallingford-House* had by this Agreement, so handsomely out-witted General *Monk*'s Commissioners, that they were very well pleas'd with their Contrivance; and therefore presently dispatch'd away their sign'd Articles by two Messengers of their own, *Wallington* and *Floyd*. But before their Arrival into *Scotland*, General *Monk* had left *Edinburgh*, intending to take up his

Quarters at *Berwick*, and was come as far as *Haddington*, where these Messengers found him *November* 18. late in the Evening, as he arose from Supper. The General having broke up the Pacquet, and perus'd the Articles, was strangely surpriz'd at the Contents of them, and did believe his Commissioners were frighted out of their Wits at *London*, or lost them by the Way, having done nothing agreeable to the Instructions he gave them. He then gave the Paper to such Officers as were then present, and (according to his usual Manner) said not a Word to them, but retir'd to his Chamber.

Nov. 18.

III. The next Morning (instead of holding on his March to *Berwick*) he retir'd again to *Edenburgh*, whither the News of the Agreement was arrived before him. So that upon the first Notice of his Return thither, there were good Store of his Officers (then quartering in the Town) ready to attend him in the usual Council Chamber. At his first coming in among them, he was very silent and reserv'd; till some of them began frankly to express their Discontent at this Agreement; others of them, that foresaw their own and the General's Ruin contriv'd by it, were ready to ask Passes to provide for themselves; and others discovered their Passion, in reflecting upon the Weakness and Imprudence of their

their Commissioners. In Conclusion, the General let them know, he lik'd the Agreement as little as any of them: But if they would all unanimously adhere to him, he was resolv'd not to confirm it. To which all that were then present did very faithfully and passionately agree. The General therefore appointed, that a Council of Officers should be conven'd to meet in the Afternoon, where they would farther deliberate upon the Means how to frustrate this Agreement. In this Assembly were present very many Officers, that (upon the late Alteration) were advanced to higher Commands in the Army, who, when they observ'd that, by the sixth Article of Agreement, a Provision was made for restoring the discarded Officers to their Places again, were implacably resolv'd against it; and, as a farther mischievous Contrivance upon General *Monk* and his Officers, this Article look'd no farther than the 7th of *October* last past: So that all those Officers who, (during the Session of the Juncto) had been displac'd by the Committee in *London* for regulating the Army, and were the best and bravest Men in the *Scotch* Army, could receive no Benefit by it, though for the present the General kept them in their Commands by his own immediate Authority. At last it was resolv'd by the General, with some others of his most intimate Counsel, that no Exception should be offer'd offer'd to any of the Articles in particular, but that in the general some Things were so express'd, as wanted a more clear and distinct Explication: And their Commissioners having fail'd in the Pursuit of their Instructions, having pretermitted several other things, which needed further to be agreed upon; that therefore they would crave Leave for the present to defer the Confirmation of these Articles, intreating their Consent for the adding two Commissioners more to the former: which should meet at *Alnwick*, or some other indifferent place, with the like Number of Commissioners from the Army in *England*, in order to a more distinct and lasting Agreement. All which was couch'd and drawn up the same Night, in a Letter to Lieutenant General *Fleetwood* and the Council of Officers, and the next Morning was dispatch'd to *London* by *Wallington* and *Floyd*, who brought down the Agreement.

IV. THE General having thus sent away these Messengers with their Letter, and ordered the Advance of his Army towards the Borders, resum'd again his Resolution for *Berwick*. So that returning from *Edenburgh*, he took up his late Quarters again at *Haddington*; from whence he march'd to *Dunbar*, where he stay'd two Days to take Account of those Forces that were quarter'd in those

those Places. Here he view'd those Hills where he had rais'd the first of his Trophies in *Scotland*, when, well nigh ten Years ago, on the third of *September*, he open'd the Way for the Conquest of the Country, by that memorable and fatal Overthrow of the Covenanters.

V. From *Dunbar* he march'd to *Berwick*, where he arriv'd about the End of *November*, and took up his Head-Quarters. By this Station he was come closer to his Business, and could better inspect the Proceedings of *Lambert*.

VI. It was about the 23d of *November* Nov. 23. when Lieutenant General *Lambert*, having before remov'd his Quarters from *York*, and kept on his Way, came to *Newcastle*, whither he arriv'd with about seven brave Regiments of Horse, and four or five of Foot. Yet in this gallant Army there were two fatal Defects: The Soldiers had no Money, and the General had no Authority. But the advancing so much nearer, began to have some Impression upon General *Monk*'s Army, especially among the Horse Regiments; whereof several Parties stole away in the Night to *Newcastle*. Major General *Morgan* having receiv'd Instructions, as we have before related, to regulate the Troops, (and
Adjutant

Adjutant *Smith* was join'd with him) had taken great Pains in fixing them to the Generaal's Resolution. But a great many of these Troops were Anabaptists, and such like Malecontents, and were more inclin'd to *Lambert*, and the Extravagancies of the *English* Army, than to the steady Councils of their own General. Yet some of these Runagates were surpriz'd before they could get off, and being unhors'd, there were Red-coats, who had been so good Husbands of their Pay, that they could find Money to buy Boots, and were mounted in their Room. General *Monk*, when he had first declar'd against the Army in *England*, was very much concern'd that he was no stronger in Horse, having had two Regiments commanded off from him by the Juncto in the Business of Sir *George Booth*. But after he found so many Traitors and Fugitives among his Troops, he was very well contented that he had no more of them to lose. His Regiments of Foot were entirely devoted to him, and were certainly, for their Courage and exact Discipline, the best Infantry in the World; and so perfectly obedient to their General, that they were resolv'd to fight in his Quarrel, if there had been no Horse at all to assist him.

VII. BEFORE this Time the Messengers with General *Monk*'s Letters were arrived at *London*,

London, where, so soon as it was known, that the General and his Officers had refus'd to sign the Agreement, it rais'd many and various Passions among them. The Council of Officers (who sat hugging themselves in the Success of their Politicks) were greatly surpriz'd with this strange Frustration, after they look'd on the Business as fully concluded, and had so represented it to all their Party. The Citizens, who, about a Fortnight ago, had given up their Liberty for lost, upon the News that both the Armies were agreed, began now to entertain some Hopes of their Redemption, when they were told the Articles would not pass in *Scotland*. And the old Members of the Juncto upon this News began to recover their Spirits. Some while before they were sullen, and out of Humour, that General *Monk*, after he had so briskly declar'd for them, had yet enter'd into a Treaty with *Fleetwood* and his Officers, without advising with them; and that his Commissioners, who manag'd it in *London*, had made no Application to them. But now some of the old Council of State, who were resolv'd to make use of the Occasion, met privately together, and drew up a very kind Letter to him, which was to be convey'd to *Berwick* by a Servant of Sir *Arthur Hazlerig*. In it they greatly magnify'd the Courage and Fidelity he had express'd in his Declaration,

to

to defend the Authority of Parliaments, promising also their utmost Endeavours to concur with him therein. This was subscrib'd by *Scot* the President, and eight more of them, whereof three were joint Commissioners with him, for the Conduct of the Army. And in Testimony of their entire Confidence in him, and their Enmity against *Fleetwood* and *Lambert*, they also sent him a Commission to command as General over all the Forces of *England* and *Scotland*. But it was so artificially and slily penn'd, that if any of the former Commissioners were with him upon the Place, or at such Distance as they could conveniently be advis'd with, he was to take their Consent along with him; only they had reduc'd the Number from seven to five, having now expung'd *Fleetwood* and *Ludlow*.

VIII. Lieutenant General *Fleetwood*, and his Council of Officers, having further consider'd the Contents of General *Monk*'s Letter, were quickly apprehensive there was no very good Meaning towards them in the *Scotch* Army, by this contriv'd Delay of signing the Agreement. They therefore sent for the Commissioners of the Treaty, who were still in Town; expostulating with them this proceeding of the General and his Officers. The Commissioners had very little to say in it: But they, having sign'd those Articles,

some

General Monk. 157

some of them gave Assurance of their utmost Endeavour to procure the speedy Ratification of them, when they should next come to resume the Treaty. Which so far satisfy'd the Council of Officers, that they presently sign'd their Pass for their safe Conduct homewards, flattering themselves with the Confidence of cheating them again in the North, as easily as they had done it at *London*.

IX. But before these Commissioners could get to *Newcastle* in their Way home, the News of General *Monk*'s Demur to the Agreement had made foul Work with *Lambert* and his Officers there; who were more concern'd than any of the rest, for the speedy Conclusion of the Treaty. And though they much exceeded their Enemies in Number, and wanted not Force enough to defend themselves against them, yet they had not their usual Conveniences, nor Money to procure them. And these Soldiers of *Lambert* were a sort of pamper'd and delicate Companions, that for a long Time had known no Hardship, but liv'd at Ease in their *English* Quarters; having nothing else to do, but to eat the Fat of the Land, and to continue the Nation's Slavery. But now these cold Countries of *Northumberland* and *Cumberland*, among a coarse and hardy kind of People, made them as weary of their Quarters, as they were of the War.

X. In

X. In the midst of these, and many other ill Circumstances, Major General *Lambert* was very desirous to hasten the Conclusion of the Treaty. To which end, before General *Monk*'s Commissioners were return'd as far as *Newcastle*, he had sent Colonel *Zanchy* with Letters to General *Monk* and his Officers, (who arriv'd at *Berwick*, *Dec.* 6.) to nominate their two new Commissioners, and to resume the Treaty, but without the Addition of new Matter, that was not agreeable to the former Articles. To which the Council of Officers reply'd, that they would not recede from any Thing which their Commissioners had assented to, which was according to their Instructions; but would not hold themselves oblig'd in such Points wherein they either err'd or exceeded.

Dec. 6.

XI. The same Messenger was also directed to intercede for the Enlargement of Colonel *Cobbet*, being sent thither as a publick Messenger. To which the General warmly reply'd, that he could not accept Colonel *Cobbet* in the Quality of a publick Messenger; but that it was rather a Presumption in him to enter into *Scotland*, where he had nothing to do, and knowing the Parliament had vacated his Commission before they were disturbed by *Lambert*. And whatever could be be pretended, the General so well knew the Temper and Influence of Colonel *Cobbet*, that he was firmly resolv'd not to trust him with his Liberty.

XII. The next Morning, being *December* 7. Colonel *Zanchy* was to return with this Answer to *Newcastle*; but the same Night the Head-Quarters were alarm'd with the News, that a Party of *Lambert*'s Horse and Dragoons were broke into *Northumberland*, and had surpriz'd *Chillingham* Castle. They were in so great Streight for Money, that they made this Incursion, partly in Hopes to seize the Lord *Grey*'s Rents, which they might easily have done, but that the Bird was flown before they had spread their Nets. This Action being so directly contrary to their Agreement at the Beginning of the Treaty, did so highly incense the General, that he presently commanded Colonel *Zanchy* to be secured, and to give him Satisfaction for this Breach of the Articles. And now *Zanchy*, instead of procuring *Cobbet*'s Liberty, lost his own.

XIII. Whilst this Business was transacted with Colonel *Zanchy*, the Commissioners of the Treaty, Colonel *Knight*, Colonel *Cloberry*, and Colonel *Wilks*, return'd from *London* to *Berwick*: Where they made the best

best Excuse they could, for the ill Management of their Embassy, and with some Reflection upon the Rashness and Imprudence of each other. The General express'd some Displeasure against them all. But because Colonel *Wilks* seem'd to have led the Dance to the rest, in departing from their Instructions, and had been too forward in revealing the General's Inclinations for a new Parliament, which was to be kept to the last Pinch, he order'd his Confinement; though afterwards he was prevail'd upon to accept his Submission and Excuse with the Grant of his Liberty.

HITHERTO we have attended the Motions of our General from his first Head-Quarters at *Dalkeith*, to his second at *Edenburgh*, thence to his third at *Berwick*, and are now following him to his fourth and last Head-Quarters at *Coldstream*.

CHAP. XIV.

I. *The General marches to* Coldstream, *and takes up his Head Quarters there*, II. *For the Conveniency of its Situation*. III. Lambert's, IV. *And the rest of that Party's ill Conduct*. V. *Who deceive themselves with the*

the Expectation of an Agreement upon the Treaty. VI. *The Condition of* Lambert *and his Forces at* Newcastle. VII. *General* Monk *meets Commissioners from the Nobility in* Scotland *at* Berwick, *who offer to raise seven thousand five hundred Men for the Service of the General.* VIII. *The Levies refus'd.* IX. *Colonel* Zanchy *discharged.* X. *The General, upon his Return to* Coldstream, *receives Overtures from the Lord* Fairfax. XI. Lambert *confin'd within his Quarters by the Severity of the Weather.* XII. *The Fleet and* Portsmouth *declare for the Parliament.* XIII. *The Committee of Safety send Forces to besiege* Portsmouth, *who revolt to the Parliament.* XIV. *An Express from General* Monk *to* Lambert. XV. Lambert *in great Distress.* XVI. *The General receives the News of the Revolt of the Fleet. The Forces in* Ireland *declare for the Parliament.*

I. ABOUT two in the Morning *December* 8. the General was mounted at *Berwick*, intending to visit the Passes over the River *Tweed*, in his Way to his new Quarters. But besides the Badness of the Way, the Weather proving very tempestuous, he was enforc'd for a few Hours to put in at the Pass at *Norham*, and about Noon arriv'd at *Coldstream*,

Dec. 8.

M

Coldstream, being nine Miles from *Berwick*, where there was in Readiness only one Regiment of Foot for his Guards and Attendance. This (as most bordering Towns) was a very poor and despicable Place, and so destitute of Provision, that, for the first Night, the General was enforc'd to entertain himself with the chewing Tobacco instead of a Supper, till he was the next Day better supply'd with Provisions from *Berwick*. The House that was assigned for his Head-Quarters, had not a Room in it of tolerable Reception for one of his Serjeants; so that he was to eat and sleep in the same Chamber. To this *Prætorium*, made of a Cottage, were adjoining two Barns, whereof one was taken up by his Sutlers for his Pantry, and the other serv'd for his Chapel.

II. But this miserable Town was furnish'd with the most commodious Pass for the March of his Army over the *Tweed*, for which Reason he chose it, and was very well contented with all other Inconveniencies. It was plac'd as a central Point to all the neighbouring Villages, where his Forces all lay quarter'd about him, so that in four Hours time he could have drawn them all into a Body upon any sudden Occasion or Alarm.

III. It

III. It was some Part of the Wonder of those Times, that Major General *Lambert*, knowing how much it concern'd him to be quick in his Business, being destitute of Money to support himself and his Forces in Delays, had not all this while march'd into *Scotland*, having an Army so much superior to his Enemies, and a considerable Body of Horse fit for such a sudden Invasion: Nor had General *Monk* fully perfected his Alterations among his Officers, nor compleatly fix'd his own Army in Obedience to him. So that upon *Lambert*'s Advance among them, most of General *Monk*'s Horse would probably have gone off from him, and perhaps many others would have shewn him their Heels, had they once seen *Lambert* and his Army in their Country.

IV. And indeed had the Armies in *England* and *Ireland* been well resolv'd together, and gone roundly to the Work; so that *Lambert* had directly march'd into *Scotland*, and at the same time some Part of the *Irish* Forces (who had as yet dissented from the General's Proceedings) had landed there, which might easily have been done in any Part of the West of *Scotland*; they would shrewdly have broken and disorder'd all his Resolutions, nor was he of sufficient Force to oppose them.

So that (though the General had omitted no Part of a wife and prudent Man) yet it is manifest he was still under a Conduct and Providence greater than his own, which did so far infatuate the Counsels of his Enemies, as they frequently overlook'd those Advantages upon him, which the Difficulty of Affairs had sometimes given them.

V. But to avert this Hazard, there was seasonably thrown out to them (from *Scotland*) a Treaty to make play with; which was entertain'd with very probable Hopes of concluding the Difference. Nor were they willing to believe, that the Army in *Scotland* would be forward to engage against their Brethren in *England* and *Ireland*, who were every Way too many for them. *Lambert* had also consented to a Cessation of all Hostility during this Treaty; and though haply he might have gone forward with more Advantage, by going back from his Word; yet he was a Person of more Generosity than many among them, and was not willing to prevaricate his Promise, whilst there was still any Hopes of coming fairly to an Agreement.

VI. But the greatest Impediment to the invading of *Scotland*, was really from among themselves. There being so many, and so different Interests and Inclinations in *Lambert's bert*'s Army. Some of those whom he took up by the Way, that had lately march'd with him against Sir *George Booth*, had been so practis'd on by him, that they were wholly at his Service. But there were many among them that had a great Inclination to *Fleetwood*; and having entertain'd a Jealousy of *Lambert*'s Ambition, were no Ways hasty to rush into the War, which, if it had succeeded with Victory, would have given *Lambert* an entire Possession of the Government. There were also some Regiments brought out of *London*, that had formerly been Guards to the Parliament, and therefore had no Stomach to engage earnestly against those, who now declar'd themselves their Restorers. Neither was there wanting a considerable Number among them of the Commonwealth Party, who, upon better Consideration, began to part with their Suspicions upon General *Monk*, for bringing in the King, and apprehended now a great deal of Reason and Justice in his Declaration for restoring the Parliament: Under whose Authority the Quarrel at first began, and no other Government could justify or maintain them in it. All these different Interests among them were very well known to General *Monk*, who wanted not Espials upon them, even in their own Head-Quarters.

VII. But

VII. But the General having spent now almost a Week, in settling himself and his Army in their new Quarters, was mindful of the Appointment he had made with several of the Nobility in *Scotland*, and their Commissioners from the Shires and Boroughs, to meet him at *Berwick*, *December* 13. on which Day he accordingly hasten'd thither from *Coldstream*, being attended with some of his best Colonels, and Dr. *Barrow* the principal Physician, who about this Time was made Judge Advocate of the Army. The General had held a former Consult with the *Scotch* Commissioners at *Edenburgh* in *November* last, which we purposely omitted in its Place, that the Reader might not be perplex'd with too many Particulars, which came so thick upon us, and having reserv'd both these Conventions to be related together. In the former the General acquainted them with his Resolution to march into *England* for restoring the Parliament, and therefore desir'd that the Arrears of Assessment for his Army might be speedily paid; which they all very chearfully undertook for, and at their Return into their several Shires it was exactly perform'd. And this was the Sum of what was then done at *Edenburgh*. But in this Convention at *Berwick*, where were present the Marquiss of *Athol*, the Earls of *Glencarn*, *Rothes*, *Roxborough*,

Dec. 13.

Roxborough, Weams, and several other of the *Scotch* Nobility, divers Things were propos'd by them to the General: That for the present they might be allow'd to have a standing Council in each Shire, with Power to raise some small Proportion of Horse, for the securing the common Safety, and that they might be furnish'd with Arms out of the General's Stores at the usual Rates; with Liberty also to wear their Swords, which had been hitherto deny'd them; and that in Case the Treaty did not take Effect, they might proceed to make greater Levies for the Assistance of the *English* Army, and their own Defence. And in particular they propos'd to raise presently for the General's Service six thousand Foot, and one thousand five hundred Horse. The General presently advis'd in private with some of his Officers upon these Proposals, where there was some Variety in their Opinions; but in Conclusion it was resolv'd, That though there was need enough for the General to encrease his Forces, yet for the present by no Means to grant any Commission to the *Scotch* Nation for raising of Arms; which would so alarm the *English* Army, as they would presently run into a Distrust of their Officers, or would take Occasion to think themselves suspected. And how unwillingly their own Soldiers would comply with a Mixture of that Nation, they had lately made an Experiment, in those Discontents that arose upon allowing some of the *Scotch* Officers to fill up their Companies with *Scots*.

VIII. Upon a further Conference therefore with the Lords, the General consented to some Part of their Proposals; but for raising Regiments he desir'd their further Patience, till he saw what Conclusion the Treaty (which they were now again to resume) would produce. And some of them were very well assur'd, that if the War did go on, the General would not then be scrupulous in admitting the *Scots* to a Conjunction with him. And both their Lordships and the other Commissioners had entertain'd such Opinion of his Generosity and Justness, that, though they were not gratify'd at present in all their Desires, yet they took Leave of him with a very perfect Satisfaction and Confidence. Some of these Lords also, and divers of the General's own Officers, had so far look'd into his Proceedings, that, though they had the Discretion to conceal their own Apprehensions, yet were they very well assur'd, that all this Bustle was not made only to restore a few hated and inconsiderable People into a Condition of doing more Mischief; but there was some greater Design in Hand than the Restitution of the Juncto Parliament.

IX. The

GENERAL MONK. 169

IX. THE General had receiv'd Intelligence before he came from *Coldstream*, that *Lambert* (to pacify his Displeasure, and to restore the Treaty) had recall'd his Forces out of *Northumberland*; and therefore General *Monk*, before he left *Berwick*, sent for Colonel *Zanchy*, who was a Prisoner; and having discharg'd him from his Confinement, sent him back to *Newcastle* with this Message to Major General *Lambert*, that he would speedily send him his further Resolution in order to the Treaty.

X. ALL Matters being thus concluded at *Berwick*, the General return'd again to his Head-Quarters at *Coldstream*, where, with much Difficulty and Hazard of the Enemy's Army, there came to him a Messenger from the Lord *Fairfax*; one Mr. *Fairfax* his Kinsman, who inform'd him, that, by the Interview between Commissary *Clarges* and his Agent Mr. *Bowles*, he was so well satisfy'd with the Justness and Reason of his Intentions, that he was very willing to join with him therein; and to that End was employing his Interest among the Gentry and Soldiery of *Yorkshire*, and the adjacent Counties, for the forming of a Party to rise with him, which would be in Readiness about the Beginning of *January*, to fall upon *Lambert*'s
Rear;

Rear; by which Action his Lordship was likely to recover that Honour in pursuing the Army, which, when he was formerly their General, he had lost by leading it. He also receiv'd from Commissary *Clarges*, and his other Intelligencer at *London*, such an Account of the Factions and Disorders beginning in the City, that he was resolv'd to make no Haste in proceeding further to the Treaty, which hitherto with much Artifice had been delay'd.

XI. Nor was there any Fear of *Lambert*'s further Advance or Assault upon the *Scotch* Army, the Weather having already prevented his March, through abundance of Snow, and a most severe Frost, which lasted for many Weeks, so that in an uneven and hilly Country cover'd with Ice, *Lambert*'s Horse (wherein was his Strength) could neither march, nor fight; and there being now more than forty Miles of Snow and Precipice between them, General *Monk*'s Quarters were as secure from *Lambert*'s Army, as if the *Atlantick* Sea had divided them. He was also so well inform'd concerning their Condition, that he very well knew their Money melted faster than the Snow, and would therefore compel them to break before the Weather.

XII. But

XII. But whilst General *Monk* held *Lambert* and his Army to hard Meat in the North, the restless Members of the late Juncto were as busy in making Parties and Disturbances against *Fleetwood*, and his Officers, and their Committee of Safety in *London*. Some of them had so far tamper'd with the Soldiery, that a great Party among them, finding they had mistaken themselves, in supporting an Interest that was not able to pay them, were willing to submit to their old Masters the Parliament. Others of the Juncto had got down to Vice-Admiral *Lawson*, and the Navy; where they told their own Tale so effectually, that the Fleet was contented now to declare with General *Monk*, for restoring the Parliament. And about the same Time Colonel *Whetham*, who commanded the Garrison at *Portsmouth*, discover'd his Inclination to join with General *Monk*, and his Army, in Defence of the Parliament. This Gentleman had formerly been of the Council of State in *Scotland*, where he began that Estimation and Friendship with the General, which led him now willingly to join his Interest with him.

XIII. Upon this Information, there were dispatch'd down to him *Hazlerig*, *Morley*, and *Walton*, who were not only Members of the late Juncto, but were also three of the five Commis-

The LIFE of

Commissioners appointed by them for governing the Army. These three Persons had so bestirr'd themselves at *Portsmouth*, that several Forces thereabouts came in to them. But to reduce this Defection there, General *Fleetwood* and the Committee of Safety commanded away a Party to besiege the Town, who, reflecting upon the declining Estate of those who sent them, and that the Play would no longer pay for the Candle, threw up their Cards, and, as soon as they came there, instead of reducing these Revolters, increas'd their Number by joining with them. So that now, by the Union of these Parties together, (besides General *Monk*'s Army in the North) there was a considerable Force in the South, resolving to restore the Parliament.

XIV. Of all these Circumstances General *Monk* had a speedy Account from his sure Intelligencer Commissary *Clarges*, who presently made use of them as a decent Contrivance for dissolving the Treaty. Thereupon he dispatch'd away Major *Bannister* to *Newcastle*, with an Express to Major General *Lambert*, acquainting him, that himself and his Officers were preparing to enter again into the Treaty, but in the mean Time he had receiv'd Advice, that three of those five Commissioners appointed with himself by Authority of Parliament, for the governing of the Army,

were

GENERAL MONK. 173

were now at *Portsmouth* in the actual Discharge of their Trust, without whose Consent and Direction (according to the Intent of his Commission) he could not proceed alone in so weighty an Affair; but did therefore desire of him a safe Conduct for this Messenger, his Officer, to pass quickly for *Portsmouth*, and to bring back from those other Commissioners such further Instructions, for the Management of the Treaty, as he and his Officers might accordingly be enabled to proceed upon.

XV. At the reading of this Letter *Lambert* express'd some sort of Displeasure, telling Major *Bannister*, that the General and his Officers had not us'd him well. The Business at *Portsmouth* was no News, having been known at *Newcastle* before it could come to *Coldstream*. But by that he easily foresaw the Treaty was at an End, and his own Forces. And now, as *Hannibal*, when it was too late, grew angry with himself, that he had not led his Army, hot and bloody, from the Battle of *Cannæ* to the sacking of *Rome*; no less did *Lambert* accuse his own Delay, that he had not, instead of staying at *Newcastle*, march'd his Army into *Scotland*, where he might have been able to command that Submission from his Enemies, which now he must be enforc'd to make to them.

XVI. But

XVI. But since the Messenger's Journey to *Portsmouth* could not be of any Use to the Treaty, he was resolv'd it should serve for no other Design; and therefore refusing to grant him any pass, commanded his Return again to *Coldstream*, whither he brought the General better News than that he had carried to *Newcastle*. For, during his Stay there, the Intelligence arriv'd, that Vice-Admiral *Lawson* and the Fleet had actually declar'd in the same Cause with him; having threaten'd to block up the *Thames*, and besiege their Trade, if the Parliament was not instantly restor'd. In these his uneasy and worst Quarters the General entertain'd all his best News. For about this Time Captain *Campbel* arriv'd at *Coldstream* with the Letters from *Ireland*; acquainting him, that the Army there had not only declar'd with him for restoring the Parliament, but would be ready also to send over such Forces to him, as he should have need of.

CHAP. XV.

I. *A private Conference between the General and his Chaplain Dr. Price, wherein he*

GENERAL MONK. 175

he declares his Resolution of restoring the King, with the Reasons of his former Caution and Reservedness. II. *A fine Reflection of the Author's upon this Declaration of the General.* III. *The disorder'd and distracted State of* London *at this Time.* IV. Fleetwood *submits to the Parliament which meets at* Westminster. V. *The General receives Advice, that Lord* Fairfax *was in Arms in* Yorkshire, *and that* Lambert *was upon his Retreat from* Newcastle *into that County.* VI. *The General passes the* Tweed *to the Support of Lord* Fairfax: VII. *Sending his Wife and Son by Sea to* London. VIII. *He receives a Letter from the Speaker, which is read to the Army:* IX. *Is complimented at* Morpeth *by the Sheriff and Gentlemen of* Northumberland; *by a Message from* Newcastle; *and a Letter from* London. X. *Arrives at* Newcastle, *from which* Lambert *was retir'd.* XI. Lambert's *Army revolt from him.* XII. *The divided State of it makes the General slacken his Pace. He writes to the Lord Mayor and Common Council.* XIII. *To the Speaker, the Council of State, and Lord* Fairfax.

I. THESE strange and fortunate Accidents at *Coldstream*, were variously consider'd by such Persons as attended the
General

General there, or were most intent upon his Service and Interest. Among the rest his Chaplain, Dr. *Price*, having no Opportunity in the Day-time of private Access to him, took Occasion, by the Help of a Corporal, who that Night commanded the Guards, to enter his Chamber about two in the Morning, where he found the Door only latch'd, and the General, being weary of his narrow uneasy Lodging in his Bed, was sleeping in his Cloaths, having laid himself down on a Form, and rested his Head on the Side of the Bed, with a Fire and Light in the Room. At his Approach, the General (who was never a sound Sleeper) presently awak'd, and enter'd into much secret Discourse with him; who freely represented to him, how much his Obligation and Safety were equally concern'd in complying with the Desires of the better Part of the Nation, by endeavouring their Settlement according to the ancient and known Laws. To which the General reply'd, that *he very well knew what he would have, nor should he be wanting therein, so soon as he could find himself in a Capacity of effecting it; of which he had now somewhat more Hopes than formerly.* And then kindly taking him by the Hand, very solemnly and devoutly told him: *By God's Grace I will do it.* His Chaplain then took the Boldness to let him know how much he had disoblig'd a

great

great Part of the Nation, and contracted his own Interest into a narrower Compass, by declaring so strictly for the Parliament as it sat *October* 11. To this the General answer'd with some Earnestness: *You see what People they are who are now about me, by whose Advice and Discretion several things are transacted and written. There are Jealousies enough upon me already, and the least Appearance of any Dislike would make them greater. But though* (as he told him) *he had been passive in allowing some Proceedings, yet he was resolved not to act by them.* This put an End to the Discourse, and his Chaplain, craving Pardon for this Interruption upon him, left him to the remaining Part of his Repose.

II. This, and the like Passages, though they are no essential Part of the Story, yet because the Minds of Men are best discover'd by such sudden and private Attempts upon them, they are very necessary to be inserted. And the impartial Reader may better discern the Envy and Prejudice of their Opinions, who have thought that General *Monk* did govern his Resolutions by the Events that fell in his Way, without endeavouring to bend and incline those Events to a Compliance with his own Resolution.

III. But leaving the General a little while to his Rest at *Coldstream*, we will lead our Reader back again to *London*, where nothing was to be seen but Tumult and Disorder: The Citizens sullen and querulous, their Apprentices unruly and desperate, the Forces divided and irresolute, and some of them already drawn off by their Officers that were devoted to the Parliament; the Committee of Safety no less distracted in their Counsels, and the Forces at *Portsmouth* upon their March towards *London*, to restore the Parliament. In so many fatal Circumstances Lieutenant General *Fleetwood*, who was certainly the most innocent Person among them, but altogether unfit to maintain the Place he held, or to support himself against such violent Tides as then ran against him, was able to hold the Reins of Government no longer, but dropt them from his trembling Hand.

IV. And sending his Submission to the Speaker, desired him to convene such Members as were about the Town, and to resume again the Government into their Hands, which had been so ill managed by his own, and the Committee of Safety. The Members very well knew, how far *Fleetwood* had been passive in these Contrivances, and by what Engines he had been wrought upon; so that

that they easily accepted his Excuse, being resolv'd to discharge the Torrent of their Indignation upon *Lambert*, and his more secret Accomplices. There wanted not much courting or Address to persuade the Senators to find the Way into their old Seats again at *Westminster*, who accordingly met there *December* 25. where we will leave them contriving the last of their Mischief, whilst we return again to *Coldstream*.

Dec. 25.

V. WHERE about this Time the General receiv'd a Message from *York*, informing him, that the Lord *Fairfax*, finding his Preparations were discover'd, and to prevent a Surprizal from *Lambert*'s Army, was already actually in Arms sooner than the Time he had appointed, and that *Lilburn*'s Regiment, deserting their Colonel, was brought off by Major *Smithson*, to join with him. The same Messenger brought him the first News, that the Junto was restored, and that *Fleetwood* with his Army had submitted to them: and that *Lambert* also was retreating from *Newcastle*, with Intention to march back into *Yorkshire*.

VI. THE General had a very tender Concern for the Lord *Fairfax*, and his Party, who had so generously declar'd for him; and knowing how unable they were alone to deal with *Lambert's* Army, he was resolv'd to march to their Relief, and to fall upon the Rear before he should be able to engage them. To that End, having drawn his Forces together he commanded their March over the *Tweed*.

VII. WHEN the General took up his Quarters at *Coldstream*, he ordered his Lady, and his Son, the present Duke of *Albemarle*, to continue at *Berwick*, there being no convenient Reception for them in those uneasy Quarters. But before he marched hence, he took Care they should pass from thence by Sea to *London*, and wait him there. Accordingly there was a Vessel in Readiness to attend them.

Jan. 1.
$16\frac{59}{60}$.
VIII. His Army consisted only of four Regiments of Horse, which were not compleat, and six intire Regiments of Foot. Their March was in two distinct Brigades, one whereof was led by himself, and the other by Major General *Morgan*. And on *New-Year's* Day he order'd the Advance of the Foot over the River, and the next Day following them with his Regiment of Horse, took up his first Night's Quarters at *Wellar* in *Northumberland*: Where, late in the Night, he receiv'd a short Letter from the Speaker, dated *December* 27. informing him of their Return a-

gain to the Government, with some Acknowledgment of his Prudence and Fidelity in their Service, but not one Word of Order for his March toward them. Which, tho' he prudently conceal'd, yet it did inwardly displease him. But his greatest Surprisal was from their so sudden Return into Power, when having now so considerable an Army which had submitted to them, it would lead them into a less Dependance upon himself, and before he could march to them, they would have so shifted Commissions in *Fleetwood*'s Army, and fix'd them in so perfect Obedience to the Parliament, as he should not be able to play them that Game which he had intended when he got well into *London*. But that the Juncto might be told how welcome their Letters were to him, he commanded they should be read next Morning at the Head of the Regiments, being drawn up in the Snow; and, to keep themselves warm, they made loud Acclamations for the Restoration of their Masters, resolving that they would march onwards, and have the Satisfaction to see them in their Seats.

IX. The same Day the General kept on *Jan.* 3. his Way towards *Morpeth*; but because it was too long a March for his Army in so deep a Snow, he stay'd at a Village in the Mid-way for a Night, and took up his Quarters (which were worse than those in *Coldstream*) as the Vicar's House of the Parish; and the next Day arriv'd at *Morpeth*; where he was met by the High-Sheriff and Gentry of *Northumberland*, who gave him the publick Welcome into their County. Here were also attending two Sword-bearers, one from *Newcastle* with Compliments from the Magistrates of the place, inviting him thither; and the other from *London*, who presented him with Letters from the Lord Mayor and Common Council of the City; expressing their Desires for a full Parliament, with the just Reason of their Demand, since, in the present Assembly, there was not one Member sitting to represent the capital City.

Jan. 4.

Jan. 5. X. From hence he came to *Newcastle*, where Major General *Lambert* had so long kept his Head-Quarters; but he quitted them about the same time that General *Monk* began his March from *Coldstream*. For the same Messenger that brought to General *Monk* at *Wellar* the Letter from the Juncto, with the Account of their Restoration, left also their Orders at *Newcastle*, commanding the Army presently to quit their Station there, and return directly to those respective Quarters which were assign'd them by the Parliament before their Interruption.

XI. Lambert's

XI. Lambert's Army was in a fair Way of diffolving themfelves before thofe Orders arriv'd. But fo foon as the Soldiers heard, that *Fleetwood*'s Forces in *London* had deferted their General, and fubmitted to the Juncto, they were refolv'd not to be exceeded by their Brethren in the Ways of Treachery and Falfhood; and therefore prefently all fubmitted themfelves to the Orders of the Juncto, without expoftulating one Word in behalf of *Lambert* their Leader, or once drawing a Sword for him; but fhifting away to their feveral Quarters, they left him naked and deftitute to the Cruelty of his Fortune. And fome of them thought they had acquitted themfelves civilly towards him, in leaving him Liberty to fhift for himfelf; and had not ferv'd him as the *Argyrafpides* did their General *Eumenes*, and made their Peace with the Juncto, by delivering him a Captive to their Revenge.

XII. He was in the Head of an Army good enough to have fought them both; fo that it was greatly admir'd he did not ftay and charge General *Monk* in his March forward, or turn back upon the Lord *Fairfax* and his Forces, whom he might more eafily have dealt with, before the Northern Army could have advanced to their Relief. But, befides the different Interefts and Diftractions in the

Army, there was a particular Dread among them of these two Generals, whom they knew to be the greatest and most fortunate Commanders in both the Nations; so that the forwardest of them all had no great Stomach to come to an Engagement against them. But since (by the Dissolution of *Lambert*'s Army) the Lord *Fairfax* and his Party were out of Danger, General *Monk* did somewhat abate his Pace, and staid three Days at *Newcastle*, to perfect such Instructions and Letters as he intended to send to *London*: From whence he dispatch'd back Mr. *Man* the Sword-bearer of *London*, with Letters to the Lord Mayor and Common Council, expressing more of Respect towards them, than Assent to their Desires.

XIII. AT the same time he also sent away Dr. *Gumble* with Letters to *London*; one to the Speaker of the Parliament, by him to be communicated to the House. And because the Letter from the Lord Mayor and Common Council could not be conceal'd from them, he inclos'd a Copy of their Letter, with another of his Answer to them, that they might discern he had no Correspondence, but such as he was willing they should be privy to. There was also another Letter to the Council of State, and a third to the other Commissioners appointed with him for the

governing

governing of the Army, and in his Way through *York* he was to leave another for the Lord *Fairfax*. Dr. *Gumble* was chosen as the fittest Messenger to convey these Letters to *London*, being so particularly known and intrusted by *Scot*, and others of the ruling Faction in the House, and therefore could more advantageously represent the Service and Intentions of the General, than any other about him: The Design of this Message being chiefly to remove from them those Jealousies they had entertain'd of his more secret Intentions; and to inspect their several Designs, and who among them had the greatest Power and Interest.

CHAP. XVI.

I. *The General's Arrival at* York, *from whence he writes to Sir* Charles Coot *in* Ireland, *to bring him into Measures for a free Parliament.* II. *A private Conference between him, and Lord* Fairfax, *and Mr.* Bowles, *his Lordship's Chaplain.* III. *The General receives Orders from the Juncto for his March to* London. IV. *He sends General* Morgan, *with two Regiments,*

ments, back into Scotland. V. *And leaves another at* York *under the Command of the Lord* Fairfax. VI. *Dr.* Gumble *returns from* London, *and gives the General an Account of the State of Affairs there, and the Disposition of the People.* VII. *The General advances to* Nottingham, *being met there by Commissary* Clarges. VIII. *Projects Means for removing* Fleetwood's *Army out of the City.* IX. *He is met by* Scot *and* Robinson *from the Parliament.* X. *His Behaviour towards them.* XI. *His Reception at* Leicester. XII. *At* Harborough *he is attended by three Commissioners from* London. XIII. *At* Northampton *receives more Addresses for a free Parliament.* XIV. *Which he was oblig'd to discountenance.* XV. *More Addresses to him at St.* Albans. XVI. Fleetwood *is order'd, with the Forces under his Command, to march out of* London. XVII. *The General halts for some of his Forces to come up.* XVIII. *On the second of* February *marches to* Barnet. XIX. *Gives Orders for the more regular March of his Army.* XX. Fleetwood's *Forces removed out of* London; XXI. *Which, together with some Apprentices, begin a Mutiny, but are soon quieted.* XXII. *The General marches into* London.

I. FROM

I. FROM *Newcastle* the General ad-*Jan.* 8. vanc'd to *Durham*. Here he receiv'd Information that the Lord *Fairfax* and his Forces had summon'd the City of *York*, and were receiv'd into it; but that his Lordship, being surpriz'd with the Gout, was retir'd to his House at *Nun-Appleton*. From thence he secretly dispatch'd Sir George *Douglass* (who had long been conversant with him at *Dalkeith*) into *Ireland*, with Letters of Credit to Sir *Charles Coot*, and others, with whom he was to enter into a dangerous Treaty, for the disposing of several Parties in *Ireland* to some Union and Agreement, and then to declare for a free Parliament, as the only possible Means that could now restore any lasting Settlement to the Commonwealth.

FROM hence the General enter'd into *Yorkshire* in his way to *North-Allerton*, where the High-Sheriff of the County attended him; and the next Day to *Topcliff*.

II. FROM thence about *January* 11. he ar-*Jan.* 11. rived at *York*, where he took up his Quarters for five Days; and, by his own Authority, modell'd and dispos'd of such Forces as he found in the Country, that had belong'd to *Lambert*; whose Regiment of Horse he gave to Colonel *Bethel*, as a Reward of his Service in joining with the Lord *Fairfax*; and
the

the Regiment which had been *Lilburn*'s, he disposed to Major *Smithson*, and made him Colonel of it, he having brought it off to the Lord *Fairfax* and his Party. During his Stay here he receiv'd a Visit from the Lord *Fairfax*, with whom he had much secret Discourse, and din'd together privately in the General's Chamber, whilst the Officers and Attendants were entertain'd publickly. The same Night Mr. *Bowles*, who was Chaplain and Agent to the Lord *Fairfax*, was directed by his Lordship to confer with the General, and was privately with him till after Midnight, representing to him the Inclination of the Country, and the Force that would be in Readiness to join with him, if he would stay with them there, and at *York* declare for the King. But the General, who very well knew that such an Attempt would presently turn all the different Parties to an Union against him, and that his own Army was not yet enough refin'd in their Principles and Temper to engage with him in such an Adventure, would by no Means admit of the Proposal. The next Day he paid a Visit to the Lord *Fairfax* at his House at *Nun-Appleton*, where himself with several of his Officers and Retinue were very magnificently entertain'd at Dinner, and at Night return'd again to his Quarters at *York*.

III. Hitherto

III. Hitherto the General had march'd about an hundred Miles in length from *Coldstream* to *York*, by his own sole Authority and Discretion; but here he receiv'd Orders from the Juncto, to keep on his Way to *London*. They had taken no Satisfaction at the Lord *Fairfax* his Appearance in *Yorkshire*, though he had prefac'd his Actions with Authority of Parliament, being very well assur'd that he had other Designs in it beyond their Safety. Nor could they be pleas'd with General *Monk*'s Stay in that County, where he might probably receive other Impressions than those he had brought out of *Scotland*. And the Union of two such Persons against them, (esteem'd the best Generals in the Nation) might have given them another Kind of Disturbance, than what they had receiv'd from *Fleetwood* or *Lambert*. They had suffer'd him to advance so far, that now they could not decently command him back into *Scotland*, without some Disobligation upon the General, and Jealousy in his Army. Nor were they secure in the early Submission of the Regiments in *London*; and therefore chose rather to authorise General *Monk*'s Advance thither, than to leave him longer in *Yorkshire*.

IV. The General kept such Intelligence

over them by his Agents, that he very well knew where the Shoe pinch'd. He had already caned one of his Officers here, who had adventur'd to say: *General* Monk *will at laſt let in the King upon us*; and, to remove all Umbrage and Apprehenſion from among them, he reſolv'd here to leſſen his Army, and from *York* ſent back Major General *Morgan* to take the Care of *Scotland*, accompanied with two Regiments of Horſe and Foot. He had us'd the beſt Means in his Power to ſecure that Nation before he left it, yet was not very well aſſur'd, in the buſy Humour of the *Scots*. But the ſecret Reaſon of ſending *Morgan* back into *Scotland*, was chiefly to keep together a conſiderable Reſerve in Caſe the General ſhould have need of them, or to which he might have retreated himſelf, if he ſhould happen to take a Battle in *England*.

V. Here alſo he left another Regiment under the Command of Colonel *Fairfax*; who, being a Native of this County, and very well ally'd and eſteem'd among them, was the moſt proper Perſon to be entruſted with the Care of the City, and the Safety of the County. And now having reduc'd his Army to four thouſand Foot, and one thouſand eight hundred Horſe, he went out of *York* about *January* 16. and march'd through
the

the rest of the County till he came to *Mansfield* in *Nottinghamshire, January* 18.

Jan. 18,

VI. At this Stage his Messenger, Dr. *Gumble*, whom he had dispatch'd away from *Newcastle* to *London*, came back to him after three Days Stay in the City, and gave him a particular Account of his Message: That he deliver'd all his Letters according to his Instructions; that he had been very strictly examin'd concerning him by the Members of Parliament, but most particularly by the Council of State. He inform'd him, that several among them had an entire Confidence in him; but that among many others he was suspected to have some conceal'd Design in Reserve for bringing in the King; which was confirm'd by the confident Expectation, which the disaffected Part of the City had of his Approach. He then acquainted him with the Division in the Council, between those who had taken the Oath of Abjuration, and were his profess'd Enemies, and others that had refused it; and had some Confidence that General *Monk* being nominated a Member of that Council, (whereof there were thirty one) there would be strong Applications made to engage him in their several Parties. He inform'd him also, that *Scot* and *Robinson*, two Members of the Parliament, and of the Council of State, were upon the Road to meet him:

That

That they were sent as Espials upon his Actions, and the Temper of his Army; and that, having themselves taken the Oath of Abjuration, they would presently be very earnest to engage him therein.

Jan. 19. VII. From *Mansfield* the next Day the General advanc'd to *Nottingham*, where he was seasonably met the Day following by Commissary *Clarges*, who had privately hasten'd down to him, with a further Account of the Affairs in *London* and *Westminster*, and what Hopes or Jealousies were entertain'd concerning him among the different Interests and Parties. He inform'd him, that the Forces then in the City were much greater than his own, and commanded by such Officers as were declared Enemies to him, except *Morley* and *Fagg*.

VIII. Hitherto the General had brought all his Business into so good a Posture, that now his next and greatest Concernment was to shift *Fleetwood*'s Army handsomely out of the City, and (without Impediment or Jealousy) to bring his own in. To this End, before the Arrival of *Scot* and *Robinson*, he enter'd into a Consultation with such Persons about him as he could best trust: Where it was resolv'd, that a Letter should be drawn up to the Parliament, giving them an Account of of his March, and the Number of his Forces with him; and because those Regiments now in the City, had so lately been in Rebellion against the Parliament, and were not yet entirely settled and reduced, he was very unwilling his own dutiful and orderly Forces should mix or converse with them. He therefore besought them (for their own Safety) that those Forces under *Fleetwood* should be remov'd to distant Quarters in the Country, except the two Regiments of Colonel *Morley* and Colonel *Fagg*, who had continued in their Duty to them, which, with his own Army, would be sufficient to maintain the Guards to the Parliament, and secure the City. But this Letter was not thought seasonable to be sent till they were advanc'd near to *London*; so that they should not dare to deny him, nor have Time enough to oppose his Entrance.

IX. THE General, having staid at *Nottingham* two Days for the Rear of his Army to come up to him, on *Munday, January* 22. *Jan.* 22. marched to *Leicester*, and met *Scot* and *Robinson* on their Way towards him. Much Ceremony and Submission was here render'd by the General and his Army towards these two arrogant Commissioners of the Juncto: Insomuch that the General, who had quickly taken the Measures of that their Stay in the Army,

Army, was so punctual, that his Soldiers were oblig'd, upon all Occasions, to pay them greater Reverence than had been us'd towards himself. During their March together, *Scot* and *Robinson* had much Conference with the General upon the late Alterations, and the present State of Things: And much of their Discourse was full of Apprehension and Jealousy of every Body about them, which further confirm'd the General, that himself was not free from their Suspicions. They reflected on the late Practice of *Fleetwood* and *Lambert* with a very particular Indignation. They fell foul on the City of *London*, for their late Stubbornness and Malignancy. And though the Army in *Ireland* had declar'd their Obedience to the Authority of Parliament, yet they very well knew they were not upon the right Basis.

X. THE General was now more troubled how to temporize with these two Commissioners, than ever he had been how to oppose all *Lambert*'s Army. But because his grand Design was now upon the Anvil, for the removing of *Fleetwood*'s Army out of *London*, and the introducing his own, without which all his Travel hitherto would be lost, he was resolv'd so far to comply with their Extravagancies, as to give them an entire Assurance of him.

XI. INTO

XI. INTO *Leicester* the *Irish* Brigade saluted him, being drawn up by Colonel *Redman* and Colonel *Brett*; of whose Fidelity he was assur'd, when they were in *Lambert*'s Army, and therefore receiv'd them with a particular Friendship.

XII. FROM *Leicester* the next Day he *Jan. 23.* went to his next Stage at *Harborough*; where he met three Commissioners, (whereof two were Aldermen) sent to him from *London*, to renew the Contents of their former Letter at *Morpeth*, wherein they desir'd a new Parliament, or the filling up this present one, by restoring the Members secluded in 1648. and compleating it by new Elections. These Gentlemen deliver'd their Message with such Freedom and Resolution, as greatly incens'd the two Commissioners; insomuch that *Scot* told them, *That the Parliament had already, by their Vote, determin'd against the secluded Members; so that it was a Presumption in any private Person to mention their Admission.* The General very well knew that, for the present, it was as much the Citizens Interest, as his own, to comply with the Parliament's Commissioners against them, and so sent them away dissatisfy'd: Though afterwards some of those Persons that attended the General, took the Opportunity of giving them privately a better Understanding.

Jan. 24. XIII. The next Morning General *Monk* set forward for *Northampton*, where he met more Addresses from the Gentry of the County, for the filling up the Parliament, or calling a new one. But the cold Entertainment which the Messengers from *London* had receiv'd the Day before at *Harborough*, did somewhat discourage them in presenting their Petition, till Dr. *Barrow*, and some other Gentlemen about the General, advis'd them to go on with their Address, and to be content with such Answer as they receiv'd, in Expectation of the future Effect.

XIV. The General was greatly perplex'd how to answer these repeated Addresses, being very well satisfy'd in the Reason and Equity of those that brought them. But *Scot* and *Robinson* eas'd him of that Care; for they undertook to answer all Comers, leaving General *Monk* to the Satisfaction of his own Silence, who never lov'd to make long Speeches, nor to hear them from others. But when he was forc'd (in Compliance with the Commissioners) to disoblige those Gentlemen that offered these Addresses, by his Answers; yet he would still be careful to make them some Amends, by his Countenance

GENERAL MONK. 197

Countenance and the Kindness of his Aspect toward them.

XV. From this Stage the General kept on his March to *Dunstable*, *January* 27. and the next Day arrived at St. *Albans*, where he was again besieg'd with numerous Addresses from several other Counties of *England*, agreeing all in the same Applications, for the restoring the secluded Members, or the calling a new Parliament. *Scot* and *Robinson* had, all the Way from *Leicester* to St. *Albans*, taken up their Quarters in the same House with him; and when they withdrew from him to their own Apartment, they always found or made some Hole in the Door or Wall, to look in or listen, (which they had practis'd so palpably, that the General found it out, and took notice of it to those about him, reflecting on their Baseness and evil Suspicions) that they might more nearly inspect his Actions, and observe what Persons came to him; and also be in Readiness to answer the Addresses, and to ruffle with those that brought them. But here they were so plainly and severely reprimanded by those Gentlemen that came, that *Scot*, in great Passion, reply'd: *Though his Age might excuse him from taking up Arms; yet, as old as he was, (before this present Parliament should be entangled, by restoring the secluded Members,*

Jan. 27.
Jan. 28.

bers, or by new Elections) he would gird on his Sword again, and keep the Door against them.

AMONG the rest of his Interruptions in this Place, he was troubled with a long Fast-Sermon from *Hugh Peters*. And now being within twenty Miles of the City, it was thought fit to send away those Letters to the Parliament, for the Removal of *Fleetwood*'s Army out of *London*, which, we gave an Account, were drawn up before at *Nottingham*. It was the last and nicest Part the General had to accomplish, in clearing the City of those other Regiments before his own Entrance.

XVI. To this End Commissary *Clarges* was sent away from hence, to prepare such Members of the Juncto as he could engage, to further the Vote; and Colonel *Lidcot* was pitch'd upon to carry the Letters, being the Speaker's Kinsman, and particularly esteem'd by him. *Scot* also and *Robinson* had, in their frequent Letters to their Confidents in the House, giving so fair a Character of the General, and of the Discipline and Temper of his Army, that, in Conclusion, the Vote passed for *Fleetwood*'s Forces to retire into new Quarters in the Country, except the two Regiments of *Morley* and *Fagg*; though there were some that would have half of *Fleetwood*'s

Forces

General Monk. 199

Forces remain in the City, and but half of General *Monk*'s admitted.

XVII. Here the General made an Halt of five Days, both for the bringing up his own Forces nearer together (some whereof, for the Ease of the Country, had march'd in the other Road by *Newark*) and also to receive the Resolutions of the Parliament by Colonel *Lidcot*, and for the distributing the Quarters in *London* by the Quarter-masters for his own Army.

XVIII. And from hence, *February* 2. he *Feb.* 2. march'd to *Barnet*, which were his last Quarters upon the Road, and within ten Miles of the City. And here his two evil Angels, *Scot* and *Robinson*, that had never fail'd to quarter with him in the same House from *Leicester* to this Stage, now left him to take up his Lodging alone, and retir'd themselves to a private House in the Town.

XIX. This Night he dispatch'd Orders for the March of the Army into *London* the next Day: and that the Soldiers should be duly charg'd to behave themselves well and peaceably in their Quarters at *London*, and to pay duly for their Entertainment; which they might very well do, there

there being some of their *Scotch* Money still in the Treasury.

XX. The General being advanced so near, the Juncto were in the mean while very busy in dispatching *Fleetwood*'s Forces out of the Town; which they did, not only to oblige General *Monk*, by removing them out of his Way; but, as an Instance of their Contempt and Scorn of those Regiments for their late Defection, esteeming them as unworthy to have their Quarters in the capital City. Yet that the common Soldiers might be oblig'd to march the more contentedly, they order'd them a Month's Pay, to qualify the Disgrace of their Removal.

XXI. But these Regiments being long accustomed to a loose and lazy Life, in the Luxury of the Town, were very unwilling to exchange their old Quarters in the City, for worse and coarser Entertainment in the Country, and stomach'd the Disgrace of the Remove: Insomuch that some of these Regiments began a Mutiny in the Suburbs; and at the same time a Multitude of Apprentices, taking the Opportunity of the Soldiers Discontents, beat up their Drums in the City, declaring for a free Parliament, in Hopes the enraged and mutinous Soldiers would join with them. The Council of State, then sitting,

GENERAL MONK.

ting, were so alarm'd with the Disorders of this Night in the City, together with the Apprehension of the further Mischiefs which might happen in this unquiet Posture of Affairs, that, late in the Night, they dispatch'd away Messengers to *Scot* and *Robinson*, in the General's Quarters at *Barnet*, desiring them to hasten his March into the City, for Prevention of further Mischief. Mr. *Scot* was so affrighted out of his Sleep with this hasty News, that he could not stay to dress him, but in the Dishabit of his Night-Gown, Cap, and Slippers, hurry'd presently to the General's Quarters, where he made a terrible Representation of this Mutiny in the City, requiring General *Monk* to beat his Drums instantly, and march forward. But the General, that did not use to be alarm'd with every little Noise, or put out of his Temper by an hasty Tale, return'd him an Answer calmly, and persuaded Mr. *Scot* to return to his Bed, and put his Fears under his Pillow: That he was so near the City, that no great Mischief could be done in one Night, and that he would be with them early enough in the Morning, to prevent any greater Design. Yet, that the Commissioner might not be altogther at his Wit's End, he presently dispatch'd away some Messengers of his own, to inform him more particularly of these Commotions; who brought him News early in the Morning, that
the

the Commanders had quieted the Mutiny among their Soldiers; and that some Troops of Horse, being sent up into the City, had dispersed the Apprentices, and that the Regiments were then marching out of the Town.

XXII. So that all things being thus quieted in the City, the General took his own Time to march leisurely that Morning, Friday, *February* 3. into *London*. But before he enter'd the Town, he made a Stand at *Highgate*, where the Army, being then but five thousand eight hundred Men, came again to rendezvous, and there receiv'd Orders for the manner of their March into the City. The three Regiments of Horse first, and the General mounted at the Head of them, with his Trumpets before him, acccompany'd with the Juncto's Commissioners, and some of his own principal Officers, with several other Persons of Quality, that had the Curiosity or Courtesy to meet him at his several Stages on the Way After the Horse march'd his four Regiments of Foot: And in the Afternoon he made his Entry by *Grey*'s-*Inn-Lane*, where, at the *Rolls*, he made a Stop at the Speaker's Door; but he being not yet return'd from the House, the General went on into the *Strand*; where, being told that the Speaker's Coach was coming near, the General alighted

GENERAL MONK. 203

ed from his Horse, and, with much Ceremony, complimented the Prince of the Senate, and his legislative Mace in the Boot of his Coach. And thence, accompany'd with some of his Horse-Guards, went on to his Quarters at *White-Hall*, where the Juncto had assign'd him before-hand the Apartment commonly call'd the *Prince's Lodgings*.

Jan. 18.

CHAP. XVII.

I. *The mean Appearance of the General's Army.* II. *The Council of State tender the Oath of Abjuration to him, which he refuses.* III. *Is visited by the Heads of the several Parties.* IV. *Is introduced into the House of Commons, where he receives their Thanks by the Speaker. The Substance of his Answer.* V. *The Suspicions of the Parliament, and their Designs against his Life discover'd to Mr.* Sturdy, VI. *Who informs the General of it.* VII. *An Observation upon their Jealousies.* VIII. *The Observation continued.* IX. *A Resolution of the Common Council, to pay no more Taxes till the Readmission of the secluded Members.*

Members. X. *The Rump impute this Resolution to some Encouragement from the General.* XI. *The General order'd to take down the City Gates.* XII. *Which he complies with;* XIII. *And executes their Orders.* XIV. *The Resentment of his own Officers.* XV. *The Citizen's Complaints to him.* XVI. *An Order to break the Gates, and dissolve the Common Council.* XVII. *The Gates broken.* XVIII, XIX. *The true Reasons of the General's Compliance with these Orders.* XX. *A Petition to the Juncto for an Oath of Abjuration.* XXI. *The General's Army incensed.* XXII. *The General expostulates with the Juncto, and directs them to call a free and full Parliament.* XXIII. *He quarters in the City.* XXIV. *The City's cold Reception of him.* XXV. *The Lord Mayor confers with him.* XXVI. *A better Understanding between him and the City; and the Juncto surprised with his Letter to them.*

I. THE Citizens, that had been accustomed only to the prancing of *Fleetwood's* Troops through their Streets, which were always kept fair and wanton, and had us'd to see those well-cloath'd Red-coats sleek and trim in the Ease and Luxury of the City, had but a cold Conceit of this Northern Army as they passed by. Their *Scotch* Horse were

General Monk. 205

were but thin and out of Cafe, with long and hard Marching; and the Men as rough and weather-beaten, having march'd in a fevere Winter about three hundred Miles in length, and through deep and continued Snows; fo that all their Way they had fcarce yet feen the plain Earth of their native Country.

II. THE next Morning, *Saturday, Febru-* Feb. 4. *ary* 4. the General was invited to take his Place in the Council of State, where, prefently after his Entrance, the Oath of Abjuration was tender'd to him by the Prefident. He expected no lefs than the Offer of it, and was prepar'd with an Anfwer: That feveral others, who were nominated with himfelf as Members of that Council, had before refus'd it; and therefore he defir'd there might be a Conference between thofe who had taken the Oath and thofe who had refus'd it; by which himfelf and others who demurr'd, might be better fatisfy'd. He alfo told them, that the Officers of his own Army were very tender in taking Oaths; and that he would not oblige himfelf in fwearing to this new one, till he had firft acquainted them therewith; and fo, taking his Leave of the Affembly, return'd again to his Quarters at *White-Hall*.

III. WHERE, the next Day, being *Sunday* Feb. 5. he was vifited by the Heads of the feveral

Parties

Parties in the Juncto and Council of State, and by many other Persons of Quality in the City: All Men having a Curiosity to discern something of his Intentions, by Conference with him, who was too wary to be fathom'd by any of them all, though he was beset with the more pert and forward Discourse of some, and the more contriv'd and cunning Artifices of others.

Feb. 6. IV. But on *Munday* Morning he was brought with much Ceremony by *Scot* and *Robinson* through the Court of Wards to the Door of the Parliament House, where the Serjeant at Arms, with his Mace, receiv'd him, and conducted him to a Chair within the Bar, in which he was desir'd to sit down: Which the General refusing, the Speaker gave him the Thanks of the House for his Service and Fidelity towards them, in a set Speech, fill'd with much scriptural and pious Raillery, according to the Guise of those Times. The General, from the Back of the Chair, answered in a very wary and agreeable Reply, contrived to fit the Temper of those Ears that were to hear him. And tho' some Men that wish'd him very well, thought, by that Discourse, he had gone too far in his Compliance with them; yet the abjuring Part of the House (whose Jealousies of him were further heighten'd by his Refusal of the Oath two Days

GENERAL MONK. 207

Days before) were difpleas'd with all he faid, and arraign'd his whole Difcourfe. His interceding for the Eafe and Conveniencies of the People, they interpreted as a Strain of his Populariry, which was not to be endured in a General that ferves a Commonwealth. The redreffing of Grievances, was but a more fecret Reproach upon their Negligence or Injuftice in the Government. His Remarks upon multiplying further Oaths, was very offenfive to them, who had lately contriv'd that new one of Abjuration. His pleading for the Encouragement of the fober Gentry, they accounted as a fly Contrivance, which in Time would let in the Royal Party upon the Government. And by his frequent and fharp Reflections upon the *Fanaticks*, (from which Speech they were thought firft to have received that Name, which they have never yet wiped off) they accufed him to have invidioufly reprefented the moft ftrict and godly Part of the Nation, who, though they might happen to have been mifled by the Defigns of others, were yet to be efteem'd and cherifh'd as the beft and fureft Friends to the Government. Nor were they pleas'd with the Title of *General* given to him, calling him always, in their own Difcourfe or Orders, *Commiffioner Monk.*

V. THAT fome of them had entertain'd
great

great Apprehensions and Suspicions of him, is manifest from one Instance, which fell out just at this Time. Mr. *Scot*'s Son had lodg'd for some Time in the House of one Mr. *Sturdy*, a *Roman* Catholick, in *Ruſſel-ſtreet*; and was so well acquainted with his Landlord, that, discoursing together about General *Monk*'s late Arrival into *London*, which was then the common Talk of the Town; he told him secretly, that the Parliament had such Suspicions of him, as that it was resolv'd to remove him suddenly from his Command in the Army, and to lay him fast in the Tower, having Articles against him sufficient to endanger his Life.

VI. Mr. STURDY observing, in this miserable Confusion, that the Hopes of all honest Men were plac'd upon General *Monk* and his Army, was very much concern'd at this Relation; insomuch as, the next Morning early, he hasten'd up into the City, and found out one Captain *Morrice*, an honest Citizen of his particular Acquaintance, to whom he revealed this secret Information. The Captain thought it a Matter of so much Consequence, that he brought his Friend *Sturdy* to Mr. *Kendall* and Mr. *James Muddeford*, who were related to General *Monk*, and they two forthwith carried him to the General at *White-Hall*, where he farther attested the

Truth

GENERAL MONK. 209

Truth of this Relation. The General had other Bufinefs in Hand, than to take any publick Notice of this Information; yet gave fo much Credit to it, as he refolv'd to look more carefully to himfelf, and commanded Mr. *Sturdy* to ride in his Guards, which he continued to do for fome while after.

VII. THE General had hitherto carry'd all Things fo fairly towards the Juncto, ever fince his appearing againft the Army in *England*; had fo carefs'd their Commiffioners all the Way they march'd with him, and feem'd fo refolv'd to continue their prefent Seffion, by difcouraging all Addreffes made to him for filling up the Houfe, or admitting the fecluded Members; that it might be Matter of fome juft Wonder, whence thofe Jealoufies they entertain'd of him for changing the Government, or introducing the King, fhould poffibly arife.

VIII. FLEETWOOD and *Lambert* had both of them commanded Armies, as well as General *Monk*, and both had rebelled againft them; yet were never fo much as fufpected to have any Defign of reftoring the King. Only General *Monk*, who had alone declar'd for them; and, when he might have been fafe in his Government of *Scotland*, by a Compliance with their Enemies, had put himfelf

P into

into a manifest Hazard, by declaring for them with unequal Forces, against all the Armies of *England* and *Ireland*, yet could not secure himself from their Suspicions. But there was something in his Nature and Principles that gave them Jealousy; something was still too apparent in him, which all his Arts of Caution and half Lights, all his Dexterity of Guards and Silence, could not conceal. Nor indeed could they reasonably trust any Man, that was not involv'd in equal Guilts and Villanies with themselves.

IX. But at the same Time there fell out another new Accident that did greatly promote their Suspicion. The City of *London* had all along been querulous, and dissatisfy'd with this present Constitution of the Parliament, and had made several open Discoveries of their Discontent; but now they proceeded to that Indignation and Scorn against this Tail of a Parliament, that the Common Council of *London* had publish'd a Vote or Order of their House, declaring they would pay no more Taxes or Assessments impos'd upon their City, till the Parliament were fill'd up with equal Representatives of the People.

X. This was such an avowed Contempt of the present Authority, and of so dangerous an Example to the rest of the Nation

GENERAL MONK. 211

tion against paying Taxes, as gave an Alarm to the Council of State. Nor could they imagine any Pretence for this their present Presumption, but from some private Engagement given them by General *Monk* and his Army. They very well knew the City had been conferring with him upon this very Point of new Representatives, or restoring the secluded Members; as also in their Letter deliver'd at *Morpeth*, and afterwards by their Commissioners at *Harborough*, which led the Juncto into Suspicion of some secret Practice between them. The City had the same Cause of Provocation before, yet never dar'd to run into such violent Counsels, till *Fleetwood*'s Army was remov'd, and the Northern Forces were quartered among them, from whom they receiv'd Encouragement, and expected Support.

XI. But to prevent this Insolence in the City before it could fix it self, and become exemplary to others, as also for the better Discovery of General *Monk* and his Army, the Council of State sent for him late at Night, *February* 8. (where were present the other *Feb.* 8. Commissioners for governing the Army) and gave him Orders to march his Regiments the next Morning early into the City, and to quarter upon them till he had reduced them to Obedience; in the mean while, to secure

eleven

eleven of the most active Persons of the Common Council, (whose Names were inserted) and to take down the Chains and Posts in the several Streets, and to unhinge their Gates and Port-cullices. Nor did they allow him longer Time to deliberate upon this extraordinary Action than till the next Morning.

XII. Though the General was somewhat surpriz'd with this outragious Resolution of the Juncto, yet at the first Offer of it to him, he presently took the right Scent of their Design. And therefore, concealing his Dislike of them, he accepted their Orders, resolving to make his own Use of them. For though the Manner was not agreed on, yet the General had design'd, before he came out of *Scotland*, to put an End to the Excrescence of a Parliament, so soon as he was well settled in *London*. And this insolent Resolution they had taken up, of violating the City, would give him the fairest Advantage upon them, (not only to the City and Nation, but also to his whole Army) that he could expect. And that the Juncto might thereby lose for ever their Interest and Credit, the General was contented to adventure his own, in becoming the Instrument of their Malice and Revenge. And, to prevent all Impression upon him to the contrary, they kept him in Discourse with them, giving him particular
Instructions

Instructions for performing their Commands, till towards two in the Morning; which was so late, that such of his Attendants, who knew any thing of Mr. *Sturdy*'s Information, began to suspect some ill Design upon his Person.

XIII. But the next Morning early, *February* 9. the General commanded the March of his Army up into the City, without advising with any of his own Officers. And having plac'd his main Guards at the *Old Exchange*, and other convenient Places, he retir'd himself to the *Three Tuns* Tavern near *Guild-Hall*, where he dispatch'd his Orders to some of his Officers, for the taking up the Posts and Chains, and sent others to apprehend those eleven Citizens, whom the Council of State had commanded him to secure. This sudden Violence offered to the City, and by that Hand from whom they least suspected it, did at present rather surprize the People with Amazement at the Indignity of it, than move their Passions; so that all things appear'd as if the Town had that Morning been taken by Storm, or enter'd by a foreign Army.

XIV. But not only the Citizens, but most also of his own superior Officers were so astonish'd at this unreasonable and odious Employment, that they frankly expressed their Resent-

Resentment, and offer'd him their Commissions. The General gave them some little Light into his own Apprehensions of this infamous Service they had put upon him; but commanded them to obey his Orders at present, and to trust his Discretion with the Consequence.

XV. SEVERAL also of the principal Citizens address'd themselves to him, and with that Temper and Prudence expostulated this unworthy Usage and Indignity put upon them, as the General was greatly concern'd for the Injury they had suffer'd. So that the same Night he dispatch'd Letters to the Council, informing them, that he had obey'd their Orders in securing the Persons they commanded, except two of them, that had been too nimble for him; and that the next Morning the Lord Mayor had appointed a Meeting of the Common Council, where he hoped they would come to a better Resolution, and Temper of submitting themselves to the Authority of Parliament, without the Necessity of any further Severity upon them.

XVI. BUT the Council of State was resolved, now their Hand was in, to do their Work to purpose, and effectually to humble that lofty City. And therefore they return'd him a further Command, not only to take down their

their Gates and Port-cullices, according to their firſt Order, but alſo now to break them in pieces: And, that they might have the full Stroke of their Revenge upon the Common Council, for their daring Reſolution of paying no more Taxes, they had decreed they ſhould never meet more; and therefore inſtantly paſſed a Vote to diſſolve the preſent Common Council of the City.

XVII. THESE ſecond Orders did more deeply incenſe the General againſt the Council of State; but ſeeing them make ſuch Haſte to their own Infamy, he was reſolv'd now to execute their Commands to the full, and venture the Iſſue. The next Day therefore the *Feb.* 10. Gates and Port-cullices were taken down, and the Soldiers broke them in pieces; but with ſuch Reflection upon the Parliament in chuſing them to this baſe Employment, in making them the Executioners of their Paſſion and Revenge upon thoſe who had receiv'd them kindly, that the Citizens, being more ready to excuſe the Stone which hurt them, converted all their Indignation upon the Arm that threw it, and loudly arraign'd this Inſolence of the Juncto. They who attended the General in this Buſineſs, and were curious in obſerving the Tracks of his Countenance, found he was neither well pleas'd with his Employment, nor the Company about

bout him. For *Hazlerig* and *Walton*, (who were equal Commissioners with him in commanding the Army) and others, were continual Espials upon him, both in observing how fully he gave out the Juncto's Orders, and at what Rate they were executed by his Officers and Soldiers. Only Colonel *Morley*, who was another of the Commissioners, and at that Time entrusted with the Command of the Tower, so far dislik'd these Proceedings, as he came this Day to the General at his Quarters in the City, and offer'd to him the Assistance of his own and Colonel *Fag*'s Regiment, with the Force and Arms of the Tower, to oppose or moderate these dangerous Resolutions of the Council of State. Nor were there wanting some Members of the Juncto it self, that, apprehending the dangerous Effects of this Violence upon the City, did greatly accuse these Methods of the abjuring Party in the Council of State. But tho' the General's Displeasure went no further than his Countenance, yet several of his Officers could not conceal their Resentments, accusing the Juncto, that they had as much contriv'd the Infamy of the *Scotch* Army, as the Discharge of their own Insolence and Revenge, in commanding them to this odious Service.

XVIII. This Action of General *Monk* towards

wards the City, was varioufly cenfur'd by all that underftood not, in thofe Times, nor, perhaps, at this Day, in what Circumftances he was then plac'd. For the Orders fign'd by the Council of State, to march the Army into the City, were not directed to General *Monk* alone, but alfo to the other Commiffioners, whereof *Hazlerig*, *Walton*, and *Morley* were upon the Place, and, ever fince his Arrival into *London*, had acted jointly with him. So that, had the General refus'd his Orders, the others, being able to carry it by the major Vote, might have done the Bufinefs without him, and, by Confequence, might have put it to the Hazard of removing him from the Command of his own Army, or have recall'd *Fleetwood* and his Forces into the City, to balance or oppofe him.

XIX. General *Monk*, who better underftood all this than they who haftily cenfured his Proceedings, was refolv'd at prefent to accept whatever Orders were impos'd on him, rather than, by refufing, to hazard his Command and Intereft in his own Army. For he very well knew this prefent State of things could not poffibly hold long, but that the furious and violent Proceedings of the Juncto, and the Odium they would draw upon themfelves thereby, and the further Difcontent

content in the City and Nation, and in his own Army againſt them, would quickly give him ſome more ſeaſonable Opportunity of entering upon his retir'd and conceal'd Deſigns, of putting an End to this Seſſion.

XX. Being now poſſeſſed with the Devils of Jealouſy and Miſchief, the very ſame Day the Council of State had employ'd General *Monk* to break down the Gates of the City, they had conjur'd up a Legion of evil Spirits as bad, or worſe, than themſelves, with a Petition to the Juncto, as extravagantly miſchievous as their own Votes, and much of the ſame Stamp, requiring the Oath of Abjuration to be taken by all Perſons in any publick Employments, and other villainous Matters. This was a Contrivance of the more violent Party of the Juncto and Council of State, who were ſo jealous of the General, that he would not be a fit Inſtrument for them; that they were caballing with *Vane*, *Ludlow*, and *Lambert*, and other Officers of the *Engliſh* Army, to make a Party againſt him.

XXI. These treacherous Deſigns were not ſo ſecretly manag'd, but that General *Monk*'s Officers had taken Notice of them, and apprehended the Conſequences; ſo that (on the ſame Night he had concluded his Orders

ders in the City, and was return'd to *White-Hall*) some of them came to him, and represented the dangerous Effects of that Day's Work in the City, by which they had provok'd and disoblig'd the Metropolis of the Kingdom; and the Noise of this Action, together with their own Infamy, would quickly spread all the Nation over; that such another Piece of Work would certainly ruin them; and yet at the same time they who employed them therein, were Confederate with their profest Enemies, and contriving Parties against them; that they had very few Friends whom they could trust, and in the Parliament House, and Council of State, none at all.

XXII. NOTHING could have been more pleasing to the General than this Discourse of his own Officers, by which he found the late Proceedings in *London* had not only render'd the Juncto odious to the City, but also to his own Army; so that of themselves they had recover'd that Temper which he had so long been contriving to incense into them. For the only Reason why he had hitherto comply'd with the Juncto was, because he thought his own Officers were not yet fit for any other Impression. But now being of themselves possess'd with such Jealousies against them for their late Actions, though he would gladly have had a little more Space to deliberate

berate upon his next Methods, yet he was resolv'd to make use of this present Passion in his Officers, and adventure upon the Design out of hand, which otherwise must have cost him longer Time, and the Contrivance of some other Pretence. Having therefore such Officers about him as he could best trust, which were only of his own Army, except Colonel *Saunders* and Major *Barton*, it was agreed to declare their Apprehensions the next Morning to the Parliament in an expostulatory Letter, the Heads whereof were drawn up: That the *Scotch* Army had receiv'd just Cause of Apprehension from their late Proceedings, having entertain'd Correspondencies with *Lambert* and other Officers, who had so lately rebell'd against them: That they had admitted *Ludlow* to sit in their House after the *Irish* Officers had laid Treason to his Charge, and were in Readiness to prove it: And that they had countenanc'd and accepted a late scandalous Petition, for the obtruding new Oaths upon the free-born People of the Nation, by which the best and most sober Persons would be excluded from having any Share in the Government, and the conscientious Clergy would be disabled from their Ministry and Maintenance. They were therefore requested, so far to comply with the united Desires of the Nation, as in a Week's Time to issue out Writs for the filling up
their

General Monk. 221

their House, and, concluding their own Session by the sixth of *May*, they would then give Place for the convening a full and free Parliament. But before the General went to Bed, being resolv'd to advise no more with the other Commissioners in the Conduct of his own Army, by his sole Authority he gave out Orders for the March of his Forces the next Day into the City, and that several of his principal Officers should attend him the next Morning at his Quarters in *White-Hall*.

XXIII. His Secretaries sate up late that Night to form the forementioned Heads into a Letter, and to transcribe Copies of it, one whereof was sent away very early to the Press, and the other was to be sign'd by the General and his Officers, whereof about fifteen were come together very early, and the Letter being read to them, they all readily set their Hands to it, and it was dated *February* 11. [Feb. 11.] The General then commanded Colonel *Cloberry* and Colonel *Lidcòt* to carry it to the House. But before his Letter could possibly be deliver'd at *Westminster*, the General had left *White-Hall*, and went up into *London*, and there he led his Forces to a Rendezvous in *Finsbury* Fields, having first sent away Commissary *Clarges* and
to Sir *Thomas Allen*, then Lord Mayor, with

with an Account of his coming, desiring him also to assign Quarters for the Reception of his Army in the City.

XXIV. The Work which the General and his Forces had made among them the Day before, quickly affected the City with a near Apprehension of this his early Return among them this Morning, so that his Messengers found but a cold Entertainment, when they came to talk with the Lord Mayor about Quarters for his Army, which he had rather wish'd were further off. Nor had they any Authority to acquaint him with the Secret of the General's Letter sent this Morning to the Juncto.

XXV. But in Conclusion the Lord Mayor, having advis'd with Sir *John Robinson*, and other principal Citizens, was contented at last to receive a Visit from the General, and to discourse with him about quartering his Army. Whereupon a Messenger was dispatch'd into *Finsbury* Fields, intreating him to hasten his Return (it being now late) to the Lord Mayor's House in *Leadenhall-street*, where his Lordship expected him at Dinner. So soon as he came in, he presently observ'd, the Interview between them was not with that Countenance and Freedom as formerly, which the Lord Mayor in some Measure excused,

from

from the late Disorders which had happen'd in the City. To which the General reply'd: *That his Return this Day among them was chiefly to rectify those Misunderstandings, which had lately arisen between himself and the City; and, to that End, entreated his Lordship to dispatch away his Orders unto the Aldermen and Common Council,* (which was the same the Juncto had dissolved) *desiring them to give him a Meeting in the Afternoon at their* Guild-Hall: Which was accordingly done before they sat down to Dinner.

XXVI. The General met with better Entertainment at the Lord Mayor's Table, than his Letters had done with the Juncto at *Westminster*; who had been debating upon them all the Morning. The appointing them a definite Day for the concluding of their own Session, they look'd upon but as a more civil Way of dissolving them. But the filling up the Vacancies of the House by new Elections, did touch them in the most tender and essential Part of their Power and Being; since they very well knew, it was scarce possible to get such Persons return'd that would be as violent and mischievous as themselves: But if the People were left to their free Choice, (which could not now be hindered) they would furnish them with such Elections, as should

should be able to out-vote them in every thing, and haply call them to account for the Villanies they had committed.

C H A P. XVIII.

I. *The Juncto dissemble their Resentments:* II. *And send a Letter of Thanks to the General, for his ready Obedience to their late Orders, inviting him to return to* White-Hall. III. *The Resentments of the General's Officers towards these Messengers of the Juncto.* IV. *The General's Command of Temper.* V. *He meets the Court of Aldermen and Common Council.* VI. *His Speech to them.* VII. *Great Joy in the City.* VIII. *The General quarters at the Glass-House in* Broad-street. IX. *The Juncto has the Name of* Rump Parliament *given it.* X. *A Scheme of the* Rump Parliament *for over-ruling the General.* XI. *The Author's Observation upon the Folly of it.* XII. *The General removes his Quarters to* Drapers-Hall. XIII. *The Council of State desire his Return to* White-Hall, *and the Citizens his Continuance among them.* XIV. *Applications to him from all Parties;* XV. *But particularly*

ticularly from the secluded Members. XVI. *A general Character of the secluded Members.* XVII. *At a Conference between some of the secluded Members, and as many of the Juncto; the Juncto give their Reasons against the Readmission of the others.* XVIII. *The Answer of the secluded Members.* XIX. *One great Difficulty which obstructed their Union.* XX. *A Proposal of the General's for the Removal of that Difficulty.*

I. THE governing and abjuring Party in the House, who had all along been jealous of the General, began now to magnify their own Politicks, in the Prospect of his Defection; whilst the more temperate among them were as ready to accuse the other's violent and extravagant Proceedings, which had enforc'd him to use these Methods with them. But knowing themselves unable (having given him the Possession of the City) to deal with him by Force, they were resolv'd to over-reach him by their Dissimulation. And therefore, concealing all Resentment of his Letter, they appointed their two usual evil Angels, *Scot* and *Robinson*, to attend him in the City, where they found him at the Lord Mayor's House, presently after they had risen from Dinner.

II. THEY

II. THEY acquainted him with the Thanks of the House for his faithful Service, in securing the Peace of the City: And that, before the Receipt of his Letter, they were debating upon Qualifications of such Members as should be chosen for the filling up the House, which should be dispatch'd as speedily as their other weighty Affairs would give them Leisure: Concluding with the Parliament's especial Confidence and Estimation of him, and inviting his Return again to *White-Hall*.

III. THE Officers who were present, could not dissemble their Discontents against the Juncto, but charged them with Perfidy and Ingratitude; and that they were designing rather to put themselves into the Protection of their late Enemies, than to oblige the Army which had restored them. And those Officers especially, whose Commissions had been vacated in *Scotland* by the Juncto's Authority, (though they were yet continued in their Command by the sole Authority of the General) had not parted with their Discontents and Revenge against them.

IV. THE General, whose Cunning it was to express his own Resentments by the Passion of his Officers, was not displeased with this their Freedom, nor did he concern himself

GENERAL MONK. 227

self to moderate their Heats; but, after his grave and solemn Manner, he at last told Mr. *Scot* and Mr. *Robinson, That if the Parliament were pleased to pursue the Advice of his Letter, in issuing out their Writs by* Friday *next for filling up the House, all would be very well, nor would there be any Cause of further Suspicion among them.* But this free and smart Discourse of the *Scotch* Officers to these two Senators, was so different from those Observances which had been paid to them, when they march'd together towards *London*, that they took their Leave not over-well satisfy'd, and return'd back to *Westminster*.

V. So soon as they were gone, the General was mindful of his Appointment for meeting the Court of Aldermen and Common Council at *Guild-Hall*, whither he was conducted by the Lord Mayor, through an infinite Multitude of People, who upon the News of his intended coming thither, were assembled, in Expectation of some great Novelty from him. The Copy also of his Letter to the Juncto, which in the Morning had been sent to the Press, was before this Time publickly exposed in Print.

VI. At his coming the General having friendly saluted this Assembly of principal
Citizens,

Citizens, told them: *That the last Time he was among them, he had submitted to the most fastidious Employment of his whole Life; the Execution of which was as contrary to his own Inclinations, as the Obligations he had to their City. That being past and done, he could only be sorry for those Affronts which had been put upon them against his Will. That this Day he had resolv'd to render a fuller Answer to their Letters, than he was able to do at* Morpeth, *where he received them; and, in Compliance with their Desires then, he had this Morning written to the Parliament, to issue out their Writs, within seven Days, for filling up their House, and by the sixth of* May *next to dissolve their Assembly; and thereby to make Room for the sitting down of a full and free Parliament. In the Interim he was resolv'd to quarter his Army in their City, and to continue himself among them, till he saw how the Contents of his Letter, and the Desires of the City and Nation, were performed.*

VII. The Acclamations of that great and numerous Assembly of *Grecians* at the *Isthmian* Games, when *Flaminius* unexpectedly proclaim'd Liberty to all the Cities of *Greece*, was hardly greater than the Joy of the City upon the News of their Deliverance from the

Bondage

Bondage of this Juncto. It is not easy to say, whether the Citizens were more surpriz'd with what the General told them this Day, or what they had suffer'd by his Soldiers the Day before, when their Posts and Chains were remov'd, and their Gates and Port-cullices broken down. But the Hopes of seeing so speedy an End put to the Parliament, and the convening of another, was so welcome News, that all Places were presently fill'd with an universal Joy and Exultation; and Quarters were presently set out for the General's Regiments, which hitherto had stood all Day on their Arms, but now Meat and Drink was sent to them from almost every House in the City.

VIII. The General, having done his Business at *Guild-Hall*, took Leave of the Citizens, who expressed a very particular Satisfaction and Confidence in him. And from thence he went to the *Bull-Head* Tavern in *Cheapside*, where he order'd the Quarters of his Forces, and the settling the Guards that Night, for the Security of the City. From whence he went very late to quarter, for the present, at the Glass-House in *Broadstreet*; which having only Accommodation for his own Person, his principal Attendants, and some Officers that were always near him, were forced ed to sit up all Night, and watch with his Guards.

IX. But before this, the Apprentices and common People, in Detestation of the Juncto, (to whom they had given, this Night, the lasting Name of the *Rump* Parliament) had set all the Bells in the City on ringing, and kindled Bonefires in every Street, which continued till Morning; and this *Saturday* Night, *February* 11. was called the roasting of the *Rump*.

Feb. 11.

X. But leaving now the General in his Quarters, and the Citizens to their Jollity, we will retreat a little while, (though late) to *Westminster*, and see what this new named Rump Parliament had, this Afternoon and Evening, been doing there. When their Messengers, *Scot* and *Robinson*, return'd from the General out of the City, they gave the House an Account of his Actions there, and with what Discourse they had been entertain'd by his Officers, which led them into further Jealousy, both of the General and his Army; insomuch that they call'd for the late Order of their House, appointing five Commissioners for the governing of the Army, to be read to them; whereupon they struck out *Overton*, because, being absent at *Hull*, he could be of no Use to them, and put in Colonel *Alured*,
who

GENERAL MONK. 231

who was upon the Place. Three of these five were to make a *Quorum*; but it being mov'd, that General *Monk* might be always one of the three for the *Quorum*, upon the Vote it was carried against him: So that, though they durst not take away his Commission *in Terminis*, yet in Effect and Consequence they had done it. For Sir *Arthur Hazlerig, Alured*, and *Walton*, were at any Time sufficient to over-rule General *Monk* and Colonel *Morley*. And thus they thought they were even with him, for enforcing them to fill up their House, and to determine their Session at a Day.

XI. The present Age has sufficiently expos'd the Villanies of these Men, but Posterity will laugh at their Follies also. For tho' the little Foplins of their Party have magnify'd them as the prime Politicians of the World, yet this was an Instance of their weak and impotent Malice, by so foolish a Revenge to provoke a great and powerful General, who had an Army so much at his Devotion, and was possess'd of the City, where he had been too nimble for them, by recovering in an Instant his Estimation among the People, and leaving the Odium of what he had done upon themselves. So that now he was in a Condition to baffle them, and all the Commissioners to boot; and to despise the

the Weakness of their Rage, in shewing their Teeth when they durst not bite.

But though the prevailing Faction of the Rump Parliament had been so inconsiderate as to disoblige him, yet the General was too discreet to take any publick Notice of it at present, having many other Irons in the Fire; nor was his own Army (though in a good Tendency towards it) yet fully brought to that Resolution and Temper he aimed at.

XII. But this Discontent, arising between the Juncto and General *Monk*'s Army, was very welcome News to those other Forces under *Fleetwood* and *Lambert*, who now esteem'd their own Insolencies justify'd, when they discern'd the Army from *Scotland*, which the House had so much rely'd upon, were likely also to quarrel with them. Nor were they without Hopes, if the Jealousies should encrease, to make their own Advantage thereby, and that their old Masters would be enforced to seek Protection from them against General *Monk*; who yet was more wary and considerate, than to let things run to such Extremity, as should give any other Party Advantage upon him.

We had left him in his strait Quarters at the Glass-House; but now, the following Week, he remov'd thence to *Drapers-Hall*, where,

GENERAL MONK. 233

where, with the Addition of another large House (of Alderman *Wale*'s) adjoining, he had Convenience enough for the Reception of all his Attendants, and for the quartering of his Guards.

XIII. AND now the Rump Parliament finding they were too weak to deal with him either by Tricks or Force, continued their further Applications and Messages to him. The Council of State also, *February* 13. invited *Feb.* 13, him again to assist them with his Presence and Counsels; to which he return'd Answer the Day following: *That till the Oaths were withdrawn, he could not possibly attend them; but, for the present, his Continuance in the City was further necessary, because of those Discontents there, which were occasioned by themselves, having distributed seven thousand Arms out of their Stores into the Hands of* Anabaptists, *and other dangerous* Fanaticks; *and that his own Forces were greatly alarm'd, till these Arms were again recall'd.* But the Juncto, and Council of State, were not more importunate to recover him again to *White-Hall*, than the Citizens were to persuade his Continuance among them, as being most for his own Safety, as well as theirs. At the same Time he was also inform'd of several ill Practices against him, contriv'd by some in the Council of State, in
sending

sending several Male-contents, and other violent Sectaries, about the Counties where *Fleetwood*'s Army quartered; possessing them with Jealousies against General *Monk* and his Forces; that they had enter'd into secret Designs with the City of *London*, to alter the Government, and to introduce the King. Some of these Reports he took publick Notice of; others he contemn'd.

XIV. During his Abode in his Quarters at *Drapers-Hall*, he was continually beset with Applications to him from the several Interests in the City, and from the Heads of the Presbyterians and Independent Parties; to whom he return'd such Answers as the Condition of his Affairs would allow.

XV. The Messages also from *Westminster* were still daily continued: But, above all the rest, that Interest in the City and Country, which the General could best trust, had now begun very powerful Addresses to him, for the restoring the formerly secluded Members. The General had before resolv'd to accomplish his Design of introducing the Monarchy by other Methods; but finding it to be the universal Inclination of a powerful Interest to readmit the secluded Members, he began to approve of it, as the most safe and easy Step he could possibly make forward at this

General Monk. 235

this time. Only he very well knew the Juncto, now sitting, would be rather willing to fill up their House by new Elections (a great Part whereof might probably be New-comers) than consent to the Return of these secluded Members, whom they had formerly disobliged by so impudent and injurious a Seclusion. He consider'd also, that the *English* Army, who had been the Instruments of that Violence, would grow very apprehensive upon the News of their Return: Nor was he perfectly well satisfied in the Inclination of his own Officers. But resolving to make some Essay, how far the Contrivance would go, he was contented to receive Visits from several of those secluded Members, having still order'd the Business so, that some of his Officers should be present at the Discourse.

XVI. These Gentlemen were mostly of the Presbyterian Interest, and some of them had been busy enough in beginning the Misfortunes of their King and Country; but were now grown wiser, by the Experience of their Mistakes, and the Miseries of a Civil War, which had ended in almost their own undoing, as well as the Death of the King. Some of them also were Persons of good Estate, and Quality, and easily apprehended the Insecurity of their Condition and Fortunes, whilst a violent Juncto of Robbers and Republicans
govern'd

govern'd at *Westminster*, and were supported by an Army of needy and boisterous Fanaticks. They now saw clearly there was no way left to settle the Nation, but by restoring the Monarchy; only they would first fit it to their Church Discipline, and melt down the Crown into a new Form, and reduce the Sceptre to a Length of their own. For the Prosecution of these Ends, they were as eager to be again fingering the Government, as the Juncto, then sitting, were to keep them out of it. But being Men of much better Morals and Principles than most of the other; they had the Prudence to propose their own Readmission with that Moderation and Temper, as was very acceptable to the General and his Officers. They assur'd them, that their Return would not interfere with the General's Declaration in *Scotland*, in behalf of the Parliament as it sat *October* 7. for it was still the same Parliament that would be continued. They convinc'd them that having, by the same Declaration, undertaken to subject the Military Power in Obedience to the Civil, they had oblig'd themselves to secure their Readmission, since they had been remov'd from their Places by the Violence of the Army.

XVII. The General and his Officers were so well satisfy'd with this Proposal, that, in the next Place, they were resolv'd to hear
what

General Monk. 237

what could be alledg'd against them. To that Purpose it was agreed, that some of these secluded Members should meet at a Conference with a like Number of those now sitting, which was accordingly done on *Saturday Feb.* 18. the General and his Officers being present. Where it was pretended by those now sitting, that since the Removal of the secluded Members, so many things had been done, both as to Change of the Government, Liberty of Conscience, and the Sale of publick Lands, as was likely to be all interrupted and disordered again, by the Return of these Members, to the further Prejudice, and retarding the Settlement of the Commonwealth.

Feb. 18.

XVIII. To this the secluded Members reply'd: That they would not bring with them their Passions nor Revenge into the House, nor concern themselves in any Man's Property, nor lose Time in reflecting back upon what had been done in their long Absence; but would direct all their Thoughts forward, in pursuing such Counsels as might lay a better Foundation of Settlement to the Commonwealth; and leave things in some good Order, for the further Endeavour of the Parliament which should succeed them. Most of those Gentlemen from the Juncto, were of the moderate Party in the House, who were weary'd with the Extravagances of their Fellows,

Fellows, and would be contented to strengthen their Interest by the Accession of the secluded Members. But because the Inclination of the House could not be given but by their Vote in Parliament, they parted on both Sides without coming to any final Agreement.

XIX. WHEN they were withdrawn, the General enter'd into further Discourse with his Officers, where several of them were inclinable enough to restore the secluded Members. But others among them, of the Independent Persuasion, (who had been tamper'd with by the Heads of their Party) began to demur upon it, unless those Members would give Security, to declare for the Government of a Commonwealth, and Liberty of Conscience, and that they would consent to a further Act for Confirmation of publick Sales.

XX. To satisfy these Scruples in those who offer'd them, the General appointed three Persons of his principal Trust, to debate these Points further with some of the secluded Members, in a Conference next Day; which *Feb.* 19. was to be held at Mr. *Annesly*'s House, the present Earl of *Anglesey*. The secluded Members were not willing to depart from their first Length; but, upon a further Debate, gave them fresh Assurance, that they would

would make no Alteration in the present Government, but leave that Point wholly to the next Parliament. And for an Act to confirm the Sale of publick Lands, they were not yet resolv'd to pass any Act at all. But, that there might be no Jealousy upon them, they were content to be limited in the chief Points they should consult upon; and, in one Month's Time, to conclude their Session.

CHAP. XIX.

I. *The General resolves upon the Admission of the secluded Members, upon certain Terms;* II. *Which they submit to.* III. *They are admitted into the House.* IV. *The Behaviour of the Juncto upon their Admission.* V. *The Lords also desire to be restored to their Seats.* VI. *The General declares that he has no Intention to alter the present Constitution of a free State, or Commonwealth, in order to set up* Charles Stuart, *or any single Person.* VII. *He is made Commander in Chief of all the Land Forces, but in the Navy* Mountague *is joined with him.* VIII. *Sir* George Booth

Booth *and others discharg'd from Imprisonment, and* Lambert *imprison'd.* IX. *The Oath of Abjuration voted down, and the Council of State, another being appointed, most of whom were well affected to the King.* X. *Mr.* William Morrice *admitted as a Domestick in the General's Quarters.*

I. ALL this while the General was very uneasy in the present State of things. From the Juncto now sitting he expected no good. The *English* Forces in the Country began to be mutinous; and some of his own Officers, by long deliberating, were grown more unsettled. So that he was now resolved, without further Ceremony, to put some Stay to the Course of things, by admitting the secluded Members. To that End, Mun-*day, February* 20. he desired a Meeting again with them, and had appointed four Articles to be drawn ready, which should be subscribed by all that were present, and by those also who were absent, before they were admitted into the House.

FIRST, *To settle the Conduct of the Armies in the three Nations, so as might best secure the Peace of the Commonwealth.* Secondly, *To provide for the Support of the Forces by Sea and Land, and Money also for their*

Feb. 20.

their Arrears, and the Contingencies of the Government. Thirdly, *To constitute a Council of State for the Civil Government of* Scotland *and* Ireland, *and to issue out Writs for the summoning a Parliament to meet at* Westminster *the* 20th *of* April. Fourthly, *To consent to their own Dissolution by a Time that should be limited to them.*

II. So soon as they were assembled, the Articles were read to them, and willingly subscribed by all then present, who were so very well satisfy'd with this Method he had taken, that they promis'd to give him a Commission of General over all the Forces in the three Nations, both by Sea and Land. Which indeed at this Time was also a seasonable Offer; for his old one granted by the Juncto being confin'd to the 22d of *February*, was to expire within two Days.

At their parting with him, the General intreated them to meet him the next Morning at his late Quarters in *White-Hall*.

The next Morning early he left the City, [Feb. 21.] and his Head-Quarters, to which he never return'd more, and hasten'd to *White-Hall*, where he met the secluded Members, whom he entertain'd with a short Speech, recommending to them the Care of the Nations, and to keep their Word with him, assuring them, he should impose nothing new upon them; which was punctually perform'd by him during their whole Session. And then order'd Major *Miller*, who commanded his Guards, to conduct them into the House of Commons, and divers also of his other Officers attended them to the Door.

IV. THIS Resolution of admitting them that Morning into the House, was so privately carry'd, that the old Juncto were infinitely surpris'd and disorder'd when they saw them enter. The violent and abjuring Party presently found, that it would not be worth their while to keep their Seats, and therefore resign'd them to these new Comers, and quitted the House, some of them muttering their Discontents against the General, as they went out of the Door. But the more moderate Party among them congratulated the Return of the secluded Members; and both Sides presently apply'd themselves to their Business.

V. BUT whilst the secluded Members of the House of Commons were thus earnestly treating with the General for their Readmission, some of the Nobility, and particularly the Earl of *Strafford*, were as importunate with him for the restoring the Lords also to their Session. But the wary General thought the

Return

Return of the Commons was as fair and safe a Length as he durst adventure to go at one Step, reserving the Admission of the Peers to a further Consideration, and the Temper of that Parliament that was to succeed.

VI. THE General having thus placed the secluded Members again in their Seats, and fearing what Disorders the News thereof might raise among the distant Forces of the *English* Army, was resolv'd to satisfy them presently with the Reason and Necessity of what he had done, before they should receive any worse or different Impressions from others. And to that Purpose he commanded the same Day a Council of his Officers to attend him, and to draw up a satisfactory Letter to all the remote Forces and Garrisons of the three Nations, concerning the Readmission of the secluded Members; assuring them, that nothing was thereby intended to alter the present Constitution of a free State or Commonwealth; that without restoring these Members the present Constitution of the House could raise no Money for Support of the Army and Navy, which now would be speedily rais'd and sent to them, and the succeeding Parliament, which was to meet within two Months, should further confirm all publick Sales and Dispositions of Lands in the three Nations. They were then further desired to send an Officer from their several Regiments and Garrisons, that might give the Lord General *Monk* an Account of their Compliance with him herein. And, that they might apprehend no Design of Alteration upon them, they were also strictly requir'd to look after all Persons designing Disturbances in Favour of *Charles Stuart*, or any other single Person, or intended Authority, and to give an Account of them to the Parliament or Council of State. This Letter was dated *February* 21. and sign'd by the General, with twelve of his Colonels, five Lieutenant Colonels, eight Majors, and some few Captains, and presently so many Hands were employed to transcribe the Letter, that the same Night there were Copies enough sign'd, and sent away to every Regiment in *England*, and to all the Commanders in chief in *Scotland* and *Ireland*.

VII. This Night the General left *White-Hall*, and settled his Head Quarters at St. *James's*, which, being a Place somewhat distant from the City, would less expose him to Visits, and Observations upon him, and where he might more privately make ready those farther secret Contrivances, which were next to come upon the Stage. Here he receiv'd an Account, what Vote the House had pass'd that Day; having first raz'd and expung'd all those

those Orders in the Journals, which had been made to authorize their Exclusion. Next they constituted his Excellency General *Monk*, Commander in Chief over all the Forces at Sea and Land, in *England, Scotland*, and *Ireland*. But in the Trust of the Admiralty, they admitted General *Mountague* to an equal Authority with him, which was the first false Step this newly re enter'd Parliament made with their Restorer, having assur'd him of the supreme and entire Command, both in their Armies and Navy, without a second Person to share with him in either. But of this the General took no notice, being very well satisfied of the Worthiness and good Intentions of his Collegue, and having now, besides the Conduct of his own Forces, the Care also of those two other Armies in *England* and *Ireland*, which were likely to give him Trouble enough.

VIII. The House also appointed the Release of all those Citizens, who had been committed by Order of the late Council of State, and discharg'd Sir *George Booth* from his Imprisonment in the Tower, with all those other Gentlemen also that had been confin'd with him upon the same Account, and order'd Major General *Lambert* to be imprison'd in their Room. And about the same Time Dr. *Wren*, Bishop of *Ely*, who was Fellow Prisoner

soner with General *Monk*, in the Tower, was releas'd alſo at the General's Mediation, after his almoſt twenty Years Confinement there.

IX. THE Houſe having voted down the late Council of State, with the Oath of Abjuration, they appointed a new one, (conſiſting of thirty one Perſons) to ſucceed. Moſt whereof for their Character, and good Inclinations towards the King's Service, were accounted of the very Choice and Flower of the Aſſembly, and of this Council the General was one.

X. THE Fame of reſtoring the ſecluded Members was quickly ſpread all over the Nation; and they who were already enter'd, diſpatch'd the ſpeedy Advice thereof to their Acquaintance that were abſent in the Countries, who accordingly haſten'd their Return into the Houſe. Among the reſt Mr. *William Morrice* of *Devonſhire* came up to *London*, who being ally'd to the General, and alſo particularly recommended to him for his great Learning and Prudence, by his Brother Mr. *Nicholas Monk*, was retain'd with him as a domeſtick Friend in his Quarters at St. *James's*, where he became an Inſtrument of ſeveral extraordinary Services, which will follow hereafter to be related.

CHAP.

CHAP. XX.

I. *The General's great Care to secure the Obedience of the Army, and Garrisons.* II. *The Condition of* Ireland. III. *Colonel* Overton *mutinies at* Hull, *but submits, and the Garrison is given to Colonel* Fairfax. IV. *An Act for raising one hundred thousand Pounds a Month for the Support of the Army and Navy.* V. *Another Act for settling the Militia.* VI. *The House offers to settle* Hampton Court *upon the General and his Heirs.* VII. *As also the Government.* VIII. *Both which he rejects.* IX. *The Engagement vacated.* X, XI. *Some Officers propose a Declaration against Monarchy.* XII. *The Design frustrated.* XIII. *Colonel* Okey's *Speech for a Commonwealth, without any House of Lords.* XIV. *Which is effectually answered by Commissary* Clarges. XV. *The General forbids any more Assemblies of Officers without his Leave.*

WHILST the Parliament were earnestly consulting for the Settlement of the State, General *Monk* begins to exercise the Authority of his new Commission, in regulating the Armies, now all united under his Command. And because the publick Safety was so much included in his own, he was prevail'd upon to encrease and settle his Lifeguards, and gave Colonel *Philip Howard* the Command thereof. And being inform'd that Colonel *Rich* was practising some Disturbances with his Regiment quartered at *Bury*, he sent down Colonel *Ingoldsby* to fix those Troops, and gave him the Command of the Regiment. *Desborough*'s Regiment, which the late Juncto had given away to Colonel *Walton*, the General entrusted to Colonel *Charles Howard*, now Earl of *Carlisle*, and made him Governor of that Place. And to Major General *Morgan* he dispatch'd a more authentick Commission for the Government of *Scotland*, and afterward sent him more Forces, for the further Security of that Nation. Neither did the Garrisons and Castles in *Wales* escape his Thoughts. He extended his Care to the Security of the more remote Western Counties of *Devon* and *Cornwal*, and from thence back again to the furthest East, in the Settlement of *Norfolk* and *Suffolk*; all which, though not done together, we have yet conjoin'd, for the greater Clearness and Ease of the Reader.

II. In the interim *Ireland* gave him no Trouble for the present, where all Things went very well through the Care of Sir *Charles Coot*, and Sir *Theophilus Jones*, and
others.

GENERAL MONK. 249

others. *Ludlow* was abſent in *England*, and Sir *Hardreſs Waller* was quickly after ſecured.

III. This extraordinary Providence of the General, together with the ſeaſonable and prudent Letter, which he had diſperſed before to the ſeveral Forces, had hitherto kept them in ſome good Order, till Colonel *Overton* at *Hull* fell into his Fits of Mutiny and Diſtraction; who being a zealous Bigot of the fifth Monarchy, and confident of the Strength of the Place, had diſperſed ſeveral Copies of a ſeditious Letter among the Officers and Regiments in the North, one whereof was ſent up to the General by Colonel *Fairfax*, then Governor of *York*. General *Monk* was not ſo much concern'd about the Danger of the Man, as the Quality of the Place he held, and therefore acquainted the Council of State with theſe Practices and Letters, who, together with the General, ſent down Colonel *Alured* and Major *Smith* with their Letters, commanding him, upon the Receipt thereof, to attend them forthwith at *London*, and there to give them an Account of his Fears and Jealouſies. *Overton* found himſelf ſurpriz'd much ſooner than he expected; ſo that he was enforc'd to ſubmit, and deliver up the Garriſon. This was a Place of impregnable Defence and Strength, whither if *Lambert*

bert had retreated with Part of his Army, after his Quarters were broke up at *Newcastle*, he might have given all of them Trouble enough, before they could have been able to reduce him. The General was therefore resolv'd to intrust this Garrison in a sure Hand, and committed it to Colonel *Fairfax*.

IV. Hitherto he had secured the Submission of the Armies by an extraordinary Prudence, which now the Parliament took care to confirm, by a Vote of their House; and knowing nothing could so much oblige the Obedience of Soldiers as the Assurance of their Pay, they passed an Act for the raising of one hundred thousand Pounds *per Mensem*, upon *England* and *Wales*, which was to continue for six Months, towards the Support of the Army and Navy.

V. But though they had thus provided for their Maintenance, yet they were resolv'd also to take Care for their own Safety. They forgot not that the *English* Army had been train'd up in Sauciness and Insolence; that they had been accustom'd to shew Tricks at *Westminster* in disturbing, or dissolving former Parliaments; and therefore, to prevent the like Violence upon them again, they passed another Act for raising the Militia in the City and Nation, which was so vigorously carried

carried on in *London*, that they had presently settled six good Regiments of Foot, and one of Horse, besides the auxiliary Forces, being in all twelve thousand fighting Men. The like Care was also used in the several Counties for the settling the Commands of their Train'd-bands and County Troops.

VI. THE Entertainment of the Soldiers being thus provided for, it was next thought reasonable to pass some Vote for rewarding also the Service of their General. And to that End those Commonwealth's Men, Members of the late Juncto, that still kept their Places in the House, being desirous to oblige the General to their Side, or that nothing might be left to support a single Person, propounded to settle, by Act of Parliament, upon him and his Heirs, the Manour and Honour of *Hampton Court*, with the Parks and Lands belonging to it, which the Villanies of those Times had not yet swallowed; having been reserv'd from their Jaws by the late Usurper *Cromwel*, for his own Convenience. And tho' the secluded Members, who had been restored by the General, could not decently refuse the Proposal, yet himself utterly declined the first Motion of it. But the House having gone so far in it, they then engaged to gratify him with the Sum of twenty thousand Pounds.

VII. THOUGH

VII. Though he had refus'd the Gift of the Crown-Lands, yet some of those who had been concern'd in the Murder of the late King, and others who had cut themselves large Thongs out of the Royal Demesns, had the Confidence to tamper with him about assuming the Government in his own Person. And, among the rest, Sir *Arthur Hazlerig* (to preclude the Restoration of the King) offered him one hundred thousand Hands that should subscribe to his Title.

VIII. It may seem strange, that they who every where discovered their Jealousies against him, for restoring the King, should now think he might be persuaded to set up himself. But since they could not interrupt his Design by suggesting the former, they had secretly contriv'd his Ruin by the Offer of the later. And they who thus officiously complimented his Advancement, would have been the first Rebels against him. But the General, who was immovable in his secret Resolution and Allegiance for restoring the King, abhorred the Thoughts of this Proposal, and gave them so close and positive an Answer, as he was resolv'd should put an End to all further Addresses of that Nature.

IX. The House was all this while busy in
settling

settling the Affairs of the Nation for the Convenience of the succeeding Parliament, and, among other things, about the 13th of *March* March 13. they vacated the Oath called the *Engagement*, which about ten Years before, was imposed upon the People, and to be taken by all Members of Parliament before their Admission to sit in the House. But the solemn League and Covenant (the Engine or Sacrament of so many Mischiefs) still hung upon the Wall of their House, as the Palladium of the Place, where most of them present might read their own Names subscribed to it, till a succeeding Parliament two Years after, went backward, and covered the Shame of their Predecessors, by a Vote of their House, commanding it to be taken down, and dissolved the Charm it had put upon the Nation, by burning the Witch.

X. Though the Proceedings of the Parliament and the General were managed with a very extraordinary Caution, yet the unquiet Officers of the Army began to be jealous and apprehensive of their own Danger. They were highly alarmed with two late Votes of the House. The Act for settling the Militia throughout the Nation, they esteem'd a Design to balance or master the Power of the standing Army; and their late Order for dissolving the Engagement, which hitherto had been

the

the Basis of the Constitution of the Commonwealth, seem'd to them as a preparatory Contrivance for changing the Government. Nor were they better contented with the late Methods of the General, in declining so fair an Offer of the Crown-Lands, and afterwards of the Government it self. Their own Ambition and Avarice would have skip'd at a much lower Bait; which led them into a deeper Suspicion of the General's Refusal, as a Contrivance of going to a better Market, by restoring the Monarchy; which would certainly put an End to their insolent Dominion over Parliaments and People, and expose their Necks to answer for their Guilt and Villanies, in murdering the King, and changing the Government.

XI. Such Apprehensions as these had so far possessed these discontented Officers, that they had appointed a Meeting thereupon; where it was unanimously resolv'd to draw up a Declaration, which should be first sign'd by the General and themselves, and then offer'd to the Parliament. The chief Point whereof was, to declare against Monarchy, and the Dominion of any single Person under whatsoever Title or Pretence, but that the Government of these Nations should continue and remain as a Commonwealth and Free-State; and that the present House should pass
an

an Act to establish this fundamental and unalterable Constitution, in such manner as no succeeding Parliament should presume to change or alter it, otherwise they would not hold themselves oblig'd to protect their Authority. Some of them presently attended the General with this Paper, desiring his Consent and Allowance. Upon the Perusal whereof, it is hard to say whether he was more displeas'd or surpriz'd. But resolving to conceal his own Dislike till he could frustrate the Effect of it, he only told them, that to Morrow there would be a general Council of Officers at the Head-Quarters, where he desired their Paper should be further examined and considered.

XII. THIS Declaration of the seditious Commanders was so directly levelled against all the General's next Contrivances, as greatly concern'd him. So that he presently advis'd with his usual Confidents, how to prevent the Progress of this Design; and thereupon commanded all his own Officers that he could best trust, to be present, and over-rule it. He had before made Mr. *Morrice* a Member of the Army, by giving him the Government of *Plimouth*, designing thereby to employ his Prudence and Temper in moderating these Assemblies. But being a Gentleman that had spent his Time in the Silence of his Books
and

256 *The LIFE of*

and Studies, it render'd him uneasy in the Company of such rude and clamorous Conventions. Commissary *Clarges* was also directed to be present, who, by his long Employment, had so practis'd the Conversation, that he was not easy to be run down or impos'd upon by those violent Hucksters. So that amongst those many extraordinary Services which the Commissary had perform'd in all this Design, the Management of this Day's Conference was very considerable, wherein he proceeded with that Reach and Dexterity, as silenced the Jealousies of those People, and baffled the Contrivance.

March 15. XIII. The next Morning, being *March* 15. a considerable Party of the Officers were ready at St. *James's*; and Colonel *Okey*, (who could better use his Sword than his Tongue, in Defence of their Commonwealth) began a long and querulous Story of their Fears and Jealousies: *That their good old Cause was like to be left in the Lurch; and such Designs were now on Foot for changing the Government, as must necessarily determine in restoring the King. But, to obviate these growing Evils, there was no other Way, but to oblige the present Juncto to declare instantly for the unalterable Continuance of a Free-State, without any House of Lords; or, upon their Refusal, to take some*

some other *Methods for the Safety of the Commonwealth:* So great a Statesman was this Chandler of *Billingsgate* grown.

XIV. To all which Commiſſary *Clarges* anſwer'd in a cloſe and well-wrought Reply: *That their preſent Jealouſies and Apprehenſions were only imaginary; that they had taken their Meaſures wrong, if they thought to make any Advantage of this Parliament, by ruffling with them, who had formerly boldly withſtood them, when they had leſs Power than now, when the Nation is more on their Side, and wholly reſolv'd againſt the Government of an Army: That the General had oblig'd himſelf to give the Houſe no Diſturbance in their Councils during their Seſſion; and that if he ſhould break this promiſe with them, they had yet Power in their Hands to deal with him, and ſuch other Officers, as they pleas'd, by voting away their Commiſſions: That by ſuch an Addreſs the Houſe would be ſo incenſed, as preſently to paſs a Vote for their own Diſſolution, without taking care of iſſuing out Writs for the ſucceeding Parliament. All which would preſently bring them into ſuch a Labyrinth of Diſorder and Confuſion, as they would not eaſily know where to turn them; unleſs they would meanly ſubmit themſelves again to* Richard Cromwell, *whom they had ſo greatly provoked.*

ed; *for, as for his Excellency here present, they knew his Mind already, so that (let them take what Course they pleas'd) he was resolved not to be concern'd in meddling with the Government.*

XV. The General, according to the usual manner, kept his own Part for the last Scene; and, having gravely put them in mind of the Inconveniencies which they had before brought upon themselves by disturbing former Parliaments, he told them *the present House was so near its Conclusion, that no evil Consequents could be feared from them. And the succeeding Parliaments would be called under such Qualifications as must necessarily secure the Government. In the interim, he advised them to remember their Duty, and how contrary it was to the good Discipline of an Army, to intermeddle in the Civil Government; and then strictly commanded them all to hold no more of these Assemblies without his Direction.* But, during this Conference, he took so particular Notice of such Officers as were most forward and turbulent, that he was resolv'd to worm them out of their Commissions by the first Opportunity.

CHAP.

CHAP. XXI.

I. *The Presbyterians encouraged by the General, for having good Inclinations towards the King.* II. *A remarkable Instance of his Favour to that Party.* III. *A Design in the Parliament to restore the King; which obliges the General to hasten their Dissolution.* IV. *Two remarkable Votes.* V. *The Parliament dissolved.* VI. *The Council of State continued: They publish a Proclamation: The Army sign an Engagement of Obedience to their General.* VII. *The Royal Party quietly wait the Event of these extraordinary Proceedings.* VIII. *Only Sir* John Greenvil *now resolves to execute his former Commission from the King to the General.*

THE short Session of the secluded Members had already made a very considerable Alteration in the late governing Interests; so that now the Presbyterian Party began to come aloft. The General was not now to be taught the Temper and Principles of the Presbyterians, having seen enough of their Way in those Petulances between the Resolutioner and Remonstrator in *Scotland*, during his long Command among them, and therefore had taken a just Length how far to intrust or employ them. He very well knew their Power and Interest in the City of *London*, and that there were also very many Persons among them, who, out of Hatred to the late Tyrannies, and Affection to the King, did very passionately desire his Restauration, as the best Remedy for saving their Country, and therefore were very likely to co-operate with him towards his own Ends. And observing how absolutely this People were govern'd by their Clergy, he had receiv'd several Visits from the chief of them, and frequently heard some of them preach, especially Mr. *Calamy*, the Superintendent of their Party; with whom he so far comply'd, as to entertain only such Chaplains to preach before him every Sunday in the Chapel at St. *James's*, as Mr. *Calamy* should please to send him, who was hourly contriving to possess the Ears of the General with the continual Air and Breath of Presbyterianism, and to plant it in his Family, to the further Advantage and Reputation of the Party.

II. But his domestick Chaplain Dr. *Price*, who knew nothing of this Intrigue, being desirous to introduce some of the principal Clergy of the Church of *England* to the Favour and Estimation of the General, had, one *Sunday*, desired Dr. *Pearson* (the present Lord Bishop of *Chester*) to preach before him,

him, who was accordingly there present. In the interim arrived two Ministers sent from the Head of their Order, to perform the Service; but in the bad Way by the Park Wall, their Coach happen'd to make so unlucky a Trip, that all came together into the Dirt, so that neither of them were in any Condition for a Pulpit, till Dr. *Price* had set them to rights again in his Chamber, intreating one of them to preach that *Sunday*, and the other on the next. The General being inform'd what Persons were there ready to preach, would by no Means accept Dr. *Pearson*, though he very well understood the Value of the Man, and was persuaded to it by his domestick Confident Mr. *Morrice*, but accepted of the Presbyterian Preachers. So careful he was, even in this little Instance, not to disoblige the Party, till he had fully done his Business with them.

III. The General having thus palliated the Discontents of his Officers, expected no further Rubs in the Current of his Affairs, when presently he found himself incumbred with a new Trouble from the Parliament it self, where several of the Members, being unwilling to hear of a Dissolution at the Time prefix'd them, began to contrive Delays for the Continuance of their Session; and foreseeing the necessary Restoration of the King, were desirous to mend their own Markets, in voting home the Son, who had first voted away his Father in the Beginning of the War. The General was acquainted with their daily Proceedings by the nightly Accounts of Mr. *Morrice*, whom he had particularly instructed, by all possible Arts of Diversion, to stave off this present Session from meddling with any Alteration of Government. For the General had at first restored them, rather to prevent the Mischief of the other Parties, than for any great Good they could have done by themselves, having placed his main Hopes upon the Effects of the Parliament which should succeed them. But finding them as willing to hear of their Death, as their Dissolution, he was enforc'd to take the Boldness of putting them in mind of it, by quickening their Pace.

IV. But now the Day for concluding their Session being near at Hand, the House began to make ready for it, having first issued out Writs for chusing the succeeding Parliament against *April* 25. which, by their Agreement with the General, should have been conven'd five Days sooner. And, that they might have an Army at hand, to justify all they had done in the late War, and a succeeding Parliament of their own sanguine Complexion, they concluded their Session with two such Votes

Votes as gave Entertainment and Discourse to the Nation; one whereof was, that no Commission should be granted to any Officer in the Army that did not first acknowledge and declare, that the late War, raised by the two Houses of Parliament in their own Defence against the late King, was just and lawful. The second was, that whatever Person had advised, abetted, or assisted in any War against the Parliament, since the first of *January* 1641. neither they, nor their Sons, should be capable of being elected into the next Parliament, unless they had before given some Testimony of their good Affection to the present Parliament.

V. AND thus having resolved to make their End agreeable to their Beginning, on the long desir'd 17th of *March* this unhappy and fatal Parliament, having been twice excluded, and twice dismember'd, was at last dissolv'd by their own Act, after they had continued thro' various Interruptions, for almost twenty Years, in the Practice of such publick Mischief and Confusions, as will ever be remember'd with Horror.

VI. BUT though the Parliament was at an End, yet the Council of State (most whereof were of the soundest and most generous Part of the House) continued still their Session, being appointed by the Parliament to put in Execution, after their Recess, the Act they had past for the Election of Members to serve in the next Parliament. They were also instructed to settle more effectually the Militia of the Nation, and to assist the General in securing the Temper and Obedience of the Army. To this End they put out a Proclamation, for the apprehending all Persons that should endeavour to make Parties, or raise Jealousies, among the Soldiers, or withdraw them from their Duty, to the Disturbance of the publick Peace. And whoever should discover or apprehend any such Offenders, should have the Reward of ten Pounds for their Pains. But because no Means was thought effectual enough to bind and secure the Obedience of an Army that had been so long accustomed to Misrule and Violence, it was contrived by the General, and some of his more secret Council, that all Officers in the several Armies should presently sign an Engagement, declaring their entire Submission to all the Commands of his Excellency the Lord General, and to the Orders of the present Council of State, and that they would yield all Obedience to the Resolutions and Councils of the succeeding Parliament. This Engagement was readily subscrib'd by all the Officers of General *Monk*'s Army, and by most also of the others; and they who refus'd

were

GENERAL MONK. 265

were presently remov'd from their Commands, which gave the General the fair Opportunity which he had so long desir'd, for introducing several Persons of Honour and Quality into Commands in the Army, in the Place of those he could no longer trust.

VII. HITHERTO all things had been manag'd by the Power and Influence of the Parliamentary Party, whilst the Royal Interest (that were to reap the sole Advantage of the succeeding Change) having entertain'd some secret Hopes or Confidence in General *Monk*'s Proceedings, contented themselves to sit still, without raising any farther Jealousies upon themselves or him, by making further Applications to him.

VIII. ONLY Sir *John Greenvil*, (his near Kinsman) who had, the last Year, been practising upon the General's Allegiance in *Scotland*, by sending his Brother *Monk* thither, of which we have given the Account before, was resolv'd to make some further Attempt upon him, especially now, observing him to be in a much better Capacity of answering his Ends, than when he had first dealt with him in *Scotland*.

1660.

CHAP.

CHAP. XXII.

I, II. Sir John, *by the Means of Mr.* Morrice, *though with much Difficulty, gets a Promise of a private Conference with the General, who knew Sir* John's *Business.* III. *Sir* John *is introduced to the General, to whom he opens his Message and Credentials.* IV. *The General's seeming Surprise, and Sir* John's *great Presence of Mind and Resolutian.* V. *The General receives him and his Message with great Kindness.* VI. *The Author's Observation upon it.* VII. *The General declares himself to Sir* John, *in the Presence of Mr.* Morrice. VIII. *Sir* John *offers the General, from the King, a great Reward, which he refuses.* IX. *His Caution in not writing yet to the King.* X. *His Instructions to Sir* John, *upon his Return to the King.* XI. *Sir* John *arrives at* Brussels, *and gives the Account of his successful Message to the General.* XII, XIII. *His Majesty's great Hopes, and Removal to* Breda.

I. TO this purpose he made frequent Visits to the General at St. *James's*, but in the Croud of so many Suitors and Attendants, he could never yet meet with a vacant
Oppor-

Opportunity of Conference with him; tho' he had several Times staid late, hoping the Retirements of others, would have given him an Advantage to surprize him alone. The General very well knew his Business, and the Reason of his so frequent and late Visits: But because he thought his own Station not yet secure enough to receive his Message; he was resolv'd still to prevent any Address to him; either sometimes calling his Secretaries, and resuming Business, or else rising from his Chair with a *Good Night, Cousin, 'tis late,* and so retiring to his Bed-chamber. But after so many Frustrations, Sir *John Greenvil,* being impatient till he had perform'd his Majesty's Commands, was resolv'd, since he could not make his Way to the General by himself, he would attempt it by the Mediation of another. And to that purpose finds out Mr. *Morrice,* to whom he was very well known, both as being ally'd to him, and also a Trustee for his Estate, by the Disposition of his Father, Sir *Bevil Greenvil*'s Will. Him he engag'd to take the first Opportunity of informing the General, that he had Business of great and secret Importance to acquaint him with, intreating his Excellency to allow him the Favour of a private Conference. It was not long before Mr. *Morrice* found an Occasion to communicate all this Discourse to the General, who reply'd: That his Cousin *Green-vil*

vil was so well known in the Town, and so noted a Royalist, that he could not, with Security or Concealment, admit him to a private Interview in the Head-Quarters, but that, in a Time of so much jealous Observation, some ill Apprehensions would be raised from it. He therefore desired Mr. *Morrice* to go to Sir *John Greenvil* in his Name, with Assurance, that he had given him full Trust to hear his secret Business, and that by him he should also receive the General's Answer. Mr. *Morrice* presently acquainted Sir *John Greenvil*, at his own House in *Covent-Garden*, with this Direction from the General; who utterly refus'd to communicate his Business to any other Person except his Excellency himself. But the General was so little satisfy'd with this Answer, that he afterwards sent Mr. *Morrice* back again, more earnestly desiring him that he would trust him with the Conveyance of this secret Affair. But Sir *John* was still resolv'd to treat only with the General, and though he had securely intrusted Mr. *Morrice* with his Estate, yet he could trust no Man but himself in this Business; assuring him, that this Affair related only to the General himself, whom it so nearly concern'd, that if his Excellency would not grant him the Favour of a private Access, he must be forced to acquaint him with it where-ever he next met him. Upon the Return of this Answer,

swer, the General was exceedingly pleas'd with the Resolution and Wariness of his Kinsman. For now he found he was to deal with a Man of Secrecy, which was all he aim'd at. And therefore the next Day Mr. *Morrice* was sent back to let him know, that the same Evening he would give him a Meeting in Mr. *Morrice*'s Chamber at St. *James*'s.

II. It cannot be imagin'd, but the General very well knew Sir *John Greenvil* could have no other Business with him of so much Secrecy, but what he had before begun in *Scotland*, the King's Restauration; nor can it be thought his Excellency would so much concern himself (in sending so many Messages) to be told that which he had no Mind to hear.

III. Sir *John Greenvil* was very careful to attend the Minutes of this Appointment, and accordingly came in the Evening to the Chamber, where he found Mr. *Morrice*; and presently after the General, by a back Stairs, entered the Room at another Door. So soon as they had saluted each other, Mr. *Morrice*, knowing it to be an Interview of Secrecy, withdrew to the Door, resolving to secure the Room from any other Interruption upon them. Whereupon Sir *John Greenvil* began to compliment the General for the Favour he
had

had done him, in giving him this Opportunity to discharge a Trust, which had long remain'd in his Hands, and was of so great Concernment both to his Excellency, and also to the whole Nation: That hitherto he had been unhappily prevented in his Endeavours from obeying the Commands of the King his Master; and thereupon presented the General with his Majesty's Letter, and also produced his own Commission from the King, by which he was enabled to treat with him in this Business.

IV. THE General having receiv'd the Letter and Papers into his Hands, stepp'd back in a kind of Surprizal, and then with some Emotion ask'd him, *How he durst adventure to treat with him in a Matter of this Nature, without considering the Danger of the Attempt?* To which Sir *John* reply'd, *That he had so long been accustomed to daily Hazards of this Kind in pursuing the Commands of the King his Master, that they were grown familiar to him: But now he was the more encouraged, by observing the Methods which his Excellency had taken, and from whence his Majesty had also entertain'd some particular Confidence of his good Affection and Inclination towards his Service.*

V. THE

V. The General could not longer conceal himself, but with some Passion (like that of *Joseph* to his Brethren) he embraced his Cousin *Greenvil*, giving him Thanks that he had with so much Prudence and Secrecy convey'd his Majesty's Letter to him; which he did more gladly receive from his Hands, being his nearest Kinsman, and a Descendant of the Family to which he owed so many Obligations. That he was very well pleas'd in observing his Resolution, not to reveal this Secret to any Man after his Brother; otherwise he should not have thought him a Person fit to be talked with in Business of so great Concernment.

VI. And here let it be noted with a Point of a Diamond, that the same General *Monk*, who was naturally so wary and considerate, that he would find Ways to deliberate upon the least sudden Proposal made to him, yet entertain'd presently this great Affair the first Minute it was offer'd him. So congenial and agreeable was the Address of Sir *John Greenvil* to his own secret Inclinations. And they who have render'd this great and illustrious Person a kind of Property led on by the Conduct of others, may here meet with their own Conviction. For though no Man knew better than himself, how to make use of those

about

about him; yet in this great Concernment, which was the most nice and tenderest Part of all his Business, he advis'd with none of them all, nor made them privy to it.

VII. The General then read his Majesty's Letters, and look'd over Sir *John Greenvil*'s Commission, and thereupon further reply'd, *That he was much oblig'd to his Majesty for this good Opinion he was pleas'd to entertain of him, and for the Assurance his Majesty had given him (by his Letter) of his gracious Pardon. That indeed he had been cast into the Society of his Majesty's Enemies, but his Heart was always faithful to him, and he had still kept an Eye upon his Service, whensoever he should be in a Condition to attempt it; unto which he had now, in some good Measure, arrived, through manifold Difficulties and Disappointments; being resolved to endeavour his Majesty's Restauration with the Hazard of his own Life and Fortunes.* And, that there might be further Witnesses of these Resolutions, he would call that honest Man from the Door. Mr. *Morrice* was accordingly call'd to the rest of their Conference, and assisted therein.

VIII. Sir *John Greenvil* acquainted the General, that he had Authority from his Majesty to assure him of an hundred thousand
† Pounds

Pounds *per Ann.* to be annually paid to him and his Officers for ever, with what Title of Honour he should chuse for himself, together with the Offer of Lord High-Constable of *England.* All which his Excellency as generously refused, telling Sir *John Greenvil: There was sufficient Reward in the Conscience and Satisfaction of serving his Prince, and obliging his Country. That he would not sell his Duty, nor bargain for his Allegiance; so that for any Regards towards him, he was wholly resolv'd in to the good Pleasure of his Majesty.*

IX. Sir *John Greenvil* then moved the General to write some Answer to his Majesty's Letter, and to send a Messenger of his own to attend him; which his Excellency declin'd, telling him, *That he had none about him that as yet he could trust with such a Secret.* And though Sir *John* mentioned the Names of some particular Persons about him, yet he refused, for the present, to adventure a Letter to his Majesty, which, if it should happen by any Accident to be intercepted, would raise such Jealousies and Apprehensions in the Army, (not yet fully wrought to his Mind) as it should hardly ever be again in his Power to compose them. He therefore desir'd Sir *John Greenvil,* as he had receiv'd from him the Commands of his Majesty, so he would also return his Answer; and that since he could not securely write, a Messenger of his own without Letters would be to little purpose; but his Majesty would believe his own Agent, though he brought no Letter of Credence. Sir *John Greenvil* then told the General, that he would begin his Journey to the King the next Evening, who thereupon appointed to meet him again the following Day in the same Place, where he should receive his Instructions.

X. The next Evening Sir *John Greenvil* attended the General in Mr. *Morrice*'s Chamber, where his Excellency desir'd him to take his Instructions in Writing, the Heads whereof were:

" That since by the long Civil War and
" Change of Government, the Minds of the
" Soldiers in general, and a great Part of the
" People would be alarm'd with the Appre-
" hension of his Majesty's Return, it was his
" humble Advice, that he would be graci-
" ously pleas'd to proclaim his free and gene-
" ral Pardon to all his Subjects, except to
" such as the Parliament should esteem inca-
" pable of it. That he would prepare the
" Minds of the Army, by declaring his Rea-
" diness to consent to such Acts as should se-
" cure the publick Sales and Dispositions of
" Lands, and the Payment also of their Ar-
" rears.

General Monk. 275

" rears. And becaufe nothing was more like-
" ly to run the People into Frenzies, than
" the Fear of Reftraint in their feveral Reli-
" gions, he did further befeech his Majefty
" to declare his Affent for a Toleration and
" Liberty of Confcience to all his Subjects,
" who fhould fo employ it as not to give any
" Difturbance to the Civil Government. He
" was alfo inftructed to defire his Majefty to
" retire from the Dominions of the King
" of *Spain* into fome convenient Place be-
" longing to the States of the united Pro-
" vinces, where, with more Freedom and Se-
" curity to his Perfon, he might treat further
" with his Parliament and People. And laft-
" ly, he was ftrictly cautioned not to give
" his Majefty any Interruption, by offering
" Propofals to him for the Reward of his
" Service." The General then defired him
to perufe his Inftructions catefully, and to fix
them throughly in his Memory; and then,
receiving the Paper from his Hand, threw it
into the Fire before them, and intreated him
to keep thefe Particulars in his Thoughts as
he travelled, and by no means to commit
them again to Writing, till he was firft arriv'd in *Flanders*, nor to acquaint any Perfon with his Bufinefs except his Majefty only.
They then privately took Leave of each o-
ther; and the fame Night Sir *John Greenvil*,
fpeeding fecretly through the City, began his
Journey

Journey towards *Dover*, where, the next Day, he seasonably found the Lord *Mordaunt*, who was then going over to the King, and had hir'd a Vessel to himself, in which he was very joyful to accommodate his old Acquaintance Sir *John Greenvil*, and engage together in the King's Service; but in all their Voyage to *Ostend*, they knew nothing of one another's Business. When they came to *Brussels*, the Lord *Mordaunt* resolv'd to go directly to the Court, and Sir *John Greenvil* to his Lodgings; desiring his Lordship to acquaint the King, that he was come to Town, and where he lodged.

XI. So soon as his Majesty was inform'd of Sir *John Greenvil*'s Arrival, he expected from him some extraordinary News from *England*; and the rather, because he came not to Court, but retir'd himself so privately. The same Night therefore his Majesty went alone in his Coach to his Lodgings, where, being private together, he gave his Majesty a distinct and particular Account of all his Proceedings with General *Monk*; with what Readiness he had embrac'd his Majesty's Service, and with what Care and Prudence he had run through a thousand Difficulties and Disappointments to arrive at his present Station; and by which he hop'd he should be able to accomplish his Majesty's Restauration.

He

He then descended to the Relation of those private Instructions he had received from the General; which, when his Majesty had further considered and debated with Sir *John Greenvil*, they found it impossible to comply with General *Monk*'s Desire, in managing this secret Affair by themselves alone, without admitting some others to a Share in their Counsels. And therefore his Majesty resolv'd that, the next Day, the Marquiss of *Ormond*, the Lord Chancellor *Hide*, and Sir *Edward Nicholas*, should be acquainted with it; who accordingly attended his Majesty privately, together with Sir *John Greenvil*, and received this News from General *Monk* with a kind of joyful Astonishment.

XII. AND now his Majesty began to entertain some nearer Hopes of recovering the Throne of his Ancestors, than he had done by those former Attempts, which had been made for him in *England* or *Scotland*. For this was a Method that had never yet been try'd, and the Conduct of it was in the Hands of a wary and valiant Man, that wanted not Prudence and Courage to go through with it. Nor did his Majesty and the honourable Counsellors forget to reflect upon the extraordinary Service of Sir *John Greenvil*, with what Pains and Industry, through how many Dangers and Hazards, he had carried on this secret Trust for almost three Quarters of a Year, and had at last so happily concluded it with the General.

XIII. At this Conference it was resolv'd to pursue the well-advised Counsel from General *Monk*, for the removing of his Majesty out of the *Spanish* Territories. And accordingly some few Days after he went privately to *Breda*, where he settled his Court; and in this Place were made ready all those Packets and Dispatches, which Sir *John Greenvil* was to carry back into *England*. A Declaration was also formed and signed by the King, containing all those very Points which the General had propos'd by his Instructions to Sir *John Greenvil*.

CHAP. XXIII.

I. *A Commission drawn up for constituting General* Monk *Captain General of all his Majesty's Forces, with Letters by him to be communicated in* England. II. *Some of the late Parliament are for imposing very dishonourable Terms upon the King, in order to his Restoration.* III. *They send a Letter a Letter to the King to that Purpose, and represent the General as complying with them.* IV. *Sir* John Greenvil *returns to* England *with the King's Instructions.* V. *What passed betweeen the General and him upon his Return.* VI. *The Election for a new Parliament.* VII. *An Insurrection.* VIII. Lambert *escapes, and joins them in* Warwickshire. IX. *The General resolves, if Occasion should be, to publish the King's Commission, and declare openly for him.* X, XI. Lambert *is taken Prisoner, and recommitted to the Tower.*

I. BEFORE his Majesty took any Care about the Disposal of his own Affairs, he was first considering how to reward the Service of the General, and was advising with Sir *John Greenvil* hereupon; who told him, he had already acquainted the General with his Majesty's Proposals, according to his former Instructions, which the General had wholly refused; and that, among his other Instructions from the General, there was this particularly inserted, "that he should move " nothing to the King about any Reward." So that Sir *John Greenvil* did now offer it as his humble Advice to his Majesty, to intermit, for the present, the Care thereof till his own happy Arrival into *England.* Wherefore at present his Majesty only commanded

a Com-a Commission to be drawn up for General *Monk*, to command as Captain General over all the Forces of *England, Scotland*, and *Ireland*; which was sign'd by him, and put up with a private Letter to him from his Majesty, written with his own Hand. There was also another Letter directed: *To our trusty and well beloved General* Monk, *to be by him communicated to the President of the Council of State, and to the Officers of the Armies under his Command*, with a Copy of the forementioned Declaration enclosed. And because the new and auspicious Parliament (upon whose Councils the Hopes both of the King and People did so much depend) were suddenly to meet, Letters were drawn up to be delivered at their Assembly by Sir *John Greenvil*, directed by the King: *To our trusty and right well-beloved the Speaker of the House of Lords*: And another, *To our trusty and well-beloved the Speaker of the House of Commons*; In both which were also Copies of his Majesty's forementioned Declaration inclos'd. There was also a Letter directed: *To our trusty and well-beloved the Lord Mayor, Aldermen and Common Council of our City of* London; In the contents whereof the Lord *Mordaunt*, who was also to return with Sir *John Greenvil*, was mentioned. And another to General *Monk*, and General *Mountague*, to be by them communicated to the Fleet.

II. BUT

II. But whilst these Letters are making ready at *Breda*, we will return a while into *England*, where all Parties were exceeding busy in the Pursuit of their particular Interests, upon the Prospect of this great Revolution, which some of them hop'd for, and others equally fear'd. So that General *Monk* was perpetually beset with many and different Addresses from those who were curious to discover his Sense and Inclination, or to propose their own. But, among the rest, there was a most mischievous and villainous Application made to him by some Members of the late Parliament; who persuaded him, that if the next Session should resolve upon restoring the ancient Government, and bring home the King; yet his Return should not be safely admitted, but upon the same Articles which, twelve Years before, had been offer'd to his Father in his last and greatest Extremity in the Isle of *Wight*, and would have made him no better than *Magni Nominis Umbra*. By which Concessions the Militia of the Kingdom, with the Disposal of all Places of Trust, and all Officers, must have continu'd in the Hands of the Parliament; and the Presbyterian Government be establish'd at least for three Years, with the fair Probabilities of a longer Lease; and his most faithful Servants be dealt with as Delinquents.

quents. So that, upon these Terms, the Parliament would not have been less Masters than before, nor his Majesty a much greater Prince than in his present Exile.

III. THE General having before sent away Sir *John Greenvil* privately to his Majesty with Assurance of his Allegiance, and Resolutions for his Service, without the mention of any Limitation, was somewhat concern'd how to make good Work with these Gentlemen. Nor were they ordinary People, but some of them Persons of Quality, and all of them Men of Parts and Eminency among the Parties where they sway'd. So that the General thought it most safe at present to entertain them with some Appearance of his Consent; and having (as they thought) thus fasten'd the Trick upon him, their next Contrivance was to perfect this Juggle with the King. To that purpose a Letter was sent to him, relating their *earnest Desires and Endeavours for his Return; and that to that End they had held several Treaties with General* Monk, *who could not be prevail'd with to consent to his Restauration, otherwise than upon his Father's Concessions in the Isle of* Wight; *beseeching his Majesty to accept thereof, rather than, by his further Refusal, to hazard a total Exclusion from his Crown and Kingdom.* This Letter was deliver'd liver'd to his Majesty, whilst Sir *John Greenvil* was attending upon him, to whom it was also shewn. But, upon farther deliberating among themselves, the Artifice was quickly discover'd; so that his Majesty pleasantly reply'd: *I perceive these People do not know that I and General* Monk *stand upon much better Terms, which he has so generously proposed to me, and Sir* John Greenvil *has so industriously transacted, and faithfully rendered me the Account of.* And these Persons when they came afterwards to find, that the General had, by Sir *John Greenvil*, enter'd into secret Correspondencies with the King, tho' they had the Discretion to conceal their Discontent, yet were ever afterwards secret and implacable Enemies to him.

IV. By this Time all the Letters and Instructions were made ready, and deliver'd by the King to Sir *John Greenvil*, together with his Privy-Seal and Signet, to be intrusted with General *Monk*; by which he was authorized to chuse a Secretary of State for his Majesty's Service. And after four Days Stay at Court he took Leave of his Majesty, and return'd for *England*.

V. At his Arrival he privately attended the General at St. *James's*, and deliver'd to him his Majesty's Letter written with his own Hand,

Hand, together with his Commission of General over all the Armies of *England*, *Scotland*, and *Ireland*. The General perus'd the Letter, and kept it with him; but, for the present, he would not trust his own Cabinet with the Commission; which was therefore deliver'd back to Sir *John Greenvil*, who secur'd it in a private Place in the Floor of his Bed-chamber, where he had us'd to lay up Letters and Commissions from the King; where also this lay till after the King's Return, and was then deliver'd to the General. And for those other Letters, it was here resolv'd, that Sir *John Greenvil* should keep them privately till the opening of the Parliament, and then deliver them according to his Instructions. The General also here deliberated with Sir *John Greenvil*, about the Disposal of his Majesty's Seal and Signet; where it was agreed, that, in Regard Mr. *Morrice* was the only Person that had been privy to this secret Affair, and had so faithfully assisted therein, they would recommend him to the Trust: Which, so soon as the King returned, was accordingly done by the General, when, at the same Time, his Excellency was offer'd ten thousand Pounds to procure the Place for another. And now, for the present, all Interviews between the General and Sir *John Greenvil* were but seldom, and always private.

VI. All

VI. ALL this while the People were every where very bufy in chufing the Members for the approaching Parliament; but with fo little Regard to thofe Qualifications appointed by the former Affembly, that no Man ever took Notice of them. The Presbyterians were very induftrious for the introducing again Men of their own Party; but were fuccefsfully prevented by the Royal Intereft, which at this Time began to appear, yet with great Moderation and Temper. And the People (from the Memory of their paft Miferies) were generally fo averfe to that Sort of Men, that few of them found their Way into this approaching Parliament.

VII. WHOSE Seffion was now fo near, that General *Monk* (having already fo fuccefsfully enter'd into a Treaty with his Majefty) began to entertain himfelf with the Approach of his own and the Kingdom's Safety: Till, on a fudden, he was furpriz'd with the worft and laft of his Encumbrances, being the expiring and foul Effect of the fanatick Rage. For the defperate Crew of Murtherers, and other mifchievous Male-contents, having of late turn'd every Stone in vain; and finding they could not continue the Tyranny of the Rump-Parliament, nor compliment the General to fet up for himfelf, nor raife thofe Jea-

loufies

lousies in the Army to any Height, as they had frequently attempted, were now resolv'd with a Push to venture at all, by breaking forth into a new Rebellion; for which they would quickly have found another Name, if it had succeeded.

VIII. But, to bring this about, it was resolv'd to contrive Major General *Lambert*'s Escape out of the Tower; which was quickly after effected, by the Treachery of two or three common Soldiers in Colonel *Morley*'s Guards. So soon as he was escaped, the General had speedy Notice of it, and where he was lodged, so that he miss'd him very narrowly. And tho' the Search after him was carefully continued, yet he heard no more of him, till Colonel *Streater* (who, upon the Distribution of *Fleetwood*'s Army, was quartered with his Foot Regiments at *Northampton*) gave the General the first Account of him. For *Lambert*, finding that the General had so settled the Militia of the City, as no good was to be done among them, quickly left the Town, and hasten'd towards *Warwickshire*: having first agreed with his Confederates to meet at a Rendezvous there, whither he hop'd the Regiments of the *English* Army, quartering in those Countries, would quickly repair to him. Upon this News, the General presently dispatch'd away Colonel *Ingoldsby*, with his

GENERAL MONK. 287

his Regiment of Horse quartering in *Suffolk*, to hasten through *Cambridge* to *Northampton*, and there join with Colonel *Streater*, and pursue *Lambert* where-ever he could be heard of; and more Forces were sent after, commanded by Colonel *Howard*, to prevent the Motions of any other Forces, quartered in those Countries, from joining with *Lambert*.

IX. AT the same Time his Excellency sent also for Sir *John Greenvil*; and, upon private Conference with him, told him, *it was not certain what might be the Issue of this Insurrection, if* Lambert *was not presently reduced, and the Army should revolt from him: But that he would publish his Commission from the King, and by it would raise all the Royal Party of the three Nations into Arms, rather than suffer these furious and hair-brain'd Sectaries to domineer within the Kingdom; desiring him to be always in Readiness for receiving further Orders from him, which should be communicated by him to such Persons about the Town, as he knew were most fast and devoted to his Majesty's Service.*

X. COLONEL *Ingoldsby* had, in four Days time, got his Regiment together, and arriv'd at *Northampton* by *Saturday* Night, where
he

he found a good Troop of Gentlemen, and others, whom the Earl of *Exeter* had brought in to the Affiftance of Colonel *Streater*.

XI. On the next Morning early, being *Eafter-Day*, the Scouts brought in News where *Lambert* was; and accordingly the Forces were drawn out to follow him, and found him near *Daventry*, having drawn out his Men in an open plow'd Field. The Force with him was but fmall, being only feven broken Troops and a Foot Company. Colonel *Okey* alfo, finding the Bufinefs would not be done by fpeaking at St. *James*'s; and *Cobbet*, whom we left laft in *Edenburgh* Caftle, had found their Way thither, together with Colonel *Axtel*, and fome few Captains. Thefe Forces having fac'd each other for four Hours feem'd not greatly inclin'd to a Combat, having fpent moft of the Time in Meffages and Parleys, till Colonel *Ingoldsby* advanced, and commanded to fire upon them. Whereupon *Lambert*'s Party were fo irrefolute and unwilling to endure the Charge, as fome of them came over to *Ingoldsby*, and the reft fled, and the Commanders began prefently to fhift away for themfelves. But Colonel *Ingoldsby* had his Eye ftill upon *Lambert*, and came up fo clofely, that he took him Prifoner; nor would he be prevail'd with to connive at his Efcape, tho' others of them offer'd themfelves

Prifoners

Prisoners in his stead. *Cobbet* also and *Creed* were here taken with better Luck than *Axtel* and *Okey*, who escaped; but not long after were brought to another Reckoning. *Lambert*, *Cobbet*, and *Creed* were presently carry'd off with a Guard; and on *Easter Tuesday* were brought to *London*, and secured again in the Tower. And thus was this little Cloud seasonably dispers'd, which otherwise might have brought upon the Nation the Tempest of another Civil War.

CHAP. XXIV.

I. *The Grounds of the General's Fear of this new Insurrection.* II. *Before the Suppression of which he wrote to the King, in Answer to one from his Majesty.* III. *The too great Forwardness of the General's Officers to restore the King.* IV. *Which he discourages.* V. *The secret and vile Practices of the old rebellious Party, in order to frustrate the General's Designs.* VI. *The new Parliament meets, and thanks the General for his Care and Conduct.* VII. *Remarks of the Author upon the General's Proceedings.* VIII. *The King's*

King's Letter to the Council of State deliver'd to the Parliament by Sir John *Greenvil.* IX. *A Motion for the Commitment of Sir* John, *which the General prevents, by answering for his Appearance.*

I. THE General was very joyful at the speedy and seasonable Suppression of *Lambert* and his Party, suspecting the *English* Army would presently have fallen off to him. For though he had always a very ordinary Opinion of *Lambert*'s Conduct, yet he knew several of the Officers with him, especially *Okey* and *Cobbet*, were bold and daring Men, and would adventure to the utmost. But though there wanted not seditious and urgent Spirits among them, yet the *English* Forces did not seem over-forward at present to join in this new Attempt. They had lately bit on the Bridle by following the Passions of their Officers, and were now well and warm in their Quarters, whither the Parliament had lately sent them their Pay; and the Government, during their Obedience, had taken Care for their Support. Those Regiments also which *Lambert* had the last Year wheadled into the North, had no Stomach to dance after his Pipe into such another Misadventure, wherein they were to encounter the same Army, and the same General, that
had

had baffled them before. Nor was the General less fortunate in the Choice of Colonel *Ingoldsby* for this Service; who, besides his Faithfulness to the General, was exceedingly belov'd by a great Part of the Enemy's Army, who would not be readily drawn to engage against him; and had also Courage and Resolution equal to the best of them.

II. We have before given Account of his Majesty's Letter to the General, which was brought to him by Sir *John Greenvil*, to which the General was so concern'd to return his Answer, with further Assurance of his Duty and Faithfulness to his Majesty's Service, that he would not defer it till the Conclusion of *Lambert*'s Insurrection; but, before ever he knew what would be the Effect of this Man's Mischief, or whether he might be able to make good his Word, he resolv'd to write back to his Majesty; and because Sir *John Greenvil*, who was to be ready at the opening of the Parliament now at Hand, could not be spar'd from that Attendance, that this secret Trust might still be continued in the Family, the General sent his Letter by Mr. *Bernard Greenvil*, a younger Brother to Sir *John*.

III. AND now *Lambert* being again laid fast in the Tower, and his Party wholly defeated,

feated, to the utter Ruin and Frustration of that Interest, the General had no more to do, but to discharge a great Part of his Care into the Bosom of the approaching Parliament, which now, within very few Days, was to sit down. But, before their Meeting, he was interrupted with an importunate and unseasonable Address from some of his own Officers, who, observing how all things concenter'd towards the King's Restauration, were very earnest with his Excellency to anticipate the Counsels of the Parliament, and assume the Glory and Advantage of the Action to himself and his Army, whereby they might fairly now oblige his Majesty, and mend their own Fortunes. They undertook also to engage the rest of the Officers, and the whole Army, to a Concurrence in the Design.

IV. But the General, who had otherwise resolv'd and lik'd his own Methods as most safe and honourable, calmly declin'd the Proposal; telling them, *They had before declared their Resolution to keep the Military Power in Obedience to the Civil; and that lately they had engaged themselves, by their Subscriptions, to submit to the Resolutions of this approaching Parliament, both which Obligations would be treacherously frustrated by such an Attempt.*

V. AND now no open Force durst any ways appear against the General's Proceedings. But, where the desperate and seditious were prevented in their publick Confederacies against him and his Party, they were contriving, by secret Mischiefs, to scatter Jealousies and Suspicions among the Soldiers. And, to that End, several villanous Libels against the King and the Royal Party were dispersed at Night among the Guards, and other Practices set on Foot to raise Misunderstandings between the General and those he most trusted, as also among themselves. To abate the Zeal and Industry of Commissary *Clarges*, it was represented, that Mr. *Morrice* had got the start of him in the General's Opinion and Confidence, and that all things were govern'd by his Counsels; so that if the King were restored, Mr. *Morrice* would triumph alone in the Glory of the Action. And, to ruin Mr. *Morrice*, it was whisper'd, that he had complained of the General's tenacious adhering to the Government of a Commonwealth, in Opposition to the King, and with what Difficulty he had wrought him to a Consent to his Restauration. But the known Artifices and Falshoods of those People, prevented the Evil Effect of their Designs. Yet these rebellious and seditious Persons, though they had so often fail'd in their Chymistry, would not give over the Experiment. For, with the like Artifices, they were practising upon their elder Brethren the Presbyterians; expostulating their vain Credulity, and Over-forwardness for restoring the King, which must needs conclude in their own Slavery. As for them, though they had no Dominion over other Mens Consciences, yet they had the free Possession of their own: But with the King's Return, Prelacy, their old Adversary, would return also, together with its Accessaries and insufferable Attendants, Arminianism and Popery, with such other injurious and stale Pretences as, twenty Years before, had usher'd in the Rebellion. And now they began to discharge all their Satire and ill Reflections upon the General also; accusing him for prevaricating with them, and that they had been deluded by him; who had never promis'd them any thing, otherwise than in Compliance with the Resolutions of a free Parliament. But they were the People that had cheated all the World that had the Folly or Misfortune to trust them. They had taken up Arms for the late King's Defence, and yet murthered him: They own'd themselves Servants to the Parliament, and yet utterly destroy'd one House, dismember'd the other, and at last dissolv'd it; justifying all their Villanies by Enthusiasm, and their Treachery by Necessity and Providence.

VI. But

VI. But now the 25th of *April* being come, the Houses of Lords and of Commons were assembled at *Westminster*, who, though they were not called by the Royal Authority, yet the great and memorable Actions done by them, in restoring his Majesty, and settling the Nation, will ever entitle them to the honourable Appellation of a *Parliament*. For the House of Lords the Earl of *Manchester* was chosen Speaker, and for the House of Commons Sir *Harbottle Grimstone*. Into their Assembly the General was elected by a double Return, both from the University of *Cambridge*, and the County of *Devon*; but, having civilly acknowledg'd the Respects of the former, he chose to serve for his native Country of *Devonshire*. In the Beginning of their Counsels the House was pleas'd to give to the General their publick Acknowledgments of his Prudence and faithful Service, in preserving the Peace of the Commonwealth, and so effectually opposing the Enemies thereof, whereby they had now the Privilege of assembling together in Parliament with Liberty and Freedom.

April 25.

VII. And here we will make a seasonable Stand, and a while rest the wearied Reader under the shady Contemplation of some particular

ticular Remarks upon the General's Proceedings.

He had now passed from one Tropick to another, by so gradual and easy Steps, that the Alteration he made, stole upon the People as insensibly as the lengthening of the Days, and Changes of the Year and Seasons. He embraced a most plausible Pretence of opposing the endless Extravagancies of the *English* Army, by declaring for the Rump Parliament; and then corrected the Furies of that Juncto, by the Mixture of the secluded Members. By their own Hands he buried that fatal Parliament, never to rise more, which otherwise pretended to an immortal Power, like the Crowns of Princes, who never dye. From their own Ashes he produced this present and better Session; so that he had now silently shifted three Scenes, to make way to his last Act.

By the like Gradations he proceeded in regulating his Armies. When he first began his Design in *Scotland*, he cleared his Hands from all his Anabaptists, by the Ministration of the Independents. At his Arrival into *London*, he attemper'd his Independents by introducing the Presbyterians: And now, at last, had let in the Royal Party, which he could only trust, to the Exclusion of both. So that all good Men were as much delighted with the Order of these Proceedings, as with the Variety. VIII. But

VIII. But the Parliament being met, it was now agreed by the General and Sir *John Greenvil*, that those Letters which he had brought over from his Majesty, should be deliver'd according to the several Instructions. And because it was not yet seasonable, that those secret Cabals and Conferences between the General and Sir *John Greenvil*, should be publickly known, it was resolv'd, that the Letter directed *to the General, and by him to be communicated to the Council of State, and Officers of the Army*, should be openly deliver'd to him at the Council Chamber in *White-Hall*. Accordingly next Day Sir *John Greenvil* stood ready at the Door, intending, by the next Member that went in, to let the General know he was there. And Colonel *Birch* happen'd to be the Man who receiv'd Sir *John*'s Message; and, upon Intimation to the General, his Excellency came to the Door; where Sir *John Greenvil* told him, he had Letters to him from the King, which he deliver'd into his Hand in Sight of the Guards; and the Business was so contriv'd, that the General receiv'd him as a Stranger whom he had never seen before, and with some Surprizal at his Business. He then desir'd him to stay there till he receiv'd his Answer, and commanded his Guards to look after him. The General then carried the Letter to the Council, opening the Seal, and delivering it to the President: And the Superscription being read, the Style of it made them all know whence the Letter came.

IX. THE Council being surpriz'd with the Receipt of these Letters, fell into an earnest Debate about them; so that Colonel *Birch* (though there was no Fear that this Business would hurt his Reputation) endeavour'd to clear himself by his Protestation, *That he neither knew the Gentleman that deliver'd the Message to him, nor any thing of his Business*. And without doubt he was believed by those that heard him. It was then resolved, that the Letter should not be open'd till the Parliament met again, which was then adjourn'd for three Days; and Sir *John Greenvil* was then call'd in, where the President examin'd him strictly about the Letter, and how he came by it. To which Sir *John* reply'd: *That the King his Master deliver'd it to him at* Breda *with his own Hand*. It was then debated to send him into Custody, till the Parliament should determine therein; but General *Monk* then told the President, *That though he had not seen Sir* John Greenvil *for many Years, yet he was his near Kinsman, so that he would undertake for his Appearance before the House*; and thereupon he was dismiss'd by the Council.

CHAP.

CHAP. XXV.

I. *At the Meeting of the Parliament Sir* John Greenvil *attends both Houses with the King's Letters: Their Resolution thereupon.* II. *The King's Letters communicated to the Army by the General.* III. *The Reception of them.* IV. *The House of Commons pass a Vote for presenting the King, and Dukes of* York *and* Gloucester, *with sixty five thousand Pounds; and five hundred to Sir* John Greenvil. V. *An honorary Grant from the King to Sir* John Greenvil. VI. *The Parliament send Sir* John *to the King with their Answer to his Letters.* VII. *General* Mountague *directed to carry the Fleet to the* Dutch *Coasts.* VIII. *Sir* John Greenvil'*s Arrival at* Breda. IX. *An Address from the Army to the General.* X. *Which is carried to the King.* XI. *The King proclaimed by a Vote of both Houses:* XII. *Attended at the* Hague *by Commissioners from them.* XIII. *Sir* Thomas Clarges *returns from the King.* XIV, XV. *General* Mountague'*s Arrival at the* Hague *with the whole Fleet.*

I. ON the Day the House met again, *May* May 1. 1. was Sir *John Greenvil* accordingly ready; and meeting in the Lobby, the Lord

Commissioner *Tyrrel*, then entering the House with whom he was acquainted; he entreated him to inform the Speaker, that he attended at the Door with Letters to the House from his Majesty. When the Lord Commissioner came in, he found the President of the Council of State giving the House an Account of Letters from the King; which so soon as he had ended, Commissioner *Tyrrel* acquainted the Speaker with Sir *John Greenvil*'s Message. But whilst the Commons were debating of this Letter, Sir *John* was retir'd from the Door, and hasten'd to the House of Lords, where he first enquir'd for his Grace the Duke of *Buckingham* and the Earl of *Oxford*: And being inform'd, that the Duke was not yet come, but that the Earl of *Oxford* was then sitting; he sent in a Message to him, upon which his Lordship came forth; and Sir *John Greenvil* inform'd him, that he had Letters from the King, which he was commanded to deliver to the Speaker of the Lord's House, intreating his Lordship to acquaint the Earl of *Manchester* therewith. This Relation was very welcome to the Earl of *Oxford*, who, besides his Descent from a Family of old and uninterrupted Loyalty, had, for several Years, faithfully assisted in those secret Counsels for the King's Restauration. He presently acquainted the Speaker with the Arrival of his Majesty's Letters.

Thereupon it was first debated in what manner they would receive them; and accordingly the Lords voted, *to attend their Speaker to the Door of the House*, where Sir *John Greenvil* met them, and deliver'd his Majesty's Letter; and, having receiv'd the Thanks of the Lord's House, he hasten'd presently back again to the House of Commons, where his Majesty's Letters were equally welcome, tho' they receiv'd them with less Ceremony, not being so well acquainted as their Lordships, in the Usage of Kings. Sir *John* was then called in, and deliver'd his Majesty's Letter to the Speaker. And upon the Perusal of these Letters, the Lords voted, *That, according to the ancient and fundamental Laws of the Kingdom, the Government is, and ought to be, by King, Lords, and Commons.* And after his Majesty's Letter and Declaration inclos'd had been read by the Commons, the like Vote was passed in that House also.

II. The General then desired Leave of the House to communicate his Majesty's Letter, which had been deliver'd at the Council of State, to the Officers also of his Army, which was accordingly there read. About the same time the Lord Mayor and Aldermen receiv'd the King's Letter from the Lord *Mordaunt* and Sir *John Greenvil*; and afterwards Sir *John Greenvil* deliver'd also his

Majesty's Letter to General *Mountague* and the Fleet.

III. The Lords and Commons then voted, *That they would return Answer to his Majesty's Letters by Messengers from their several Houses.* And the Lord Mayor and Common Council appointed twenty of their principal Citizens to return their Answer to his Majesty's Letter, with their Present to the King, and the Dukes of *York* and *Gloucester*. But General *Mountague* and the Fleet being resolv'd to carry their own Message themselves to his Majesty, sent no Messenger.

IV. And because his Majesty had been so long dispossess'd, not only of his Kingdoms, but Revenues, the House of Common's pass'd a Vote for the presenting him with fifty thousand Pounds, and ten thousand Pounds to the Duke of *York*, and five thousand Pounds to the Duke of *Gloucester*; which Sums (because of the present Dispatch) were to be instantly borrowed of the City of *London*, till the Money could be afterwards raised at Leisure from the rest of the Kingdom. And, that it might appear how joyfully they received his Majesty's Letter, they voted five hundred Pounds to Sir *John Greenvil* for bringing the Letter, to buy him a Jewel, which he was desir'd to wear as a Memorial of the Thanks

and

General Monk. 303

and Respects of the House to him. And accordingly the said Sum was brought to his Lodgings the next Day.

V. And having mention'd the Gratitude of the House of Commons to this Gentleman, we will here seasonably also take notice of the Estimation and Value, which his Majesty set upon his Service, as appears from his Majesty's Royal Grant or Warrant to him, which we have transcribed from the Original, and have added in the Collection at the End of this History.

VI. The Parliament then proceeded to the Nomination of such Persons from their several Houses, as should attend upon his Majesty with their Answer to his Letters, and ordered also the Instructions to be drawn up for them; and that General *Mountague* with the Fleet should be in Readiness to attend them. But because these Proceedings of the Parliament would take up Time, and the General was altogether uneasy, till his Majesty was actually return'd, he resolv'd to send Sir *John Greenvil* again to him, to acquaint his Majesty with the Reception of his Letters; and that he would be pleas'd to expedite his Return into *England*. He also further consider'd, that, in regard his Journey into *England* could not be decently set in

Order,

Order, till the Money were remitted thither; The General so far prevail'd with the Lord Mayor and Citizens, that the fifty thousand Pounds voted by the House of Commons for a Present to his Majesty, was instantly raised, to be conveyed to him by Sir *John Greenvil*, whereof ten thousand Pounds in Gold he carry'd with him in Coaches to *Dover*, accompanied with a Convoy of Horse; for the rest he had Bills of Exchange, which were afterwards paid at *Amsterdam* upon Sight. With Sir *John Greenvil* went over, to his Majesty the Lord *Lauderdale*, being released from his Imprisonment in *Windsor* Castle, where he had been confin'd ever since the Battle at *Worcester*, together with divers others.

VII. WHEN his Excellency dismiss'd Sir *John Greenvil*, he directed him to acquaint General *Mountague* with his Desire; that, for the more speedy Expedition of his Majesty's Return, he would forthwith carry the Fleet to the *Dutch* Coasts. Accordingly General *Mountague*, having first accommodated Sir *John Greenvil*, for the quicker Dispatch, with the *Mary* Frigat (then called the Speaker) and left a good Convoy in the *Downs* to bring over the Commissioners, order'd the rest of the Fleet to put under Sail for the Shore of *Holland*.

VIII. THE

VIII. The next Day Sir *John Greenvil* landed at *Flushing*, and then attended the King at *Breda*; where he acquainted him with the welcome Entertainment of his Majesty's several Letters, and that all things did concur in *England* to hasten his Restauration; to which End he had brought over fifty thousand Pounds from the House of Commons for his Majesty's present Occasions. And Resolutions began now to be taken in order to his Removal.

IX. The General had before communicated his Majesty's Letters and Declaration to the Officers of his Army who were near him; by whom they were so joyfully receiv'd, that they presented a publick Address to the General, to testify their Duty and Allegiance to his Majesty. The Copies of which Letters and Declaration, together with the Copies of the Address, were dispatch'd away to all the remote Garrisons and Regiments; where they were entertain'd with the like Readiness and Submission. The General had, by his former Methods, so effectually regulated his Army, that there was no Report made of any one Officer that refused to sign the Address.

X. This Address from the Army, toge- *May 5.* ther

ther with the General's Letter, was sent to his Majesty by Commissary *Clarges*; and gave a further Assurance of the Army's Obedience and Submission. His Majesty had before receiv'd an Account of this Gentleman, and of the Service he had render'd him, by his constant and faithful Correspondence with General *Monk*, in order to his Restauration. So that he entertain'd him with a particular Kindness, and presently knighted him, being the first Person who receiv'd (and deservedly) any Title or Mark of Honour from his Majesty upon this Service.

May 8. XI. UPON the same Day (*May* 8.) on which Sir *Thomas Clarges* presented to the King the Army's Address at *Breda*, his Majesty was, by a Vote of both Houses, proclaim'd at *London* with all the usual Ceremonies, but with an Affection that certainly was never so manifested towards any of his Predecessors. In this Solemnity the General joyfully assisted, following in his Coach the Coaches of both the Speakers. And such was the publick Festivity of this Day, that it seem'd as the Shadow of the King's Approach, or like the first Light of the Morning that looks over the Mountain's Tops, and ushers in the Sun.

XII. BY This time the Parliament had perfected

General Monk. 307

fected their Instructions for their Commissioners from both Houses that were to attend his Majesty at the *Hague*, whither he had remov'd from *Breda*, in order to the receiving them there. And the *English* Fleet was already arriv'd near him in the Bay of *Scheveling*, where they lay at Anchor, in Readiness to receive his Commands. On the 16th of *May* the Commissioners attended his Majesty at the *Hague*; and, according to their Instructions, they acquainted him: *That, before their setting forth, the Parliament had already proclaimed him in his City of* London, *which was already done in all the rest of his Dominions. That, for the Success of his Arrival and future Happiness, they had order'd the Prayers,* for the King's most Excellent Majesty, *to be restored in the publick Office of the Church; and had prepar'd the Way for his Arrival, by erecting the Royal Arms in the Place of those set up by the late usurping Commonwealth. They were also further to supplicate his Majesty to hasten his Return; and that the Houses might receive timely Notice in what manner he would please to be received.*

May 16.

XIII. THE same Day the Commissioners arrived at the *Hague*, his Majesty, in the Evening, dispatch'd Sir *Thomas Clarges* back for

for *England* to the General, with News of his intending to land at *Dover*.

XIV. By the Arrival of the honourable Commissioners, and several other Persons of Quality, that hasten'd to proffer their early Duty at the *Hague*, the King began even in a foreign Country to have the Splendor of a Court, and appear'd like the Monarch of *Great Britain* in the morning Rays of Royal Majesty. The Presence of these Commissioners was very welcome to him; but when he came to view his Fleet, the Prospect was like that of *Joseph*'s Waggons to his Father *Jacob*; both whereof were sent on the same Errand, and had the same Assurance.

XV. But in the midst of this Festivity some of the Commissioners could not conceal their Resentments; being displeas'd that General *Mountague* had left them only a Convoy, and that they had not the whole Fleet to attend them in their Voyage. But, to pacify this Displeasure, an antedated Order was secretly procured under his Majesty's Hand, to authorise General *Mountague*'s Arrival.

CHAP.

CHAP. XXVI.

I. *The King lands at* Dover, *and is received by the General.* II. *At* Canterbury *the General is made Knight of the Garter.* III. *The King is received by the Army drawn up at* Black-Heath. IV. *His Entrance into* London. V. *The Magnificence of it.* VI. *He is congratulated at* White Hall *by both Houses.* VII. *The Places and Honours conferred on the General:* VIII. *And Sir* John Greenvil. IX. *The General made a Commissioner of the Treasury, and afterwards Lord Treasurer.* X. *He is created Duke of* Albemarle, *and has seven thousand Pounds* per Annum *settled upon him and his Heirs. His great Temper and Humility shewn in the upper House. He promotes the Act of Oblivion.* XI. *His Moderation in general.* XII. *A special Instance of it, in his Consent to the disbanding the Army.* XIII. *An Instance of his exact Discipline, in the Readiness of the Soldiers to be disbanded.* XIV. *The King advises with him about the Government of* Scotland: *The happy Effects of his late administration there.* XV. *His publick Cares and Service: A just Reflection of Sir* Edward Nicholas *upon them.*

I. AND

I. AND now all things being in Readiness for the King's Removal, he went on Board his Fleet, *May* 23. where he first took Possession of his Dominion at Sea, and then arrived at *Dover*; where the General was ready to receive him on the Shore. At his landing, and after the Sight of his Majesty, many there present had a particular Curiosity to observe their Interview; which was perform'd by the King with extraordinary Kindness and Affection; and on the General's Part, with that Duty and Prostration, as if he had come this Day rather to ask his Majesty's Pardon, than to receive his Thanks.

May 23.

II. From hence he attended his Majesty to *Canterbury*, where he receiv'd the first honourable Mark of his Favour, being there made Knight of the Garter, which was the Foundation of those further Dignities which were to be conferred upon him. And the most illustrious Dukes of *York* and *Gloucester* put upon him, with their own Hands, the Ensigns of his Order.

III. In all the Way of the King's Progress towards *London*, the General had much Freedom of Discourse with his Majesty, and was admitted to all his private Hours. At *Black-Heath* he led his Majesty to view that Part of the Army, which was then drawn up to

offer

General Monk. 311

offer their Address and Service to him: An Army of such clear Courage and exact Discipline, that, being united into one Body under such a General, it would have shaken any Crown in Christendom, not accepting his who is now thought so much superior to his Neighbours.

IV. From hence his Majesty begun his triumphant Entrance into *London* on the Anniversary of his Nativity; on which Day, thirty Years before, he was born in this his native City of *Westminster*. In this glorious and magnificent Procession, the General rode next before his Majesty. The rest of its State and Order is so sufficiently known and describ'd, that we will not tire our Reader with the particular Recital. *May* 29.

V. In the Splendor and Acclamations of this Day's Triumph, his Majesty exceeded all his Royal Ancestors. For neither the Reception of *Richard* the Ist from the *Holy Land*, and his Captivity in *Germany*; nor of *Henry* the Vth from the Conquest of *France*, nor of *Henry* the VIIth to his Coronation from the Battle of *Bosworth*, had any thing comparable with this Day's Magnificence: In which his Majesty also greatly out-shin'd his Grandfather King *James*, when he came to *London* to unite the Crown of *England* with his own native Diadem.

VI. AFTER the Glories and Festivities of this Day, the General having seen his Majesty safely lodged in his Palace at *White-Hall*, and congratulated there by both his Houses of Parliament, retir'd to his Apartment at the *Cockpit*, whither he was now remov'd, to be nearer the King's Presence and Counsels. And when his Friends and Attendants began to renew their Thanks and Acclamations to him for his great Service and Faithfulness, in producing the Effects of this Day; he was so far from being exalted with any Opinion of his own Merit, that he declin'd them all: Telling them, *he had all along been beset with so many Difficulties and Jealousies upon him, as all Thanks and Acknowledgments must be only paid to the Miracle of the Divine Providence.*

VII. PRESENTLY after his Majesty's Restauration, he settled his Privy-Council, chosen out of the chief Officers belonging to the Crown, and other principal Nobility; of which Number General *Monk* was one, and was continually admitted to all Counsels of the most interior Trust and Concernment. He was also made Master of his Majesty's Horse, and one of the Gentlemen of his Bed-chamber.

By the first he had a considerable Station in the Court, and the other gave him the constant Opportunity of Access to his Majesty's Person and Converse.

VIII. AND having mention'd here his Majesty's Favour to the General, we are seasonably to inform the Reader with those Rewards placed upon that honourable Person, who did first and principally co-operate with the General in this great Affair, *viz.* Sir *John Greenvil*; who, upon his Majesty's Return, was made first Gentleman of the Bed-chamber, and Groom of the Stole, and afterwards, against the Solemnity of the Coronation, was created Earl of *Bath*, Viscount *Greenvil* of *Landsdown*, Baron *Greenvil* of *Biddiford* and *Kelkhampton*. Nor were the Services of Mr. *Nicholas Monk* forgotten, being made Provost of *Eaton*, and afterwards Bishop of *Hereford*; in which Dignity he dy'd some Years after.

IX. AND because, in this present State of things, nothing requir'd greater Care than the Management of his Majesty's Exchequer, the General was chosen one of the Commissioners for the Treasury. But that Office was some time after intrusted in the Hands of a single Person, the late just and upright Earl of *Southampton*; after whose Death, both

the

the King and People were so perfectly satisfied with the General's Care and Faithfulness in that Trust, that he was called to it again, and in which he continu'd to the Day of his Death. To this Employment he brought very congenial Virtues, both by his unquestionable Integrity and natural Frugality; so that he was a greater Husband in the King's Expences, than in some of his own.

X. Nor did the Current of his Majesty's Favour and Gratitude to the General stop here, but within a little more than a Month after his Restauration, he was, by Letters Patents under the Great Seal of *England*, made Duke of *Albemarle*, Earl of *Torrington*, Baron *Monk* of *Potheridge, Beauchamp* and *Tees*; and, for the better Support of this high Dignity, besides the Pensions recited in the Letters Patents, his Majesty settled upon him seven thousand Pounds *per Ann.* out of the Royal Demesnes, to him and his Heirs for ever. He was also summon'd by Writ into the House of Lords; and tho' the Commons were very sorry to part with so dear and considerable a Member from their Body, yet, in Testimony of their great and particular Estimation and Respect towards so great and illustrious a Person, most of them attended him to the Door of the Lord's House: Whither he brought with him the same Temper and
Mode-

Moderation, the same Silence and Humility, which he had practis'd in the House of Commons; applying himself always to such Counsels as did most promote the King's Service, and the publick Benefit. To that End he much furthered the Progress of the Act of Oblivion and general Pardon, which was then under Debate, and had taken up so much Time in both Houses; and did privately move his Majesty to quicken their Proceedings therein, as being so very considerable and effectual to his own Security, and the Quiet of his People.

XI. THEY who have had the good Fortune and Abilities, by great Services, to oblige Kings and States, may be easily thought not to want Spirit or Inclinations enough to reflect upon their own Merits. And therefore such as knew not the Virtues and Caution of the Duke of *Albemarle*, expected he would now have put that Value on himself, as to have govern'd the publick Counsels, to have over-rul'd the Opinions or Methods of others, or have render'd himself the Head of an Interest; or, with *Mutianus* (whose Services to *Vespasian* had rather some Resemblance with the Duke's, than an Equality) have made himself a Companion with his Prince, and shar'd the Government. But, instead thereof, as he had possess'd his Majesty's Favour by his great Prudence, so he us'd it with equal Humility. And he that had many Years commanded Armies, which usually makes the Temper of Generals violent and presuming; he that for several Years, as an absolute Prince, had govern'd *Scotland*, knew now as well how to obey, and be a dutiful Subject in *England*. Nor was he less careful of his just Regards and Observances towards all the Nobility and Ministers of State, who, though they had frequent Emulations among themselves, yet held good Correspondence with the Duke of *Albemarle*; who invaded no Man's Province, nor engrossed Business or Power to himself, nor was ever the Author of extreme Counsels. Though he wanted not early Enemies, even among those who had but lately come to eat assured Bread by the Benefit of his Prudence and Faithfulness, and who began to accuse the Virtue which kept some of them from starving. The Ambitious envy'd the Greatness of his Merits, and the Covetous the Rewards of them.

XII. Though a very considerable Part of the Duke's Interest lay in the Army, and the disbanding of them would greatly lessen his Power and Influence; yet when the Parliament had voted their Discharge, no Man did more readily assent to it than the Duke of *Albemarle*; and, to that End, had beforehand introduc'd several of the Nobility into Commands

Commands in the Regiments, by whofe Authority and Example they might more readily fubmit.

XIII. His Majefty had been very juft to thofe Forces, in the full Payment of their Arrears, and very kind alfo in the Gratuity given them over and above out of his Royal Bounty. Yet, that Pofterity may fee how much the good Difcipline of an Army prevails to the disbanding of them, as well as the keeping them up; the Duke had inured them to fo exact an Obedience, that, when they faw their Continuance would be unneceffary to the Nation, they laid down their Arms without Murmur, and betook themfelves to other Employments; to which they were enabled, by a very indulgent Act of Parliament that gave them their Freedom, to exercife their Trade in all Cities and Towns Corporate. This was a Temper very different from that in the Army of the late Ufurper *Cromwel*, who were fo infolent and reftive, as they would only march at their own Pleafure, and pick and chufe their Employment, and had frequently mutiny'd againft their Mafters upon the leaft mention of disbanding.

XIV. It pleafed his Majefty about this Time to confult with the Duke about the Government and Affairs of *Scotland*, and the
Choice

Choice of Officers of State; in all which he advis'd with great Experience and Prudence; though many things were afterwards altered by the Influence and Importunities of others. But, as an Instance of those true and exact Measures, which, in the Time of his own Command, he had taken, for settling the Peace of that Country; the Effects thereof continued many Years after he had left it: So that no Rebellion, nor any considerable Disturbance, was form'd any more in *Scotland* during the Duke's Life.

XV. AND now every Man had a greater Share in the Delights of this happy Change, than he who had the greatest Share in effecting it, who could only enjoy the Satisfaction of it without the Diversions, being always beset with continual Cares of publick Trust; which made Sir *Edward Nicholas* (who had been Secretary of State to two Kings) say, *That the Industry and Service which the Duke of* Albemarle *had paid to the Crown since the King's Restauration, without reflecting upon his Service before, deserved all the Favour and Bounty which his Majesty had been pleased to confer upon him.*

CHAP.

CHAP. XXVII.

I. *General* Monk's *Candour in the Tryal of the Regicides; with a particular Act of Generosity to Sir* Arthur Hazlerig. II. *An Insurrection in* London: III. *But immediately suppressed by the General's own Regiment.* IV. *Which is continued.*

I. HITHERTO we have survey'd the Endeavours of the Duke of *Albemarle* against the Enemies of the Crown, and now we shall find him employ'd in the Punishment of them. For the Parliament having now perfected the Act of Indemnity, and general Pardon, with their Exceptions to those particular Persons who had been concern'd in the Murder of the late King; his Majesty accordingly granted his Commission of Oyer and Terminer, under the great Seal of *England,* directed to several of the chief Nobility and Judges of the Land, for the Tryal of those Regicides, which was begun *October* 9.*oa.*9. In the Number of these Commissioners the Duke of *Albemarle* was one, wherein he gave the World one of the greatest Instances of his Moderation. For though he knew more of the Guilts and Practices of these Criminals, than most of those who sat on the Bench, and some of them had been his greatest and most

inveterate

inveterate Enemies; yet he aggravated nothing againſt them, but left them to a fair Tryal, and the Methods of their own Defence, when he could have offer'd Matter againſt ſome of them that would have preſſed them harder. And, by a like generous Way of forgiving Injuries, he had a little before ſaved the Life of Sir *Arthur Hazlerig*, and afterwards procured his Eſtate alſo, by owning of a Promiſe made to him; when there was no Man among them all had more maliciouſly expos'd and traduc'd him; and, after the Aſſurance given, he had done enough to diſengage the Duke from the Performance of it.

II. ONE might reaſonably have thought, that ſuch an Act of general Pardon as has been lately paſs'd, might have oblig'd the Minds of all People to a Submiſſion, and Satisfaction in the Government; but that Hereſy and Fanaticiſm are not to be cured by Balſams. For about this Time began ſuch an Inſurrection, as it is not eaſy to tell, whether the Fury or the Folly of it were the greater Ingredient. His Majeſty being then gone out of *London* to *Portſmouth*, whither he accompany'd the Queen-Mother and Duches of *Orleans* in their Journey towards *France*; a ſmall Company of the Fifth-Monarchy Zealots having arm'd themſelves in
their

GENERAL MONK. 321

their Meeting-Houſe, where uſually their Villanies are firſt hatch'd, broke out into an actual Rebellion in *London*. Their Teacher was alſo their Captain, one *Venner*, a Wine-Cooper, who had preach'd his Diſciples to a Degree of Madneſs and Extravagancies, beyond the Force of all the Wine in his Cellar.

III. This Irruption was ſo ſudden as did greatly ſurprize the City; and tho' their Number was contemptible, yet Men believ'd they would not have ventur'd on ſo deſperate an Attempt, but upon Confidence of a greater Party in *London* to join with them. Many of them had been Soldiers in *Cromwel*'s Army, and, being poſſeſſed with the Height of fanatick Rage, laid about them at a rate not uſual. Nor was any effectual Reſiſtance made againſt them by the City Arms, or the new-rais'd Guards; till the Duke of *Albemarle* brought his own Regiment of Foot (not yet disbanded) up among them, who, being old Soldiers that had been long accuſtom'd to this kind of Work, quickly put a Check to their deſperate Madneſs, having kill'd and wounded ſeveral of them upon the Place, and diſperſed the reſt.

IV. Upon this Accident (though timely ſuppreſs'd) it was repreſented to the Duke by ſome of his Officers, of how little Service

Y   Train'd-

Train'd-bands, or new-rais'd Guards, would prove upon any sudden Disturbance; and how necessary it were, both to his Majesty's Safety and the publick Peace, to keep up his Grace's own Regiment, and some other small Force, against such hasty Attempts. To which the Duke reply'd, *That his Endeavour to continue any Part of his Army, would be obnoxious to much Misinterpretation, that he would by no means appear in it;* but being further importuned, *that he would not hinder their Endeavours therein,* he made no Answer. But, by these Applications to his Majesty and Council, that Regiment was still kept up.

CHAP. XXVIII.

I. *The King's Coronation.* II. *The Duke grows inclinable to a private Life.* III, IV. *A War with* Holland; *the Duke of* York *and Prince* Rupert *command the Fleet.* V. *An Engagement.* VI. *the* Dutch *beaten.* VII. *Our Fleet pursues them as far as the* Texel. VIII. *The Loss the* Dutch *sustained.* IX. *The Bravery of the Duke of* York. X. *The Plague breaks out in* London; *upon which the King goes to* Oxford. XI. *The Care of the City committed to the Duke of* Albemarle: *His Tenderness and Compassion to the Poor.* XII. *He is assisted by the Archbishop of* Canterbury *and the Earl of* Craven. XIII. *An Encampment in* Hyde-Park. XIV. *The Multiplicity of Affairs wherein the General was involv'd.*

I. THE following Year begins with his Majesty's Coronation; which was perform'd with greater Ceremony and Magnificence, than we can meet with in the Inauguration of any of his Royal Predecessors. The preparatory Ceremony began *April* 22. with his Majesty's triumphal Passage through the City from the Tower of *London,* to his Palace at *White-Hall*; attended by his domestick Servants, the Judges, and Nobility, with the chief Officers of State, and passing thro' those four triumphal Arches, which the Citizens had erected, to do Honour to the Solemnity of the Day. In this Ceremony the Duke of *Albemarle,* as Master of the Horse, followed his Majesty's Triumph, leading the Horse of State. The next Day his Majesty was solemnly crown'd at *Westminster,* in the Abbey Church, with all the usual Ceremonies. In the Procession from *Westminster-Hall* to

1661.

April 23.

the Abbey, the Regalia were carried before the King by the chief Nobility, and, among the rest, the Sceptre and Dove was born by the Duke of *Albemarle*. In the Time of the anointing, he was one of the four that held up the Pall of Cloth of Gold over his Majesty's Head; whilst the Archbishop of *Canterbury* perform'd the Unction. And afterwards he, and the Duke of *Buckingham*, did Homage for themselves and the rest of the Order of Dukes in *England*.

II. And now his Majesty being perfectly settled in the Government, actually crown'd, and the Army disbanded; the Duke of *Albemarle*, for some Years, betook himself to Privacy: So that we find no very publick Action of his Life for some Years, save that he carefully attended at the Privy-Council, advising with his Majesty upon all Occasions, and was constantly present at the House of Lords in the several Sessions of Parliament.

III. At home all things were quiet and orderly, excepting some little Plots and Contrivances among the Seditious; which were still so timely discern'd, that they were as easily prevented. Nor had his Majesty any Quarrels abroad, having renewed Alliances with all his Neighbours, till a War begun 1664. with the *Dutch*: Who refusing to give Satisfaction

General Monk. 325

tisfaction for old Injuries, and contriving the Practice of new ones, rais'd such a Multitude of Complaints against them by the Subjects of this Crown, that his Majesty (having first in vain sought Reparation by Treaties and Messages) resolv'd at last, with the Advice of his Privy-Council, to enter into a War with the *States:* Which was seconded by a brisk and unanimous Vote of the Parliament then sitting, for the raising of Money proportionable to maintain it. So that by the following Spring his Majesty had made ready a Fleet of near an hundred Ships of War, furnish'd with above thirty thousand Mariners and Soldiers. And his Royal Highness the Duke of *York*, being also Lord High Admiral of *England*, undertook the Conduct of them, accompany'd with the most illustrious Prince *Rupert*, who commanded a Squadron, the late General *Mountague* (since Earl of *Sandwich*) being Vice-Admiral. But, before his Royal Highness went on Board the Fleet, he left the Care of the Admiralty to the Duke of *Albemarle*, to provide for the Stores and Provision of the Navy, which was all attended with a very particular Industry.

IV. About the 22d of *April* this Fleet set *April 22.* Sail from the *Downs* to the *Dutch* Coasts, and came to an Anchor about the *Texel*; where they continued for almost a Month,

expecting

expecting daily the coming out of the *Dutch* Fleet, and provoking them to a Battle, by taking daily several of their Ships. But, being wearied with so long Delays, and having in a Month's Time, exhausted much of their naval Provisions, his Royal Highness brought back the Fleet toward their own Shores, from whence they might be again more speedily supply'd. But, whilst he lay at Anchor in the *Gun-fleet* near *Harwich*, he receiv'd Advice that the *Dutch* were come out to Sea, consisting of more than one hundred Ships, and proportionably mann'd, led by the Admiral *Opdam*, and four Vice-Admirals; and, in their Way had surpriz'd several *English* Merchant-men coming from *Hamburgh*, which had unfortunately fallen in among them. Though his Royal Highness had presented them Battle upon their own Coasts, yet he was not willing to receive the like Offer from them at home, but commanded the Fleet instantly to weigh Anchor

June 1. towards *Sowold* Bay, where he arriv'd *June* 1. And the same Day Intelligence was brought him, by some Ships kept out for Discovery, that they had Sight of the Enemy's Fleet. Wherefore he commanded the Fleet to weigh again, and to get farther off from Shore, for the Benefit of Sea-Room.

June 2. V. THE next Morning his Royal Highness

ness made all the Sail he could to join the *Dutch* Fleet; but they, being to Windward of him, declin'd engaging. That Night both Fleets came to an Anchor at convenient Distance from each other; so that the next Day, *June* 3. after three in the Morning, Prince *Rupert*, who commanded the Van, began the Fight. But the *Dutch* being desirous to gain the Wind of the *English* Fleet, kept off at present from all close Engagement, and made several Tracts upon him: So that his Royal Highness came at length to have his own Squadron in Front of the Enemy's Line; having Sir *John Lawson* on head of him, who bore in upon the *Dutch* Fleet, seconded by his Royal Highness, keeping still the Wind of them, to prevent the Assault of their Fire-ships, wherein they exceeded the *English* Fleet. The Duke then observing Admiral *Opdam*'s Ship to come up into their Line, commanded his own to bear up to him, by whose Example, and following the Motions of the Admiral's Ship, the Body of the *English* Fleet came close up to the Enemy, and ply'd their Guns on all Hands at near Distances. But his Royal Highness charg'd Admiral *Opdam* so warmly, that, after a smart Encounter, his Powder-Room was fir'd, and the Ship blown up.

VI. BEFORE this Accident the *Dutch* Fleet

Fleet began to shrink, and give Ground; but when they observ'd the Loss of their Admiral and his Ship, they made their own Misfortune this Day the greater, by an hasty and inconsiderate Flight; in which they lost the *Orange-Tree*, a Ship of seventy six Guns, second to the Admiral, which was taken and burnt; and, in this frightful Run, four of their capital Ships, falling foul of each other, were burnt by a Fireship close to them. Afterwards three more, by a like Accident, being intangled, were destroy'd by another.

VII. His Majesty's Fleet had the Chace of the *Dutch* all the Day towards their own Coasts, and in the Night kept up with them; so that, in the Morning early, they were upon them again, destroying more of their Ships, and pursuing them to the Mouth of the *Texel*; where, being better acquainted with their Road, and drawing less Water, they got in with the first Tide. And afterwards his Royal Highness brought off the *English* Fleet triumphing in their Spoils, and Victory of their Enemies, to their own Shame.

VIII. In this Fight there fell of the *Dutch*, besides Admiral *Opdam*, three Vice-Admirals, *Stillingwalf*, and *Schamp*, and about eight or ten thousand common Soldiers and Mariners, with the Loss of about twenty eight

General Monk.

eight Ships, taken and funk; with a very inconsiderable Damage to his Majesty's Navy, having lost only one little Vessel, call'd the *Mary*, taken in the Beginning of the Fight, and carried off with them; and the Loss of Men was also disproportionable. Only some honourable Persons, who serv'd as Volunteers or honorary Soldiers at this Battle, fell in it; as the Earl of *Portland*: But the Earl of *Falmouth*, the Lord *Muskerry*, and Mr. *Boyle*, second Son to the Earl of *Burlington*, were cut off together by one Shot in his Royal Highness's Ship. The Earl of *Marlborough*, who commanded a Frigat, was here slain, with Rear-Admiral *Johnson*. Vice-Admiral *Lawson* received a Hurt in his Knee, at the Beginning of the Fight, which was thought so inconsiderable, that there was not that timely Care taken of it which it deserv'd: Nor did he make so much Haste to Shore, as he should; so that in about five Weeks he dy'd thereof.

IX. In this Engagement his Royal Highness had so far exposed himself, that neither his Majesty, nor his People, were willing to adventure the next Hope of the Commonwealth, to any further Dangers and Hazards: So that, the remaining Part of this Summer, the Earl of *Sandwich*, being Vice-Admiral of *England*, commanded the Fleet. But this late

late Fight had so taken down the *Dutch* Stomachs, that, for the rest of this Year, they had neither Force nor Courage to adventure upon another Engagement.

X. WITH the Beginning of this War, began also a most fatal Pestilence in *London*, and both were of *Dutch* Original. For as they brought the War upon themselves, by their several Depredations of *English* Goods; so they sent us the Contagion in some of their own, convey'd hither out of *Holland*, where lately the Plague had very severely raged. It began first in *London*, and from thence was dispers'd to most of the principal Towns and Cities of the Nation, accompany'd with so great Mortality, as we have no Account of the like Contagion in any Age or Annals of *England*. His Majesty was therefore enforc'd to leave his Palace at *White-Hall*, and retire to *Oxford*, whither afterwards the Houses of Parliament and the Term were adjourn'd. The Nobility also, and Gentry, and principal Citizens, were dispers'd for Refuge from the Infection throughout all the Villages of *England*.

XI. BUT being the capital City of the Nation was not to be left at random, where not only the Poor, enforc'd by Necessity, or encourag'd through Liberty, might rifle the Houses of the Rich, but the Seditious also might

might take the Opportunity to practise new Mischiefs; it pleas'd his Majesty to entrust the Care and safety of the Place with the Duke of *Albemarle*, commanding his Continuance in the Town. And though his Grace might very well, with the rest of the Nobility, have consulted his own Safety, by retreating with his Majesty to *Oxford*, or to some of his own Retirements in the Country, and his past Services might have fairly exempted him from this hazardous Attendance, and throw it upon some others; yet he very willingly obey'd, and, when other Men had expos'd their Estates and Fortunes to secure their Lives, he was contented to stay and expose his own Life to secure their Properties. Nor did he only direct his Care to the Concernments of the Rich, but especially for the Necessities of the Poor, by continually inspecting the Distributions of the publick Charity, to which was also superadded a Share of his own private Bounty.

XII. In these Cares he was greatly helped by the Assistance of two other great and honourable Persons, who also remained in the City: His Grace the Lord Archbishop of *Canterbury*, who stay'd a great Part of the Time at his Palace at *Lambeth*, where, besides his own vast and diffusive Charity towards the Poor and Afflicted, he so effectually solicited

solicited the other Bishops in *England*, that several great and almost incredible Sums of Money were rais'd for Relief of the infected. And had the Factious given the hundredth Part of their Bounty, the Nation must have rung with the Noise of their Charity. With the like compassionate Care did the Earl of *Craven* continue in the Town, distributing constantly the greatest Part of his Revenue to supply the Necessities of the sick and perishing.

XIII. The Guards and necessary Forces left with the Duke for securing the Peace of the City, were, by his Order, quarter'd in *Hyde Park*, where there were Tents and Conveniences made ready for them; but, notwithstanding all his Care, and their Distance from the Infection, yet he lost a great Part of them. His own Residence he still continued at the *Cock pit* near *White Hall*, where, by his free Admission of all Persons that had Business with him, he convers'd daily with more assured Dangers, than in any of the Battles that had been fought by him.

XIV. But, besides the Hazard of this Employment, it was attended with so many Cares and infinite Importunities, as would have troubled an Head that had not been habitually accustom'd to Business like the Duke

of

of *Albemarle*'s. For his Majesty being removed to *Oxford*, the Duke was oblig'd to constant Correspondence with him, besides his assiduous Dispatches to the Lord Chancellor, and the Secretaries of State. With the Fleet he had continual Business, in ordering Supplies for them, upon all Occasions, out of the Stores in the City. His Care was endless and unceffant, both with the Admiralty, and Commissioners of the Navy, in inspecting the Management of the Prize-Office: Besides his daily Correspondencies with the Lord Mayor, for Relief of the Poor, and Security of the City; his granting Licences for Ships to Sea, and appointing Convoys to attend them. In all which, having a croud of Business, neither the Danger of his Person, nor the Trouble of his Employment, gave him any Disturbance; but his Grace was as easy and present to himself, and well pleas'd, as other Men are in their Recreations and Diversions.

CHAP. XXIX.

I. *Prince* Rupert *and the Duke of* Albemarle *join'd in Commission against the* Dutch. II.

The Duke accepts the Charge, against the Advice of his Friends. III. *Has the Care of making all the Naval Preparations.* IV. *The King returns to* London. V. *The Admirals go on Board.* VI. *The* Dutch *make an Alliance with the* French. VII. *Who assist them, and declare War against* England. VIII. *The Preparations on both Sides towards Action.* IX. *The* Dutch *Fleet appears.* X. *They come to an Engagement.* XI. *The Event of it.* XII, XIII. *Another Engagement. The Duke resolves to retreat.* XIV. *The Manner of his Retreat.* XV. *Prince* Rupert *returns.* XVI. *And joins the Duke's Fleet; the* Dutch *upon their Conjunction retiring.* XVII, XVIII. *Resolved, in a Council of War, to give them Battle again.* XIX. *Our Fleets follow them.* XX. *They come to an Engagement upon the* Dutch *Coast,* XXI. *The Duke's Courage and Conduct in this Action.* XXII. *The* Dutch *are beaten, and get off; the* English *returning home.* XXIII. *Different Reflections upon the Duke's Conduct.* XXIV. *The Opinion of the* Dutch *upon it.* XXV. *The* Dutch *put to Sea again.* XXVI. *The* English *Fleet pursues them to their own Coasts;* XXVII. *And engages them.*

I. TO-

I. TOWARDS the End of the Year, his Majesty advis'd with his Privy Council at *Oxford*, about the Conduct of the Fleet next Spring. And though his Royal Highness was very importunate to finish the War with the *Dutch*, which he had so fortunately begun; yet, since they were resolv'd not to venture his Person again to further Hazards, it was at last determin'd, that his Highness Prince *Rupert*, and the Duke of *Albemarle*, should, by joint Commission, command at Sea, and carry on the War the following Summer.

II. THE Prince, being present upon the Place, accepted the Charge; and his Majesty appointed the Duke should hasten down to *Oxford*; which he presently did by Post, and chearfully submitted to the Commands of his Sovereign; though there wanted not those about him, who dissuaded him from this Employment; alledging, that his Merits were great and unweildy already, and his Reputation higher than to need further Advance; that his Fortune had already foyl enough, and that he had now no greater Concern than to preserve himself where he was; that the ill Success of this War might perhaps be sufficient to lessen him; but the Prosperousness of it would add little to his Fame, and much to Envy. Though there wanted not some Reason in these Suggestions, yet the Duke lik'd no politick Contrivance in the Instance of his Obedience; and having staid three Days at *Oxford*, advising privately with the King about the Preparations for the War, and receiv'd his Majesty's Thanks for his faithful Care of the publick Safety, and Security of the City, he return'd back to his Charge at *London*.

III. And now, being made Co admiral at Sea, he had another Province added to the rest of his Cares, whereby he was oblig'd to give Orders for the making ready such Ships as were not yet finish'd, and the Repair of others, that had been disabled in this Year's War, besides all other naval Preparations for the following Spring.

IV. Though the Plague did greatly spread and increase in other remoter Cities and Places of the Kingdom, yet, towards the End of the Year, it manifestly abated in *London*; and the City became so clear'd from farther *Feb. 1.* Infection, that about the first of *February*, his Majesty hasten'd his Return from *Oxford* to his Court at *White-Hall*, where he might more commodiously inspect his Affairs, and advise for the further Preparations of his Fleet. The late Mortality, as it had swept away

GENERAL MONK. 337

away great Multitudes in the Suburbs of the City, so it had destroyed abundance of the Seamen in those Parishes adjoining to the River, and had done the like in other maritime Towns of *England:* Insomuch that there was some Difficulty in procuring enough of those stout and valiant People to man the Fleet. But the Duke of *Albemarle*, having formerly commanded at Sea, had so much Reputation and Influence among the Seamen, that, whilst there was any of them left in *England*, he was not likely to want their Company in his Majesty's Service. And, by the united Interest and Influence of the Prince, notwithstanding the Disadvantages of the late Plague, all things were brought into so good Readiness, as that both the Men and Ships would quickly be fit to sail, attending for their Admirals to come on Board.

V. ACCORDINGLY, *April* 23. being St. *George*'s Day, his Highness Prince *Rupert*, and the Duke of *Albemarle*, took Leave of his Majesty and the Court; and, at *White-Hall* Stairs, in one of the King's Barges, went down the River to the Fleet.

VI. NOR were the *Dutch* all this while less sedulous in preparing their own Navy. The last Year's War had so much weaken'd their Fleet, but more the Courage of their
People.

People, that they found themselves not able to continue it further without the Arms of their Neighbours. To that End they had contracted a new Alliance with *France*, from whence they were to have the Assistance of the *French* Fleet, led by the Duke *de Beaufort*.

VII. His Majesty of *Great Britain* was already so much superior to all his Neighbours at Sea, that the *French* King was greatly afraid he should grow more potent there, by his further Success against the *Dutch*. And though he hated nothing more than that People, and their Government, yet he lov'd his own Interest better than to depart from it, by denying them Assistance. He had already design'd the Invasion of their Country by Land, and therefore was not a little concerned, that his Majesty should prevent him in the Conquest, by subduing them first at Sea. And other secret Reasons led him, in Conjunction with the *Dutch*, to declare War against *England*; which was accordingly denounced back upon him into *France*.

VIII. Prince *Rupert* and the Duke of *Albemarle* had, by this Time, brought the Fleet to such Readiness, as they were come to an Anchor in the *Downs*, resolving from thence to set sail for the *Dutch* Coasts,

Coasts, and find out the Enemy. But, in the interim, his Majesty had receiv'd Intelligence from *France*, that the Duke *de Beaufort* had made equal Dispatch in getting ready the *French* Fleet, and was coming out to join with the *Dutch*. Upon which Information from thence, his Majesty, with the Advice of the Privy Council, dispatch'd away Orders to his Fleet, *That* Prince Rupert *should take twenty of the best and nimblest Frigats, and, directing his Way towards the Coasts of* France, *should attend the Motions of the* French *Admiral, aud engage him before he could join his Fleet with the* Dutch. These Instructions were presently put in Execution by his Highness, leaving the Duke, with the rest of the Fleet, still in the *Downs*.

IX. The last of *May* the Duke set sail from the *Downs*; and the next Morning early, the *Bristol*, plying about a League from the rest of the Fleet, discovered several Sail; and therefore fir'd three Guns one after another, which gave Warning to the Fleet. About eight of the same Morning, from the Admiral's Top-mast-head, they discovered about eleven or twelve Sail; and at the same time other Ships discovered about twenty or thirty Sail more, towards *Dunkirk* and *Ostend*, and presently after more of them were descry'd; so that it was out of hand concluded to be the

May 31.
June 1.

the *Dutch* Fleet. Therefore his Grace presently commanded the Flag-Officers to meet in a Council of War, where were present Sir *Robert Holmes*, Sir *Joseph Jordan*, Sir *Christopher Mings*, Sir *George Ascough*, Rear-Admiral *Harman*, and others, where it was debated, *Whether they should adventure to engage the* Dutch *in the Absence of so considerable a Part of their Fleet, then gone off with the Prince.* But, in regard *several good Ships, besides the* Royal Sovereign, *then at Anchor in the* Gun-fleet *(neither fully mann'd, nor ready) would, upon their Retreat, be in Danger of a Surprizal by the Enemy; and that such a Course might have some Impression upon the Spirit and Courage of the Seamen, who had not been accustom'd to decline fighting with the* Dutch*;* it was at last unanimously resolved to abide them, and the Fleet should presently be put in Readiness to fall into a Line. This Advice was agreeable to the Opinion and Sentiments of the Duke, who did very much undervalue the Power and Force of the *Dutch* Fleet, expecting such easy Conquests as he had obtained thirteen Years before. But the *Dutch* of late had built much greater and stronger Ships, and, by often Tryals, had learnt from the *English* the Experience of fighting better.

X. The

X. The *Dutch* Fleet was that Day esteemed about seventy six Sail, and ten Fire-ships, commanded by the Admiral *de Ruyter*, who succeeded after the Death of *Opdam*. With the Duke there was not above fifty Frigats, whereof eighteen were heavy *Dutch* Bottoms, which had been taken from the Enemy in this and the former War. About one of the Clock, about Mid-Sea, towards the Coast of *Dunkirk*, the Fight was begun by Rear-Admiral *Harman*, of the *White* Squadron, who led the Van, and bore in upon the *Zealand* Squadron, riding head-most of the Enemy's Fleet, and presently a great Part of the Ships on both Sides were engaged. But the Wind blowing high, the Force of the *Dutch* Fleet fell chiefly upon the Sails and Rigging of the *English*. The Duke was so intent upon this Charge, that he engaged far among them, till he had most of his Tackling taken clear off by the Chain-Shot, and his Standard struck down, so that he was forc'd to tack and go off to an Anchor, being reliev'd by the *Royal-Oak*. And, having speedily rigg'd again with Jury-Masts, and brought new Sails to the Yards, he stood in again, and fell into the Body of the *Dutch* Fleet, where he engaged *de Ruyter*; and, about this Time, four of the *Dutch* great Ships were sunk and burnt; but many of the Sea-men sav'd, being taken

taken up by the *English* Boats and Tenders; and *Trump* receiv'd a full Broad-fide from the *Royal Catherine*, which fo difabled him, that he was forc'd to get off, as alfo were feveral other capital Ships that drew into Harbour. Among the reft, *Van Trump*, with his Ship of eighty two Guns; *Van Ghent*, with his Ship of feventy; and *Neffe*, with a Ship of eighty Guns (befides fome others) got into the *Goree*, miferably torn and fhatter'd.

XI. Nor was it any whit better with feveral of the *English* Ships, which, by that Day's Work, were fo difabled in their Shrouds, Mafts, and Tackling, that they were forc'd to retire, and make their Way to the next Harbour. The *Henry* had three Fire-fhips upon her, yet had the good Fortune to clear them all with fome Lofs, but fo torn and fhatter'd, as fhe was fent off to Harbour. In this Day's Engagement there appeared no confiderable Damage to any of the Ships themfelves. All the Tempeft fell above Deck among the Shrouds and Mafts; and, for the Length and Fiercenefs of the Encounter, there were very few Men kill'd or wounded. His Grace receiv'd that Day a fmall Bruife in his Hand by a Splinter, and, among thofe unlucky and thick Vollies that brought down his Tackling, one of them fhot away his Breeches, but leaving the Skin untouch'd;

and,

and, by nine or ten of the Clock at Night, both Sides were well enough content to give over, and fall to mending their Sails and Rigging.

XII. The next Morning about six, the Fight begun again, and the Duke, though so much inferior to the Enemy, in the Number of Ships, was yet the Aggressor, and most Part of the Day had the Advantage of the *Dutch* Fleet, till towards two in the Afternoon; about which Time the Enemy, which was so much superior in Number before, was recruited by the Accession of sixteen fresh Ships, by which they were enabled to press very hard upon the *English* Fleet, who yet kept their Ground, and fought it out till Evening, though extremely shatter'd in their Masts, Sails, and Rigging, and many Men kill'd. The *Dutch* lost three good Ships in this Day's Engagement; and the Duke four, the *Swift-sure*, the *Eagle*, the *Loyal George*, and the *Catherine*; which two last were no Part of the Royal Navy, but Merchant-men which had been hir'd into the Service. Yet though the Ships were destroy'd, the Men were generally sav'd. This Night the Lord *Ossory*, and Sir *Thomas Clifford*, with some other Persons of Quality, came from *Dover* on board the Admiral, by whom his Grace was assur'd, that the Prince was upon his Return.

June 2.

XIII. But

XIII. But this Day's Work had so far disabled several of his Majesty's Ships in their Masts and Rigging; and their odds of Number was so extremely disproportionable, that it was resolved this Night by the Council of War, (having with unequal Force so advantagiously asserted the Honour of his Majesty, and their own Gallantry,) to make a fair and regular Retreat.

June 3. XIV. To that End, the next Morning his Grace ordered all the Men out of two or three slug Ships, which were unserviceable, and commanded them to be fired, rather than put them to the Hazard of falling into the Enemy's Hand in his Retreat. And now he had not full forty good Ships with him to make good his Retreat against about ninety of the Enemy's. But, commanding all his weak and disabled Frigats to go off before him, and placing about sixteen or twenty of the soundest and most in Heart to the Enemy's Front, he began a regular and leisurely Retreat, which was managed with so much Bravery and Courage, that the *Dutch*, though possessed with so many great Advantages upon him, had no great Stomach to the Pursuit, contenting themselves to follow a-loof off, and to fire their Guns at such Distance, as gave no Prejudice to the *English* Fleet: Till about four

GENERAL MONK. 345

four in the Afternoon, the Wind encreasing, they came closer up to the Duke in two Bodies, and spent some Broad-sides upon his Ship; but were so warmly ply'd from the *English* Fleet with their Stern Pieces, as made them contented to lye further off.

XV. The same fresh Gale which at this Time had brought up the *Dutch* Fleet, brought also the Prince with his Squadron in View of the Duke's Ships, which now appeared in the most seasonable Minute, having made all the Sail they could to come to his Relief. Nor was the Duke less willing to join the Prince and his Squadron. But, in making their Way towards him, several of the principal Ships, and among the rest, the Duke in the *Royal Charles*, came a-ground on the *Gapper* or the *Galloper Sands*, but had all of them the good Fortune to get off again; only the *Royal Prince*, a great and brave Frigat, was so deeply stranded, that it was not possible to bring her off, but became a Prey to the Enemy, where Sir *George Ascough* that commanded in her, and his Company, were taken Prisoners. And when the *Dutch* also had in vain attempted to get her off the Sands, at Night they burnt her down. This unfortunate striking of so many of our Ships upon the Sands, gave the *Dutch* so great an Opportunity of destroying the Duke's Fleet, as they have Cause never to forgive the Commanders that made no greater Advantage of it, where all might have been lost, if the Enemy had been brave enough to have adventured for it.

XVI. So soon as the *Dutch* observ'd the Approach of the Prince with his Squadron, *de Ruyter* sent over a Party of between twenty and thirty Ships to meet him, himself with the rest of the Fleet still attending the Motion of the Duke. This Squadron of the *Dutch* Fleet sent out against the Prince, seem'd to provoke him to the Combat; but because he as yet knew nothing of the State of the Fleet, he resolv'd first to send off a Vessel to the Duke, letting him know, that, if he thought it most advisable, he would keep to Windward, and engage that Party which had been sent out to brave him. But, least the Vessel should not return Time enough to prevent the Prince's Intention, his Grace first fir'd two Guns from the *Royal Charles*, to give him Warning, and made a Waft with his Flag; and presently after the Messenger return'd also, and brought his Highness Caution from the Duke, *That he should by no means bear up the Squadron, there being a dangerous Sand, called the* Galloper, *lying between them, where several of his own Ships had that Day been stranded; and, at one*

General Monk. 347

one *End of it, the* Royal Prince *was loft: That the Appearance of the* Dutch *Squadron in that Place, was only to tempt them into the Bank, and draw them into the Toil.* Upon this Advice, his Highnefs prefently bore away to the Northward, to get clear of thofe dangerous Sands, and, by the Evening, made his Way to the Duke's Fleet, the Enemy all this while, not offering them any Difturbance. But fo foon as they perceiv'd the *Englifh* Fleet to be all join'd, the *Dutch* Fleet prefently haled clofe upon a Wind, and went out of Sight.

XVII. The Duke prefently haften'd to attend his Highnefs in the *Royal James,* and gave him an Account of all Particulars in thefe three Days Action. That Night a Council of War was called, where were prefent Sir *Thomas Allyn,* Sir *Chriftopher Mings,* Sir *Edward Sprag,* and the reft; where it was agreed, *That it would be injurious to his Majefty's Honour, and the Refolution of the* Englifh *Fleet, to let the* Dutch *go off thus, and to carry home with them the Appearance of an Advantage: That the Courage of the Sea-men was ftill brave and high, and the Fleet in Heart; their Hulls being all untouch'd, and the Damage hitherto being only in their Shrouds and Tackling: That by the working of the Enemy's Fleet all this Day,*

when

when our Fleet retreated, it appear'd, tho' they were so much higher in Number, yet they were lower in Courage.

XVIII. It was therefore resolv'd, *That, the next Day, they would fall upon the Enemy; and that his Highness's Squadron, being fresh and untouched, and being the best sailing Frigats in the Fleet, should lead the Van.*

June 4. XIX. And on *Munday*, by the Morning Light, the *English* Fleet was under Sail; and, the *Dutch* being gone out of Sight, they stood their Course after them; and some while after recovered Sight of their Fleet, who made their Way at Leisure towards their own Coasts. For, besides what Damage they had themselves known and seen in the *English* Fleet after three Days Fighting, they had receiv'd from those Prisoners they had taken out of the *Royal Prince,* such an Account of the shattered and disabled Condition of the *English* Fleet, that they could not easily believe the Prince and Duke would have the Courage to pursue them; or, if they should, yet the *Dutch* had so much Wit in their Anger, as they would endeavour to fight near home, whereby, upon any Disadvantage, they might more easily run into their own Stations, whither the *English* could not easily follow them.

XX. By

XX. By eight of the Clock the *English* Fleet was got up to them; and the *Dutch*, having got the Weathergage, put their Fleet in Readiness, and fell into a Line all to Windward of the *English* Fleet; which, coming up in very good Order, ranged themselves for the Fight. Sir *Christopher Mings* with his Division led the Van, next the Prince with his Squadron, and then Sir *Edward Sprag*, having the Duke of *Albemarle* in the Rear. The Fight was begun with that Courage on both Sides, and continu'd with such Fierceness, as any one would have thought it the first Day's Encounter, rather than their fourth. In the first, Rear-Admiral *Mings*, and some other Ships were disabled, and presently enforc'd to quit the Fight, whilst the Prince with his fresh Squadron, found the Enemy Work on all Hands, succeeded by the Duke, who revengingly charged them.

XXI. One of their Vice-Admirals, being a stout Ship, boldly attempted to board him, coming up so near, that the Shroud Arms touched each other; but his Grace receiv'd him with so full a Broad-side, and pour'd upon him so smart a Volly of his small Shot, that he immediately fell a Stern, and appear'd no more, nor any other to succeed in his Room. And *Trump* receiv'd such another Broad-

Broad-side from the *Royal Catherine*, as utterly disabled him for the rest of the Day. But the *Dutch* knowing his Grace's Squadron, by the former three Days Fight, to be weaker than the rest, charged fiercely upon him, and gave him no Breath, whilst the Duke, by his extraordinary Conduct and infinite Courage, so managed the Force of his Squadron, improving vigorously such Ships as were in Heart and Strength, and warily sheltering such as were most disabled, that he still gained Ground upon the Enemy.

XXII. Both the Prince and Duke had, in this Day's Engagement, five times passed through the Body of the *Dutch* Fleet, at every Pass making some signal Impression upon them. And by this time the *Dutch* were fought so low, that Part of the Fleet began to think of securing themselves by retreating; and, among the rest, *de Ruyter*, who, to disguise his Flight, or to secure it, made Shew as if he would tack again; which being observ'd by the Prince, who, towards Evening, with eight or ten of his Frigats had got to Windward of the Enemy's Fleet, he was resolved to bear in upon them, and at one Push to compleat the Victory, by putting them to the Run. At the same Instant his Main-topmast, being terribly shaken, came all by the Board; and the Duke, who also at the same

time

time stood by the Leeward of the Enemy with his Squadron, gave Order to tack and join with the Prince, in this concluding Charge upon the Enemy. But having, in the last Pass, receiv'd two Shots in his Powder-Room between Wind and Water, they could not presently be stopped. His Main-top-mast also was so shatter'd by a Shot through it, that he was forced to lower his Top-sail; and at the same Time his Fore-mast had received so many Shots, that it was disabled for further Service at present. By which unhappy Accidents the *Dutch* Fleet gain'd a lucky Opportunity to make the best of their Way, and got off much fairer than otherwise they should have done, being pursu'd by some of the nimbler Frigats whilst their Powder and the Light lasted. In this Engagement the *Dutch* had six Ships fir'd and sunk; on the *English* Side were lost only the *Prince* (worth all the *Dutch* lost) and the *Essex*, having grappled with a *Dutch* Ship, was by others boarded and taken. Two Days after, his Highness and the Duke brought the Fleet to an Anchor in the *Gun-fleet*; but a great Part of them so miserably torn and shatter'd, that they had little else to boast of, except the honourable Marks of a severe Engagement. From thence the Fleet was distributed into several Harbours, to be refitted with all possible Speed; and the Commissioners of the

Navy were strictly obliged to inspect the Dispatch. His Highness and the Duke of *Albemarle* hasten'd then to *London* to attend his Majesty: To whom they were the more welcome, by those extraordinary Services and Hazards they had passed through.

XXIII. This Action of the Duke's, in adventuring to fight the *Dutch* after the dividing the Fleet, was by several Men variously considered. His Enemies, though they acknowledg'd his Courage and Generosity, yet did greatly accuse his Discretion; and did suggest, *That a little Allay of the Coward was a safer Ingredient in a General, than such vast and transcendent Rashness: And tho' he came off well, yet he intrusted Fortune with a greater Stock than a wise Man would put into her Hands.* But his Majesty, and all discerning Persons, had another Opinion of this extraordinary Action: *That it was grounded on the greatest Reason and Necessity, and that the Honour of the Nation was concerned in it: That he had thereby given the greatest Instance of his own and the* English *Prowess; and had raised the Reputation of his Majesty's Naval Force to such an Height of Glory, as would render him more terrible to his Enemies, and desir'd by his Allies.*

XXIV. 'And

XXIV. And, if we will hear the Opinion of the *Dutch* themselves, who, in this Instance, may be counted the best and most impartial Judges, it is manifest, that this Encounter of fifty Frigats against all the Force they could make, gave then a greater Apprehension and Dread of his Majesty's Power at Sea, than all the Victories which had been gain'd on them. So that, though the Confidence of the common People was to be kept up with Bubble and Brandy, yet their Governors discern'd their own Danger and Inability; and that his Majesty's Fleet, under an high and great Conduct, had a Force and Courage more than human. Which made the late Heer *de Wit* (accounted the wisest Man in the Nation, and who then govern'd their Affairs, and who was never guilty of much Respect to his Majesty, and the *English* Nation) acknowledge to Sir *William Temple*, his Majesty's Ambassador then to the States of *Holland*, "That, by this Engagement of the
" Duke of *Albemarle*, we had gain'd more
" Honour to our Nation, and to the invin-
" cible Courage of the Seamen, than by the
" other two Victories. That he was sure the
" *Dutch* could never have been brought on
" the other two Days, after the Disadvantage
" of the first; and he believ'd no other Na-
" tion was capable of it except the *English*."

But if his Grace was too daring in this Encounter, yet the *Dutch* were certainly much more too cowardly, in neglecting the Advantage of it. Had the Duke been possess'd of half those Advantages upon the Enemy, he would have given Security, at the Price of his own Head, to have destroy'd or taken their whole Fleet. But the *Dutch* had got off so much better than they hoped for, from this Encounter, that they were willing to fansy it for a Victory. So that it was not only owned as such by their own People, with whom such Contrivances are politickly necessary; but was puplish'd also in the Courts of foreign Princes, who, being better inform'd in the Circumstances of the Action, greatly smiled at the *Dutch* Vanity.

XXV. The States in the Interim had repair'd their Fleet with such extraordinary Diligence and Dispatch, (in which Instance only they may be thought to exceed their Neighbours) as they were again got out to Sea with about an hundred Sail; and, that they might appear to have been victorious in the late Engagement, came and lay upon the *English* Coasts: With which, not only their own People, but the Seditious and Discontented in *England*, were well satisfy'd. Yet all this was but Pretence, and a Copy of their Countenance. For the *Dutch* very well knew,

knew, that his Majesty's Fleet would not yet be ready; and so soon as it was, they presently drew off, not for Sea Room, as the *English* used to do from the Coasts of *Holland*, but, in case they were forc'd to an Engagement, to lye near the Retirements of their own Shores.

XXVI. By this Time the Prince and Duke of *Albemarle* had used such Industry, that his Majesty's Fleet was in Readiness to come to a Rendez-vous at the *Buoy* of the *Nore*, *July* the 17th, and from thence, *July* 22. sail'd to the *Gun-fleet*. The next Day they stood to *July* 23. Sea after the Enemy's Fleet, who kept under Sail before them towards their own Coasts. And on *July* 25. by six in the Morning, got *July* 25. within two Leagues of the *Dutch* Fleet, who thereupon sailing in very good Order, brought themselves into a Crescent; and the *English*, as they came up, fell into a Line; both Sides having divided themselves into three Squadrons.

XXVII. Between nine and ten in the Morning the Fight begun. The *White* Squadron, led by Sir *Thomas Allen*, rode in the Head of the Fleet; and, coming close up to the Enemy, the *Anne* began to fire, and presently the *White* Squadron was wholly engag'd with the Enemy's Van. And the *Red*

Squadron next advancing upon the Body of the *Dutch* Fleet led by *de Ruyter*, and then the *Blue* Squadron undertook the *Zealand* Division; so that by Noon all our Fleet was in with them. This Encounter, though it lasted not long, yet, for the Time of its continuance, was sharp enough: In which the *Dutch* had several Ships sunk and fir'd; and some of our own, as the *Royal Catherine*, the St. *George*, the *Rupert*, and another Ship of the *White* Squadron, were so disabled as they came out of the Line, and lay by to mend. His Highness and the Duke being both in the *Royal Charles*, bore up to Admiral *de Ruyter* within Musket Shot, and fought him hand to hand for some time, till they came out of their Line to refit their Tackling, leaving the Place to Sir *Joseph Jordan* in the *Royal Sovereign*, who ply'd him so warmly, that he shot down his Top-mast, and sunk his Fireship by his Side. In half an Hour's Time the Prince and Duke stood in again, engaging the second Time so closely with *de Ruyter*, as, having receiv'd seventeen Shot in his Ship under the Water, and double the Number in his Hull above, he was glad to give Way, and retire. All the Damage to the *Royal Charles* was only in her Tackling; where they had no Ropes nor Steerage left, but she was towed out of the Line by Boats, his Highness and his Grace removing into the
Royal

Royal James. About this Time Sir *Robert Holmes*, having lost both his Top masts, lay by a while to repair. And now the *Resolution*, being first disabled, was burnt by a Fire-ship sent upon her by *Van Trump.* Captain *Hannam*, who commanded in her, bravely clear'd himself of the Fire-Ship; but the Flame was advanced so far, as he could not possibly preserve his Ship; yet himself and Ship's Company saved themselves by Boats which were sent off to them from such Ships as lay nearest. For some Time before, the Enemy was observ'd to give Ground; between one and two of the Clock the Van was already got off with all the Wind they could make; and now, about four in the Afternoon, *de Ruyter* with the Body of their Fleet began to run; but made frequent Tacks to fetch off his shattered and maimed Ships. In one whereof he hazarded his own Safety to rescue his second; which was so disabled, as it was not possible for him to retrieve her. And now, besides what the *Dutch* had lost in the Fight, several other Ships were lost as they fled away. About seven at Night the *Royal James* took Vice-Admiral *Banchart*'s Ship of sixty Guns, himself escaping a-board Captain *de Haes.* And the *Snake* of *Harlem*, a stout new Ship of sixty six Guns, was also taken, and both of them fir'd by the *English*, being earnest in the Pursuit. All this while Sir *Je-*

remy Smith with the *Blue* Squadron stood engaged with *Van Trump* and the *Zealand* Division, till, toward Night, they also made all the Sail they could to the Northward, and the *Blue* Squadron in the Pursuit till Night parted them.

CHAP. XXX.

I, II. *The* Dutch *are beaten into their own Harbour.* III, IV. *The Loss on each Side.* V. *The Prince and Duke resolve to anchor upon the* Dutch *Coasts.* VI, VII. *Sir* Robert Holmes *makes a Descent upon the Island of* Schelling, *plunders and burns the Town of* Brandaris, *with an hundred and fifty Ships in the Harbour.* VIII. *The* Dutch *put to Sea again, and sail towards the* French *Coasts, in hopes of joining them. The* English *Fleet goes in Pursuit of them.*

I. THE *Dutch* Fleet being gone off, his Highness and the Duke this Night gave Order to Sir *Thomas Allen* in the *Royal Oak*, with two other Frigats, to keep near them,

them, and to put up Lights that might give Notice, in case the Enemy should alter his Course; which was so effectually perform'd, that, by the first Light of the Morning, Sir *Thomas Allen* found himself not much above Musket shot from *de Ruyter*'s Lee, and then tacked towards our own Fleet. This Morning early the Prince and Duke drew the Fleet into a Line, and made all the Sail they could, to get up with the *Dutch*; but there was so little Wind, that they could not possibly reach them. But while the Ships, for want of Wind, could not make sail, the *Fan-Fan*, a little Pleasure-boat built at *Harwich* for the Service of Prince *Rupert*, by the Help of her Oars, where the Frigats, for want of Wind, could not come, made up to *de Ruyter*; and bringing her two little Guns to bear on one Side, ply'd the Admiral's Ship Broadside to Broad-side for almost an Hour: The Admiral having spent several Guns to no purpose upon her, till at last he gave her two or three Shot between Wind and Water, with which she retired; having thereby let the Enemy see, at how low a Rate they valued the *Belgick Lion*, whom they had so often worried. Afterwards, the Wind a little increasing, the Prince and Duke made their Way towards *de Ruyter*, who found himself so disabled by Yesterday's Engagement, that both his Men and Ships were out of

Courage to stand another Encounter, but bore away before them. The *English* Fleet chasing them over several Banks and Flats, till the great Ships came to six Fathoms Water, and the less continu'd in Pursuit within two Miles of their own Shores. And, had there been Wind enough in this Retreat, both *de Ruyter*, and several of his Ships, had certainly been taken or destroy'd. But there being so great a Calm, the *Dutch* Ships, drawing less Water, made their Way faster than the *English* could pursue them, and so escaped into the *Harlow* Channel of *Zealand*.

II. THE same Day Sir *Jeremiah Smith*, with the Blue Squadron, pressed so hard upon *Van Trump* and his Division, that he beat them all into their own Port of the *Weelings*.

III. IN this Engagement the *Freezland* and *Zealand* Squadrons were thought to have lost the better half of their Men. In their whole Fleet were estimated about four thousand Men killed, two thousand wounded. The Commanders of Note that fell in this Fight were, *Evertson* of *Zealand*, *Termick Hides* Admiral of *Freezland*, and *Conders* his Vice-Admiral, with about twelve of their principal Captains.

IV. THE

IV. THE Loss on the *English* Side was greatly disproportionable, having lost but few in the Fight, and not above three hundred wounded, upon a strict Computation. And, among the Officers, were kill'd only Captain *Seymour* in the *Foresight*, Captain *Martin* in the *East-India, London*, and Captain *Parker* in the *Yarmouth*; Captain *Saunders* only in the *Breda* dangerously wounded. And but one Ship wanting, namely the *Resolution*, of which we have given Account before.

V. THE Day after the Fight the Prince and Duke, at a Council of War, resolv'd to send home those few Ships that were disabled, and to ply upon the *Dutch* Coasts, in Expectation of some further Advantage upon the Enemy, who could not make this Engagement Pass among the People for a Victory, when they saw every Day the *English* Fleet at Anchor in View of their Shores.

July 27.

VI. NEITHER would the Courage and Resolution of his Majesty's Fleet content it self to lye idly upon the Enemy's Coasts; but the Prince and Duke having receiv'd Information from a discontented *Dutch* Captain, how easy it was to make an Attempt upon the Island of *Schelling*, and Town of *Brandaris*, commanded Sir *Robert Holmes* to go upon that Expedition; who accordingly, taking with him eleven Foot Companies, and eight small Frigats, with five Fire ships, besides several Ketches and Boats, in the Morning early enter'd the Channel; and, being come into *Schelling* Road, Sir *Robert* and the Captains with him, observing a considerable Fleet of about an hundred and twenty Sail, riding thick and close together at Anchor in the *Uly*, with few Men of War among them for their Assistance, resolv'd to attempt the firing of them. Whereupon Sir *Robert Holmes* left the *Advice* and *Hampshire* Frigats without, to secure the Buoys, lest the Enemy should send some Vessels to take them away, and so hazard their Retreat in an unknown Channel. The *Pembroke* and three Ketches and Boats, with one Foot Company, and Sir *Robert Holmes* himself in the little *Fan-Fan* that had lately braved *de Ruyter*, with the five Fire-ships a-head, went in upon the *Dutch* Fleet, and presently fir'd two *Dutch* Men of War, and some other Ships, that, upon the Alarm, stood to defend the Fleet. The Boats then were sent to burn the rest of the Ships; which was dispatch'd with such Success, that presently all their Ships were on fire, except a *Guineaman* of twenty four Guns, and three small Privateers, that, halling together in the narrow of the Channel, preserv'd themselves,

and

and five Sail more that were behind them, so as the Boat could not possibly get up to them.

VII. The *Tyger, Assurance, Dragon, Garland,* and *Sweepstakes,* stood in *Schelling* Road with five Foot Companies, to prevent any Surprizal from the Enemy, whilst the other five Companies went on Shore upon the Island of *Schelling* for the Town of *Brandaris*; which, in half an Hour's Time, was all on a Flame, and above a thousand Houses were consumed. The Spoil and Plunder, both in the Ships and Houses, were wholly abandoned to the Seamen and Soldiers, where some of them found great Booties. And, having destroy'd more than an hundred and fifty Sail of the Enemy's Ships, Sir *Robert Holmes* returned safely, having not above twelve Men kill'd or wounded in the Action. And, being come back to the Fleet, the Prince and Duke sent Sir *Philip Howard,* who was one of those eleven Captains that went on this Expedition, to give his Majesty an Account thereof.

VIII. The Prince and Duke continued still upon the *Dutch* Coasts, intercepting their Trade and Ships; and, about the middle of *August*, returned with their Fleet to their own Shores, having spent all their Provision,

and

and much of their Ammunition; both which were to be supply'd again at home. But some Vessels for Intelligence were still continu'd on the *Dutch* Coasts; and, toward the End of this Month, brought Account, that the Enemy was coming out with a Fleet of eighty Sail; who took this Advantage of the *English* Fleet's Retreat, to get out with all the Haste they could make, and sailed towards the *French* Harbours, hoping to join with their new Ally, who hitherto had given them no Assistance.

IX. The News of the Enemy's Fleet coming forth, was quickly brought to the Prince and Duke of *Albemarle*, who made all the Haste possible to get the Fleet in Readiness to fall on them. And, about the first of *September*, came up to them, having gotten *French* Harbour in the Bay of *Staples*, where the *English* Fleet stood ready to engage them; but the Enemy kept themselves close in the Harbour. The Weather was now very tempestuous by a strong Easterly Wind, and the *English* could not conveniently weather it; and, perceiving the Enemy not willing to fight, the Prince and Duke retir'd to St. *Hellen*'s Bay, that being a safe and commodious Station, where they might intercept the joining of the *Dutch* and *French* Fleet, then lying about *Rochel*.

CHAP.

CHAP. XXXI.

I. *The Fire of* London. II. *The Duke commanded home for his Assistance upon that Occasion.* III. *No farther Action at Sea this Year.* IV. *The Methods taken next Year to bring the* Dutch *to some Action, or to Peace.* V. *The Distribution of the* English *Fleet.* VI. *The* Dutch *make an Attempt upon* Chatham, *but afterwards submit to a Peace.* VII, VIII, IX. *The Duke taken ill, his Distemper, the Course of it.* X. *He returns to* London, *grows worse.* XI. *His Advice to the Members of Parliament, and Ministers of State, who come to see him.* XII, XIII. *Marries his Son to a Daughter of the Duke of* Newcastle. XIV. *Sequesters himself from all publick Affairs.* XV. *His Death.* XVI. *Some of his most important Actions enumerated.* XVII. *His Death universally lamented.* XVIII. *His Funeral celebrated at the King's Charge.* XIX. *A physical Account of the Author's concerning the Cause of his Death.* XX. *His Body lies in State at* Somerset *House.*

I. WHILST the Fortune of *England*, by so many Naval Successes abroad, run thus high upon the Water, it was suddenly arrested by a fatal Fire at home, which about this Time (*September* 2.) began, and, in three Days Time, burnt down the greatest Part of the City; which the Citizens computed at above one thousand three hundred Houses, besides so great a Loss of Goods and Wares, as can never be duly estimated. And, after the Astonishment of this Conflagration it self, the next Wonder is, that the Minds of Men have been no ways clearly satisfied about the Beginning or Continuance of it.

Sept. 2.

II. After so great a Blow upon the Metropolis of the Nation, it pleased his Majesty to command the Duke of *Albemarle* from Sea, to be near his Person and Counsels in so distracted a Time; who accordingly came back to *London* about two Days after the Fire was quenched.

III. It might have been here expected, that the *Dutch* Fleet, now in Conjunction with *France*, would have taken this Opportunity of fighting his Majesty's Navy, which all this while stood ready for them. But the late Engagement, upon dividing the Fleet, had cost them so dear, they were not willing to try a second Experiment; and were so far from coming to a Fight after the Union with the *French* Ships, that, though his Majesty

kept

GENERAL MONK. 367

kept out his Fleet till the Seafon was over, yet the Enemy trifled away the Time without coming to Action. So that his Grace went no more this Year to the Fleet, but continued at home, affifting with the Privy-Council for rebuilding the City.

IV. AND for the next Year his Majefty, having taken other Methods, was pleas'd to excufe him from any further Service at Sea. For the *Dutch* were contriving as dilatory a War with his Majefty of *Great Britain*, as they had formerly manag'd with their natural Prince *Philip* II. to weary him with Delays. So that in *England* there was more Fear about the Continuance and Charge of the War, (efpecially after the burning of the City) than for the Event of it. This Year 1667. therefore it was refolv'd, inftead of dancing Attendance after their fighting Fleet, to turn the War upon their Trade, and intercept their Commerce; whereby the *Dutch* Fleet would be enforc'd, either to follow their Blows more roundly, or fubmit to a Peace.

V. IN order to this Refolution, his Majefty had taken Care to fecure the *Britifh* Seas, by appointing a convenient Number of Ships to lye upon the Coafts about *Scotland*, and another Squadron to ply about *Portfmouth*; fo that neither Way the Merchant-Ships

Ships should be able to pass without Hazard. The rest of his Majesty's Fleet was put into the Harbour at *Chatham*; and, for their Security and Defence, Order was given for the better fortifying *Sheerness*, at the Mouth of the River, for the planting of Guns at *Upnor* Castle, which commanded the Stream; and to secure the River *Medway* with a large and strong Chain.

VI. OF this limber and ductile Contrivance the Duke of *Albemarle* was neither the Author nor Promoter; which yet might have succeeded much better, if any Part of the Instructions had been duly prosecuted. But the *Dutch*, finding *Chatham*, and the Parts about it, unable to make a Defence, took those Advantages upon the Water, which it was impossible for the Duke of *Albemarle*, and those Land Forces, which, to the Number of one thousand five hundred Foot, and five or six hundred Horse, were sent from *London* thither under his Conduct to deprive them of. Wherefore doing as much as could be effected by Land against an Enemy at Sea, the Duke secured the Coast and the Country; and letting them know that *Albemarle* was *June.* still alive, disposed the *Dutch* to a Peace; which was concluded between his Majesty and the States not long after in the same Summer. After which, having no further Occasion

sion to use his Sword, he return'd to enjoy the Benefit of that Peace, which his Courage and Conduct had helped to procure.

VII. FROM which Time he divided himself between his Majesty's Service (which in any the least Instance he would never neglect) and his own private Affairs; till he arrived to the sixtieth Year of his Age.

VIII. AND now that firm and good Constitution of Body, that great and constant Health, which he had so long enjoyed, began to impair in him; which Decays were more hastily promoted, by the Hardships of a Soldier's Life in his younger Days; and were further advanced, by the continual Weight of publick Cares in his declining Age. His general Indisposition of Body discover'd it self in the Beginnings of a Dropsy, against which no timely Care was employ'd. For, though his Grace was very well pleas'd with the Reasons and Discourse of Physicians, yet, through an uninterrupted Health, he had a kind of Averseness to Medicines, or Methods of Physick. In this Condition he retired himself to his Seat at *New-Hall* in *Essex*, in Hopes that the fresh Air might have some good Effect upon his Body; and, by this Retreat and Recess from publick Business, he might recover his Health.

1668.

IX. WHICH,

IX. Which, proving otherwise, and his Dropsy and Shortness of Breath still increasing, he was persuaded, by the Importunity of his Friends, and particularly by one who had been an Officer in his Army, to use a Pill, which, at that Time, had some Reputation for curing the Dropsy, and was then in the Hands of a Person that had formerly been a Soldier under him in *Scotland*; and being informed, that the Remedy might be try'd without any strict Method or Confinement, he was the more inclinable to make some Experiment of it. Which, though it never effected any thing worthy the Name of a Cure, yet, upon the frequent Use thereof, it so discharg'd the Deluge of waterish Humour, as the active Parts of his Blood began again to recover; so that the Difficulty of his breathing, and the swelling in his Body and Legs, were very much relieved. And all Men, being so greatly desirous of his Life and Health, they were ready to persuade him into the Confidence of a greater Amendment than there really was.

Dr. Sermon.

1669.

X. With this Opinion, at the End of the Summer, he returned back to *London*: But, upon the Approach of the Winter, his Blood declining again with the Year, his Dropsy encreased upon him, with the same Accidents as as before. Nor could his former Remedy, which, by the Opinion of curing him before, was grown to a great Reputation, avail any thing to preserve his Grace, and its own Credit, by a second Recovery.

XI. The Noise of his Relapse, and the imminent Danger of it, being quickly spread about the Town, all his Friends and Retainers came to make their Visits to him. Several also of the House of Lords, and of the Commons, then sitting, did frequently attend him; and, having accustomed himself to publick Cares, he could not part with them in the midst of his own Difficulties; but, with that little Breath he had left to support himself, discoursed always very earnestly with them about his Majesty's Service, and the Good and Settlement of the Commonwealth; conjuring them, *to preserve always a good Understanding between the two Houses; and that his Majesty's Crown and Government ought never to suffer any Inconvenience by the Passions or Prejudice of those, who were so nearly obliged to take Care of it.*

XII. In this his Sickness (when the King sent continually, as well as the Duke of *York*, to know his State) he was frequently visited by his most intimate and principal Friend the

Earl of *Bath*, and also by the Lord *Arlington*; to both whom he recommended the Care of his Servants. For, as to his own Concernments, he had brought them into a narrow Room; having now but one mortal Care upon him, which was the Marriage of his only Son, whom he was likely to leave young, being then about sixteen or seventeen Years of Age. So that his Grace was very desirous of living so long as to provide a Match for him in some ancient and loyal Family, which were the principal Qualifications he aimed at. To that End, some Weeks before his Death he entered into a Treaty with the Duke of *Newcastle*, with whom he contracted a Match for his Son with the Lady *Elizabeth*, eldest Daughter of the said Duke, a fair and virtuous Lady. By which Alliance he united the Glories of the ancient Houses of *Newcastle* and *Dorchester*, *Cavendish* and *Pierpoint*, with his own Ducal Coronet.

XIII. And finding, by his daily and encreasing Weakness, the Approach of his Death, he made the more Haste to consummate the Marriage. To that End, *December* 27. his Grace employed the most Part of the Day in giving Instructions to his Council at Law, for the better settling his Estate upon his Son, and the assigning a Jointure upon the

the young Lady. And three Days after, being *December* 30. the Marriage was solem- *Dec. 30.*
niz'd in the Duke's Chamber; where, with
that little Strength he had, he delivered the
Bride from his own Hand into the Arms of
his Son.

XIV. When the Ceremony was ended, he
seem'd very much pleas'd that he had lived to
see the Accomplishment of it, being the last
of his human Cares. After which he sequestred himself from all mortal Affairs never to
be resumed more.

XV. And now the extreme Difficulty of
breathing, which had all along been the most
uneasy Part of his Sickness, increased so violently upon him, that he could not lye down
in his Bed, but entertained himself only with
some short Sleeps in his Chair; in which Posture
he dy'd four Days after the Marriage of his
Son, *January* 3. about nine in the Morning. *Jan. 3.*
And as he liv'd in Silence, so he dy'd with- $16\frac{6\cdot 3}{4}$.
out Noise; one easy and single Groan did the
Work of Death upon the stoutest and most
valiant Hero of the Age he lived in. In his
Sickness he had been often visited and comforted by his Grace the then Archbishop of
Canterbury; and, in those his last Minutes,
he was assisted by the Prayers of the Bishop

of *Salisbury*, who attended him to his last Breath, and closed his Eyes.

XVI. Such was the *Exit* of this high and illustrious Person. After he had survived ten thousand Hazards of War and Battels, and surmounted as many Difficulties to redeem his Country; and in his immortal March from *Dalkeith* to *London*, had led two Kingdoms in his own Triumph; after he had restored his Majesty to his Crown, and had erected the Trophies of his Courage and Prudence in his Dominion at Land, and had humbled the Pride of the stubborn Enemy, the *Dutch*, in two memorable Battels at Sea; after he had seen the Enemies of this Crown under his Majesty's Feet, and, for ten Years, faithfully assisted in the Settlement of the State; he exchanged this mortal Life for an happy Immortality, having lived sixty one Years and twenty nine Days.

XVII. The Report of his Death was quickly convey'd from his own Family to the Court adjoining, where it affected his Majesty and all Persons with a very particular Sorrow; and the News thereof was entertain'd in the City, and throughout the Kingdom, as a publick Loss and general Calamity, all Men commenting on the Fall of this their great Restorer with an universal Sorrow.

XVIII.

XVIII. And as his Majesty had always treated him with a very singular Esteem all his Life-time, so he was pleas'd to follow him with the Marks of his Royal Favour to the Grave, resolving to celebrate the Duke's Funeral at his own Charge; and he assign'd him also a Tomb in *Henry* the VIIth's Chapel, that the great Instaurator, and Guardian of Monarchy, might rest himself near the crown'd Heads, and mix his loyal Dust with the Ashes of former Kings.

XIX. January 4. his Body was opened and embalmed, in order to the Solemnity of his Funeral. But, upon the Search, there was found only a large Quantity of discoloured Matter in the Cavity of the Belly, and no considerable Alteration or Injury upon the Parts within; save only in the Heart it self, both the Ventricles whereof were fill'd with a bloody Substance, which had also insinuated it self into the Mouths of the adjoining Vessels, which had so far precluded the even Motion and Circle of Blood through his Lungs, as gave him a perpetual Difficulty of breathing. His long and habitual Dropsy had also so far disabled the Vigour and Motion of his Blood, that it was not able to entertain and assimilate the chylous Liquor offered from his Diet; which did first stick

stick among the Fibres and Columns in both Ventricles of the Heart; and, by the continued and gradual Succession of the like tenacious Matter, came at last to that Bulk as to fill up both the Cavities, and inevitably to strand the further Current of his Blood.

XX. AFTER his Body was embalmed, it was, by his Majesty's Command, removed to *Somerset* House, and there placed for many Weeks in Royal State, attended with all the Ceremonies of pompous Mourning.

THE
CONCLUSION,
Containing a
CHARACTER
OF THE
DUKE.

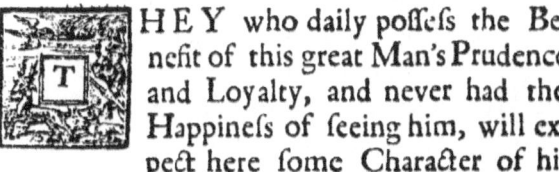HEY who daily poffefs the Benefit of this great Man's Prudence and Loyalty, and never had the Happinefs of feeing him, will expect here fome Character of his Perfon; which was indeed rather comely than elegant.

elegant. His Stature was of the middle Size, but contrived for Strength and Action. In his Countenance there appeared something very great and august, yet without Pride. His Aspect was so truly martial, that they who knew him not, might have taken him for a General, and collected the Ideas of an Hero from the Lines of his Face. His Eye-sight served him to the last upon nearer Objects, though at remoter Distances it was somewhat defective. Which Imperfection was, in some Measure, recompensed to him, with a very extraordinary Quickness of hearing; wherein he did so very far excel, that it was dangerous to whisper a Secret in the same Room with him.

His Constitution also was framed to a singular Steddiness of Temperament, which inabled him to live with a very little Sleep, and without any of those Emotions in his Blood, which most other Men find from the Want of it. Upon the same Account he was capable of enduring long and frequent Fasting, when imposed upon him, either by Religion, Necessity, or Business, without any observable Prejudice to his Health, or any other Inconvenience. In his Palate he was not curious, or at all studious how to gratify it. When he was young, he had the Small-pox; yet entertain'd them, most Part of the Time,

Time, on Horse-back, and marched every Day with his Regiment, without any of those fatal Effects, which naturally follow from the least Impression of the cold Air.

But when we come to describe the Virtues and Endowments of his Mind, we enter upon a more copious and extensive Subject. His Courage and Fortitude were beyond any hyperbolical Strains of his Friends, and were never yet questioned by his greatest Enemies. They were not, like the uncertain and occasional Impetuosity of the late Usurper *Cromwel,* taken up by Fits; but a steddy and well-advised Greatness of Spirit, separate from Rashness, and conducted by an extraordinary Prudence and Foresight. So that in those many Engagements where he had commanded, he was always attended with a smooth, uninterrupted Success, which has rarely been constant to old Generals. And, in that single Surprizal upon him by the *Dutch* Fleet, he fought them so stoutly with a very unequal Force; and afterwards secured his Retreat with so much Resolution and Bravery, that his Enemies were obliged to acknowledge, there was something in his Greatness of Mind and Conduct that was more than human.

If we consider either the Ascendant of his Courage,

Courage, or Fortune, it will not be easy to find a Parallel in his own Age, and as hardly in all Antiquity. He had restored his Country with *Camillus*, but the Sequel of his Life was more glorious. He had all the Dispatch of *Cæsar*, but none of his Ambition; the Popularity of *Pompey*, without any of his Errors, or Misfortunes; the Estimation of *Lucullus*, separate from his Luxury; the Industry of the brave *Agricola*, but in the Service of a better Master. He had equalled *Scipio*, in reducing the greater Enemies of the Common-wealth, and more faithless than the *Carthaginians*, but exceeded him in the Love of his Country, and the Glory of his End. His Command, and the Times he lived in, had the nearest Resemblance to those of *Sertorius* in *Spain*; nor were there wanting Confederates about him of *Perpenna*'s insidious Temper; but he look'd so narrowly after them, that none of them could find those Advantages against him, which were taken against that generous *Roman*.

If his Virtues had been only Military, he and his Armour might, in peaceful Times, have rusted together. But as he had the Sufficiency of a great General in War, so he had equal Prudence and Industry in Civil Business. And, when there was no more Occasion for his Sword, he became a most useful

ful and necessary Minister of State; wherein, if some few have exceeded him in Dispatch, yet none in Sureness and Fidelity. By his Prudence he baffled all his Enemies, and unravelled all the Labyrinths of their crooked Subtilty. By the same Virtue he preserved to himself the continued Affection and Kindness of his Majesty, which shined upon him to the Evening of his Life, without the Interruption of the least Cloud. By the like Quality he kept up his Estimation with his Equals, and the Ministers of State, against whom he had never given into any intriguing Schemes. And, as a Reward of his Prudence and Integrity, he had those Advantages which have seldom been known to center in the same Person; of being equally the Favourite of the King, the Court, and the People.

Nor was it the least of his Felicities, that he had the Opportunity of obliging a Prince of so generous and humane a Disposition, who could never be capable of looking upon the Greatness of his Services with Suspicion, or to esteem it a Reproach to his own Greatness and Glory, to have been restored by one of his own Subjects. He had also the further good Fortune to perform his Service to the King in the Flower of his Age, and the Fulness of his Joys, before the narrow and
suspicious

suspicious Temper, which is more incident to an advanced Age, could be supposed to discover its ordinary and too natural Effects.

His Silence and advised Taciturnity was Part of his Prudence, which grew in a great Measure upon his Nature, and became habitual to him, by a long Conversation among those whom he could neither love, nor thought it reasonable to trust. Such was his Caution and Wariness, that he would commonly contrive to be the last Man in the Company to declare his Opinion. He had those Virtues in Perfection, which the Lord *Bacon* requires in a Person in a publick Office, *viz.* " Openness in Fame and Opinion " of others, Secrecy in an habitual Conceal- " ment of himself." Because the Generality of Men are most delighted in discoursing of those Subjects wherein they excel, or have been eminently successful; some have contrived to oblige him, by making the Affairs of those Times, and his extraordinary Services in restoring the King, the Subject of Conversation in his Company; in all which he would always reply with so great Humility, and Appearance of disclaiming all Merit in himself, that there is not a Person now living, who can charge him with Vanity or Ostentation. And, perhaps, there is not an Instance

stance in History of any Man, who ever performed such great Services, and discovered so little Inclination to mention them, or to hear them mentioned by others.

Though his Grace very well knew how to expect those Regards, which were due to his Person and Quality, yet surely no Man entertained his own Greatness with less Ceremony, being a professed Enemy to the little pompous Vanities, by which Persons of the first Distinction so magnificently trifle with one another. And they who could only take the Height of a great Man, by the Length of his Shadow; by Appearances, and the Noise about him; by Formalities, and a numerous Croud of Attendants, thought they wanted something of Grandeur in his Character and Behaviour; who had indeed the Spirit of a great Hero, with the Moderation of a Philosopher; the Plainness of a good Man, with the Secrecy of a Confessor.

The Envious whom he out-shined, and the Malicious whom he had defeated, have exposed his regular and decent Frugality to the Disadvantage of his Generosity, which, if rightly considered, was one of the greatest Ornaments of his Life; and did not proceed from the Littleness of his Mind, but from the Greatness of his Wisdom. For his Grace had
taken

taken the true Measures of human Things; and esteemed it as a sure Maxim, that Power and Interest are hardly separable from Wealth. He very well knew how much Princes descend from the Footstool of their Throne, and veil their Sovereignty to their Subjects, by too frequent, and, sometimes, mean Applications to their People in their Wants: How unable the Nobility are to support their own Esteem and Order, or to assist the Crown, whilst they make themselves contemptible and weak, by the Number and Weight of their Debts, and the continual Decay of their Estates. And if the Wealth of the Nation come to centre most among the lower and trading Part of the People, at one Time or other, it will certainly be in their Power, and probably in their Desires, to invade the Government. These, and the like Considerations, had moved the Duke of *Albemarle* to become as great an Example to the Nobility of honourable good Husbandry, as he had been before of Loyalty and Allegiance.

Besides his immortal Fame, he has another Instance of posthumous Felicity, leaving behind him a Son, the present Duke of *Albemarle*, the Inheritor of his Nobility and Glories; and growing daily more to the Resemblance of him, not only in the Lineaments

of

of his Face, but in the Image of his Mind, the Worthiness of his Nature, and Height of his Courage and Gallantry. Besides his own great Example, he had given him, in his Lifetime, the early Impressions of Virtue and Loyalty; and left him, at his Death, great in the Favour of his Prince, great in the Esteem of the Nobility, great in the universal Affection of the People, and great in the Circle of human Fortune.

Such were the Felicities of the late Duke of *Albemarle*, as cannot possibly happen to any, but to those who are singularly sustained by the Divine Favour, and have pursued glorious Ends; which will make Men of rebellious and fanatical Principles afraid how they mix their Reproaches and Curses among so many Blessings of God.

Thus have we brought this Great, this Fortunate, this Triumphant Hero to his Grave.

And now may the Imperial Crown of *England* never want any thing to support it, besides its own Majesty and Greatness. But if ever it should, may there never be wanting a Duke of *Albemarle*. Amen.

Gen. *MONK*'s Pedigree.

*HE following Account of* General Monk's *Descent, was taken out of a Pamphlet (lately communicated to me) printed A. D. 1659. And I presume from the Date of it, the Design of publishing it at that Time was, to make out a Title to the Crown, which they were so importunate with him to accept of. The Pamphlet is entitled,*

The Pedigree and Descent of his Excellency Gen. *George Monk:* Setting forth how he is descended from K. *Edward* the Third, by a Branch and Slip of the *White Rose*, the House of *York:* And likewise his Extraction from *Richard* King of the *Romans*.

General Monk's *Pedigree*.

Page 10.

"*Frances*, another Daughter and Coheir of the said *Arthur Plantagenet*, was married first to *John Basset* in the County of *Devon*, by whom she had *Arthur Basset*, Knight, &c. She after married to Sir *Thomas Monk* of *Potheridge* in the aforesaid County of *Devon*; which Sir *Thomas* was the Son of *Anthony*, the Son and Heir of *Humphrey Monk* of *Potheridge*, and of his Wife *Mary*, Daughter and Coheir of *Richard Champernoon* in *Cornwal*, by the Daughter and Coheir of Sir *John Lumley*, Knight, and of his Wife the Daughter and Coheir of Sir *Humphrey Talbot*, Knight; which *Richard Champernoon* was Son to *Richard*, Son of *John*, third Son to *Richard*, Son to *Henry*, Son to *Thomas*, Son of *Richard* and *Joan* his Wife, Daughter and Heir of *Ralph Vautort*, and of his Wife *Joan*, Daughter to *Edmund* Earl of *Cornwal*, Son to *Richard* King of the *Romans*: Sir *Thomas Monk* aforesaid had Issue, *Anthony Monk*, first Son, (and several other Children) from whom is descended *George Monk*, Lord of *Potheridge*, and at this Time the famous and most renowned General.

GEORGIO MONK,

Duci de ALBEMARLE, Comiti de TORRINGTON, Baroni in POTHERIDGE, &c.

Exercituum in ANGLIA, sub Rege *CAROLO* Secundo, GENERALI, à Consiliis Secretioribus, & Nobilissimi Ordinis Aureæ Periscelidis Equiti,

EPITAPHIUM.

Luge & Mirare,

Quisquis ades.

ECCE jacet in Tumulo, qui sedere noluit in Throno;
Fatis communibus moritur, qui communibus non vixit;

Naturâ

Naturâ magnus, Fortunâ major, se ipso maximus.
　　Miles audaciâ, Secundus nulli,
　　　　Dux prudentiâ,
　　　　　　Subditus fide.
Tyrannum, & Populis & Regibus formidabilem, Solus non timuit, sed terruit;
　　Defuncto Tyranno, & Superstite Tyrannide,
　　　　Venit, Vidit, Vicit,
　　Non Armorum strepitu, sed Consiliorum alto Silentio:
　　(Genus vincendi plane novum, quod nec Voce, nec Armis!)
　　　　Tria Regna obtinuit, vel uno Die,
　　　　　　Nec proeliatus, nec locutus;
　　　　　　　　Obtinuit Tria, noluit vel Unum:
　　Sceptri enim factus Arbiter, maluit redderequàm habere;

Pluris

Pluris meritò æstimans, restituere Regem, quàm esse.
Restituit quidem, restiturumque observantissimè coluit,
CAROLO, non sibi, Victor;
Et Obedientiâ inclytus, magis quàm Imperio,
Humilitate, quàm Gloriâ;
Modestior Ipse post restitutam Majestatem, quàm post læsam alii.
Felix, qui triplici Regno Regem demeruit, & hunc Regem,
CAROLUM Secundum;
Præter injurias oblitum nihil,
Nihil Memorem præter Officia,
Nec triplici Regno, sed omni dignum.
Restituto Rege, simul omnia restauravit,
Pacem, Justitiam, Religionem.

Restauratisque

Restauratisque omnibus, decennium adhuc vixit, conservaturus quæ restauraverat,
Et conservando, quàm restaurando clarior;
Curarum nempe Vitæque prodigus, ut semel restaurata semper conservaret.
Amicos habuit *BONOS* omnes;
Inimicum neminem, nisi aut Dei, aut Regis, aut Patriæ.
Titulis, Honoribus, Divitiis, crevit supra modum, sed infra meritum;
Fortunis mutatis, nihil mutatus ipse,
Semper minor sibi, quò aliis major.
Penè inter nuptias *filii hæredis* obiit, lacrymas funeris temperaturus nuptiarum gaudiis.
Domestico tamen solatio nihil placantur publici luctus;
Nec aliquod remedium doloris est, ubi calamitas dolorem superat,
Ubi amittitur, quod nec reparatur in Hærede dignissimo;
Virtus enim Successorem non habet, quæ Antecessorem non habuit:

HEROES

HEROES toti nascuntur, & toti pereunt;
 Similem non viderat Anglia, nec Orbis videbit.
Sepelitur cum Regibus, qui Rex non fuit, sed nec voluit esse.
Quidni cum Regibus jaceat, per quem stant Ipsi Reges,
 Tumulumque accipiat, qui Solium reddidit?
Superstes, etiam post haec Marmora, futurus,
 Nobilior & recentior, dum antiquior;
Dignus planè qui celebretur mortuus, cùm recusaverit vivus;
Imò qui Cœlum mercedem habeat, cui compensando Terra non sufficit.

Hunc & Luge & Mirare.

F I N I S.

www.ingramcontent.com/pod-product-compliance
Lightning Source LLC
Chambersburg PA
CBHW031248230426
43670CB00005B/85